Women
in Iran

Women
in Iran

Emerging Voices
in the Women's Movement

Hammed Shahidian

Contributions in Women's Studies, Number 197

GREENWOOD PRESS
Westport, Connecticut • London

For Roohi and Nahid
sisters, teachers, and *friends*
with love and gratitude

Library of Congress Cataloging-in-Publication Data

Shahidian, Hammed, 1959–
    Women in Iran : emerging voices in the women's movement /
Hammed Shahidian.
       p. cm.—(Contributions in women's studies, ISSN 0147–104X ; no. 197)
    Includes bibliographical references and index.
    ISBN 0–313–32345–3 (alk. paper)
    1. Feminism—Iran. 2. Women—Iran—Social conditions. 3. Political culture—Iran.
4. Social movements—Iran. I. Title. II. Series.
HQ1735.2.S536 2002
305.42'0955—dc21   2002016101

British Library Cataloguing in Publication Data is available.

Library of Congress Catalog Card Number: 2002016101
ISBN: 0–313–32345–3
    0–313–32482–4 (set)
ISSN: 0147–104X

First published in 2002

Greenwood Press, 88 Post Road West, Westport, CT 06881
An imprint of Greenwood Publishing Group, Inc.
www.greenwood.com

Printed in the United States of America

The paper used in this book complies with the
Permanent Paper Standard issued by the National
Information Standards Organization (Z39.48–1984).

10 9 8 7 6 5 4 3 2

Contents

Acknowledgments

Many have assisted in the completion of this project, appearing in two independent yet interrelated volumes, *Women in Iran: Gender Politics in the Islamic Republic* and *Women in Iran: Emerging Voices in the Women's Movement*. I would like to thank my cohorts in the Sociology/Anthropology Program at the University of Illinois at Springfield for their support and friendship. I am also grateful to Nancy Ford, Executive Director of the Institute for Public Affairs at UIS, for her encouragement and support.

Deborah Kuhn McGregor, Michael Lewis, and Nastaran Moossavi number among the people who read both volumes. Several colleagues read chapters of these books at various stages—my thanks to them all: Ali Akbar Mahdi, Nasser Mohajer, Shahrzad Mojab, Ali Pourmand, and Robbert Schehr. Many activists inside and outside Iran read all or parts of the manuscript. They wish to remain anonymous. I would like to express my warmest appreciation to them for sharing with me their experiences, and extending their cooperation and trust. My special thanks to Ethan Lewis for believing in the importance of my work, for his warm support, insightful editorial comments, and his valuable friendship. I wish also to thank Kris Jagusch of the Center for Teaching and Learning at UIS for her editing of several chapters.

My family has been a great source of continuous love, kindness, and friendship throughout my life. To them I am particularly indebted for teaching that a passion for justice and human dignity is indispensable to a meaningful life. I am most grateful to them. Recognizing my debt, however, is surely insufficient compensation; but recognition at least testifies that I remember.

Note on Transliterations

I use Farsi, rather than Arabic, pronunciations as the basis of my transliterations (e.g., nafaqeh rather than nafaqa). For the most part, I use a modified version of the system recommended by the *International Journal of
Middle East Studies*. I have avoided diacriticals with three exceptions: (ʿ)
for ʿeyn, (ʾ) for hamzeh, and (a) for long "a" (similar to the word *car*). I
use (q) for the Farsi gheyn or ghaf. Whenever common transliterations
exist, I use them to avoid confusion (e.g., Iran instead of Iran, Hashemi
instead of Hashemi, Ali instead of ʿAli). I also use existing English spelling
for proper names when available. I transliterated Farsi and Arabic words
as they are pronounced by Iranians, not as they are written, in order to
both ease the reading for those not familiar with these languages and to
more accurately reflect how the majority of Iranians use these words.

1

Introduction: Revolution, Gender, and Cultural Politics

The joy of a raindrop
and the sorrow *of it* in a swamp.

This is how I read Esmail Khoi's "Sketch 1" to reflect upon the Iranian revolution of 1979. Or maybe it should be read as it appears in a translated anthology of his poems: ". . . and *its* sorrow in a swamp" (Khoi 1995: 42)? The translation is, of course, more loyal in its rendition of Khoi's poem, written in 1961, though I believe both versions accurately reflect the experience of many whose lives have been shaped by the historical events of the late seventies in Iran. The first version is from the perspective of an onlooker, joyously watching the life-giving raindrop, only to abruptly recognize its horrid fall into the abyss. The second narrates the same journey, but from the viewpoint of the raindrop itself. *Watching* the raindrop with exultation and sadly realizing its demise, or *being* the raindrop, happily dancing toward the earth, only to find oneself swallowed by the swamp: the difference—if in fact any—is minimal. Both are recurring metaphors in reflections upon the 1979 revolution in Iran.

I remember a celebration of the Iranian New Year (*Nourouz*, the first day of spring) in the early eighties, organized by Iranian student opponents of the Islamic Republic of Iran (IRI) in the United States. Student organizations that supported various Iranian political groups had set up literature tables, displaying books, newspapers, pamphlets, and photos published overtly or covertly in Iran. Browsing through the literature, a reprint of a collection of articles from *Kar*, the official paper of the then-popular Fedaiin, caught my attention. The title, *What Did Khomeini Say? What Did Khomeini Do?* pointed out the discrepancies between the promises and the practices of the newly established IRI. As I leafed through the pages, I noticed a middle-aged man skimming through the same pamphlet. His glance arrested mine. He shook his head in perplexed awe: "*Chi khâstim; chi shod!*"—*what did we want; what did we get!* And he hurried away. At the receiving end, however, I remained motionless. Was that an observation? A question? Or perhaps he was searching for an explanation, even a justification? Was he lamenting over what happened to us? Or asking how revolutionaries, *farzandân-e khalq*, "the children of the masses," could let the calamity of the Islamic Republic befall the people? How could *darskhândeh-hâye mâ*, "our educated folks," *roushanfekrân-e mâ*, "our intellectuals," not know what to expect from a theocracy? Were these questions really his, expressed in his disappointed facial expression, or was I only hearing and seeing them in my mind's ears and eyes?

Maybe yes; maybe no. After all, these are questions with which many Iranians have grappled for more than two decades. Both of my examples reveal the reflexive nature of the endeavors of many Iranian intellectuals and scholars. Iran of the turn of the century was the scene of a strong constitutionalist movement—a movement that sought to limit the power of the Qajar monarch, though failed to imagine bringing the monarchical system to an end. After years of weakened state power, Reza Shah, with the active support of Great Britain, established the Pahlavi dynasty in 1925 to create a strong central power.[1] That goal was unattainable without a crackdown on many progressive movements, especially the labor and women's movements. The Shah was abdicated to South Africa by the British during World War II for siding with Hitler. His son, Mohammad Reza, took the throne in 1941. The new Shah in turn had to contend with social movements that sprouted since 1941. The labor movement, predominantly under the influence of the communist Tudeh Party, and the movement to nationalize oil, headed by the charismatic Dr. Mohammad Mossadiq, culminated in the 1953 ousting of the young Shah. He managed a comeback soon after, however, thanks to a CIA-led coup. Repression grew once again, especially after the establishment of his notorious secret police, the SAVAK. Another wave of protests was crushed in the bloody June 10, 1963, uprising. The protest was mainly led by the clergy in opposition to the Shah's proposed reforms—his so-called White Revolution—which included land reform and franchise for women. The Shah's power became even more consolidated after 1963. Numerous small oppositional cells were dismembered by the SAVAK. The urban guerrilla movement of the 1970s was initiated by Mojahedin and Fedaiin in response to the increasing power of the Pahlavi state, the futility of scattered small oppositional groups, and the (perceived) impossibility or ineffectiveness of waging political—rather than military—struggles. The movement's aspiration to lead a nationwide massive warfare against the state was soon abated, however, after the death or imprisonment of its leading figures by the SAVAK—Mohammad Hanifnezhâd, Saʿid Mohsen, Asqar Badiʿzâdegân from the mujahedin, and Massoud Ahmadzâdeh, Amir Parviz Pouyân, Ali Akbar Safâʿi-Farâhâni, Hamid Momeni, and Bizhan Jazani from Fedaiin, to name but a few. In 1979, the two major guerrilla organizations had few rank-and-file members (many of them in prison), though their popularity rapidly grew. They became two of IRI's major contenders.

As the revolution approached, anti-Shah forces, particularly the Left, aspired to maximize their unity and strength. Difference of opinion, they believed, could be peacefully resolved in the happy, post-revolutionary Iranian family. So, strategic and tactical differences with the Islamists[2] were overlooked. The united happy family was dismantled shortly after the official seizure of power by the Provisional Islamic Government. From anti-women decrees to the brutal suppression of the Kurdish nationalist movement, to the violent response to the peasant councils (showrâhây-e dehqâni) of Turkaman Sahrâ, to the banning of the Âyandegân newspaper,[3] to attacking the headquarters of political organizations, to the dissolution of genuine workers' collectivities, within a few months after coming to power, the new government, step by step, attacked all the bastions conquered by the revolution and rebuilt the prisons that were damaged by the "flood" of the February uprising that put an end to the monarchy.[4]

A common set of questions has been posed after the bitter experiences of inequality, poverty, injustice, censorship, imprisonment, torture, execution, war, exile, uprootedness, humiliation, prejudice, discrimination, oppression of women, the rape and execution of imprisoned, innocent young girls and pregnant women, the mass executions of thousands of political prisoners and the suffocation of artists and intellectuals. Countless lives have been sacrificed in years of struggle against the oppressive and exploitative Iranian regimes in the past century. The fruit, however, appears to be a mere change in tyrants—a turban instead of a crown. The persisting questions, then, are: What factors contribute to the failure of Iranian activists searching for a just, egalitarian, free, enlightened, and happy society? Why is it that after decades of hard work, the destiny of a revolution, intended to attain equality, freedom, and democracy fell into the hands of those with no respect for these ideals? The need to gaze into the eyes of whatever it is we have done which condemned us to the Sisyphean punishment has directed many to reconsider Iran's cultural and political dynamics.

Inside and outside Iran, reevaluation of cultural and ideological patterns is deemed to have utmost urgency. Writing in Iran, Mohammad Mokhtâri recalls the turmoil of the Kânoon-e Nevisandegân-e Iran (the Iranian Writers' Association) immediately after the revolution. The Kânoon planned to hold a few meetings—"Freedom and Culture Nights"—to discuss the rising threat of censorship and repression. Five members, who were also active in the pro-Islamic state Tudeh Party, were opposed to holding that event, arguing that such events could weaken the revolution.[5] Before reaching a final conclusion inside the Kânoon, the five authors made the case public through party newspapers. Members of the Writers' Association voted for a six-month suspension of Tudeh'i writers. When the suspension was lifted, the Kânoon had to determine the future of these members. One motion was to extend their suspension for another six months, during which time the Association was supposed to reach a final decision. A second, presented in the form of a petition signed by, among others, Mokhtâri himself, called for their expulsion. The debate grew intense and the five authors left the Kânoon.[6] Years later, Mokhtâri ponders the whole incident—the pressure tactic of the Tudeh'i writers, the response of the Kânoon, the petition to expel. He suggests that to understand that episode, as well as much of the contemporary history of Iran, one must comprehend the "dictatorial struc-ture of the [Iranian] mind" (sâkht-e estebdâdy-e zehn). Such a structure is "an old cultural characteristic, itself stemming from centuries-old socio-historical dictatorial structure" (Mokhtâri 1992: 16). Only through a con-certed cultural analysis of Iran's history and society, he concludes, can we untangle the vicious knot of Iranian cultural politics (19).

Writing in exile, playwright and director Mohsen Yalfani makes a similar observation in more vividly political language:

The intellectual and mental conditions of Iranians abroad have changed drastically in the past few years. Following a period filled with great hopes, expectations, and collective efforts, and after living through rapid and, at times, easily accomplished changes, which themselves entailed vexing and bloody attempts and the experience of defeat, a period of stagnation, tranquillity and waiting—for what, is hard to imagine—has arrived. We felt defeated, not because the enemy was superior, but because of our own weaknesses. We felt deceived that we made our lives the bar-gaining chip of a trade-off which benefited our enemy the most; and cheated on and manipulated by an international system that is the outcome of bargains and negotiations of powerful countries which at times made us hopeful about our de-sires and expectations and at other times proceeded in their usual manner of dis-interest and profit seeking. All of these factors made Iranians pause and contemplate what has happened to them, where they stand at the present time, what their future is going to be, and what they can do about it. (Yalfani 1987: 3–4, translation modified)

The urgent need for cultural reevaluation felt by intellectuals in and out of Iran has also been augmented by the IRI's emphasized cultural task. According to the IRI's cultural politics (siyâsat-e farhangi), "the Islamic revolution is verily a cultural revolution and if not all, certainly the majority and the most significant of our efforts and abilities must be used for cultural developments in all personal and social aspects" (Ministry of Islamic Cul-ture and Guidance 1992: 7–8). Post-revolutionary Iran has been the scene

of fierce cultural struggles, of which banning newspapers, arresting journalists, and imprisoning and murdering intellectuals are only the tip of the
iceberg. A more complicated—and equally stubborn—resistance to IRI exists underneath the formal Islamic appearance, in the intricate weave of
daily life.

The increasing post-revolutionary concerns with gender politics should
be understood in this context of reassessing Iranian culture and politics.
The "woman question" is located at the crossroads of a number of key
political terrains. It is related to the development and changes of Iranian
society under the Pahlavis and the IRI. It is also pivotal in the study of
the cultural politics, particularly in relation to Islam, of pre- and post-
revolutionary social movements in Iran. Finally, the "woman question" is
crucial because it not only demonstrates a variety of explicit political beliefs
and priorities, it also reveals many deep-rooted convictions and assumptions that contribute to the formulating of questions regarding social movements' objectives.

CULTURE AND CULTURAL POLITICS

I use "culture" in this book as historically accumulated patterns of symbols and meanings. Humans utilize these patterns to produce and communicate knowledge about our world. Culture gives meaning to our
actions; without culture, social life would have been "a mere chaos of
pointless acts and exploding emotions" (Geertz 1973, p. 46). Clifford
Geertz defines culture as patterns of meanings, embodied in symbols, transmitted through generations:

Undirected by cultural patterns—organized systems of significant symbols—man's
[sic] behavior would be virtually ungovernable, a mere chaos of pointless acts and
exploding emotions, his [sic] experience virtually shapeless. Culture, the accumulated totality of such patterns, is not just an ornament of human existence but . . .
an essential condition for it. (46)

Culture shapes how we understand and organize our objective social
relations and pursue our interests. Culture interweaves objective interests
and subjective values, as Max Weber explains, "Not ideas, but material
and ideal interests, directly govern men's [sic] conduct. Yet very frequently
the "world images" that have been created by "ideas" have, like switch-
men, determined the tracks along which action has been pushed by the
dynamic of interest" (Weber 1981: 280).

Culture is neither indifferent nor benign. Social groups that control economic production and have political leverage also control the means of
cultural production. Culture in the traditional Marxist analysis is understood as a product of the underlying material conditions, which reflects the

dominant socioeconomic formation. Every mode of production relies on compatibility between the forces of production and the relations of production in order to survive. Therefore, development in the mode of production leads to a change in the culture. In other words, culture is a product of objective laws that exist independently from human will. This analysis has been the subject of criticisms and controversies.[7] Lukács distanced himself from this deterministic base and superstructure analysis in favor of a notion of totality of social life which saw societies as a complex web of interrelated practices (see Jay 1984: 81–127). Gramsci explained culture as deeply rooted in the consciousness of a society, not simply as an imposition of a cluster of values and beliefs serving the ruling class (see Bocock 1986; Mouffe 1979).[8]

Following Lukács and Gramsci, Raymond Williams proposes that in discussing the relationship between base and superstructure, we should look beyond the production of the capitalist economy and instead see "the primary production of society itself, and of men [sic] themselves, the material production and reproduction of real life" (Williams 1982: 35). From this vantage point, culture is seen as a "vital productive social force" that is blended into the totality of social life, and as a sphere of constant conflict between the dominant and oppositional cultures for gaining hegemonic power. Williams identifies two alternatives to the dominant culture: residual and emergent. The former refers to "some experiences, meanings and values, which cannot be verified or cannot be expressed in terms of the dominant culture, [yet which] are nevertheless lived and practiced on the basis of the residue—cultural as well as social—of some previous social formation" (40). The latter points to the continual creation of new forms of cultural life. Whether the dominant culture entertains either alternative depends on the interest of the dominant culture. "If the interest and the stake [of the dominant culture] are explicit," Williams writes, "many new practices will be reached for, and if possible incorporated, or else extirpated with extraordinary vigor" (43). Multiplicity of cultures creates the possibility of recognizing alternatives as not just manifestations of the ruling class culture, but also as instances of resistance to, or conflict with, the residual and dominant cultures. Besides, the multiplicity hypothesis also points to the complexity of the relationship of domination and subordination; and to the need to broaden leftist theory and practice to embrace an expanded scope of political struggle. Beyond the labor-capital conflict, this scope must acknowledge resistance to political, social, or cultural domination.[9]

Unlike a more orthodox reading of Marx that argues for a "dominant ideology" (e.g., Abercrombie, Hill, and Turner 1980), Gramsci emphasized hegemonic culture that connotes an active consent, rather than a coercive control or deceptive manipulation. Gramsci used hegemony to refer to the moral and philosophical leadership, achieved through various social and political organizations such as the law, education, parties, and the media. Several insightful analyses have been inspired by Gramsci's discussion of hegemony. Gaventa (1980), for instance, explores the silence and rebellion of Appalachian mountaineers in relation to coal and landowners. He analyzes the effects of hegemonic culture in muzzling active opposition against the powerful. Even when the powerless begin to voice their demands, their articulations are inconsistent, which in turn reinforce quiescence. Stokes (1995) similarly explains the aversion or participation of the Peruvian poor in oppositional movements by an "ethos of deference" promoted by the Peruvian state as far back as the 1930s and disseminated through the church and political parties present in working-class neighborhoods. Only after profound "transformation of the settings in which Peru's urban poor were socialized to political life" (115) did the poor become effectively involved in politics:

The rise of the "classist" labor movement, the injection of the "critical idea" of Peruvian history and society into public school curricula, the arrival in the shantytowns of legions of outside organizers with new messages about the sources of poverty and possibilities for change—all of these, direct or indirect results of military government policies, transformed the worldviews of large segments of the urban poor. (116)

A key criterion for hegemonic cultural leadership is that it should be attained through the active consent of a major segment of the population: "people should freely, autonomously and rationally understand and participate in the cultural, economic, and political affairs of their society" (Bocock 1986: 58). Since hegemonic leadership is gained through consent, certain fundamental beliefs about society, economy, polity, morality, and culture appear as "natural" to people. Gramsci writes:

It is essential to destroy the widespread prejudice that philosophy is a strange and difficult thing just because it is the specific intellectual activity of a particular category of specialist or of professional and systematic philosophers. It must first be shown that all men are "philosophers," by defining the limits and characteristics of the "spontaneous philosophy" which is proper to everybody. This philosophy is contained in: 1) language itself, which is a totality of determined notions and concepts and not just of words grammatically devoid of content; 2) "common sense" and "good sense;" 3) popular religion and, therefore, also in the entire system of beliefs, superstitions, opinions, ways of seeing things and acting, which are collectively bundled together under the name of "folklore." (Gramsci 1971: 323)

Here Gramsci directs us to search in people's daily lives for the persistence of hegemonic cultures. Common sense, popular beliefs, and language appear to be crucial elements in social struggle. For social movements, popular beliefs are not benign notions that could evolve over time, much less soon after the victory. Beliefs must be challenged constantly, *before* any movement can claim victory. By the same token, ordinary language should be an important means for permeating hegemonic culture. Thus, no challenge to hegemonic cultures could be successful if it relies on existing languages. Language is not merely a communicative device; it has a "prosthetic function" also, as Shotter (1993: especially 78–79) proposes. Words do not merely tell us "what is out there;" they also tell us "what to *see* out there." Embedded in words are sophisticated belief systems that are reproduced as words are utilized. The language of a movement, then, has a profound impact on how its political ideas and objectives are articulated. It has a crucial role in how activists understand their goals and construct their movement. It also informs how activists understand the objectives of other movements and where they locate their similarities and differences. Moreover, social movements are understood and evaluated by *others* through the language of the movement, the concepts and beliefs utilized in order to communicate with the public. This approach situates the battleground of revolutionary movements not merely in the politico-economic sphere, but also in the realm of daily life, where symbols, meanings and ideas are experienced, defined, and negotiated.

The concern about the extent to which social movements may uncritically borrow from hegemonic culture is especially acute insofar as the ideology of the movement is concerned. By ideology, I mean here both the domain of ideas (culture) and that of political culture, that is, acceptable ways of politicking, shaped through the complex interaction of such factors as class, gender, race, ethnicity, religion, and culture. The ideology of a movement articulates not only its ideals and objectives, but also the means for achieving its goals. Prosthetic lexicons of the ideology can then both communicate it to others—that is, "tell" others what to look for in the movement—and guide subscribers in what to look for "out there."[10]

Following Gramsci, some scholars such as Scott (1985) have drawn our attention to the everyday forms of class struggle and resistance and, like Stokes (1995), have cautioned us against assuming a total consent to the hegemonic culture by the oppressed. These scholars suggest instead that the oppressed strategically interpret existing conditions and shrewdly choose a line of action that best suits their interest. This analysis, I believe, could be further broadened if one considers the oppressed not as a homogenous group with one set of common interests, but rather a heterogeneous construct of people with both convergent and divergent interests. "Cultural politics" is the contested process by which social actors articulate values, norms, symbols, and meanings. This struggle is launched both at the highly formal political confrontations and in informal daily expressions.

Though Gramsci's discussion of hegemony takes us beyond the simplicity of the "dominant ideological thesis," we must not overlook "dominance" as a possible form of social relationship. While hegemony involves consent, that is, subscription to a "common conception of the world" (Gramsci 1971: 349), dominance is achieved through overt and covert coercion. To be sure, dominance and hegemony are not permanently distinct. A dominating culture does not necessarily mean an alien one, imposed from without; it can be indigenous. A dominant culture borrows from the existing culture; it indeed uses indigenousness as a basis for claiming legitimacy. Yet it also proposes—or, more accurately, imposes—values fundamentally different from, or opposed to, popular consensus. Despite using brutal force, cultural dominance may prove too weak to withstand popular resistance. Yet dominance can also lead to passive consent. Coercion, along with repeated representation of dominance as inevitable, enables dominant groups to "persuade" subordinates that "whatever they may think of the social order, and however much they may be alienated from it, there is no alternative to it" (Miliband 1995: 11). As a result of hegemony by "resignation" (to use Ralph Miliband's terminology), individuals give up—albeit only temporarily—searching for alternative social orders.

BARGAINING WITH PRIVATE AND PUBLIC PATRIARCHY

I fashioned my analysis of the developments in patriarchal relations in pre- and post-revolutionary Iran around Sylvia Walby's distinction between private and public patriarchy in Britain (see *Women in Iran: Gender Politics in the Islamic Republic*, hereafter *Gender Politics*). Examining alterations in six patriarchal institutions (the paid labor force, domestic labor, the state, sexuality, culture, and male violence), Walby (1994) highlights a structural shift from private to public patriarchal relations in the nineteenth and twentieth centuries. Women experience sexual domination in both private *and* public spheres under both arrangements, but the two forms of patriarchy are distinct as far as the primary agencies of sexual dominance and the dynamics of domination are concerned. Private patriarchy is characterized by the family being the loci of control over women, that is, specific men controlling and appropriating women's labor, sexuality, and access to culture. In a public patriarchy, women's public participation increases. As workers, employees, and students, women come more under the control of social institutions than that of the specific men in their lives. Public patriarchy does not exclude women from the labor force, politics, or culture; rather, it segregates them within these, hiring them in certain fields with limited opportunity for upward mobility. Walby particularly underlines the adaptability of patriarchy, contending that what patriarchy loses in battles over one institution, it can compensate for in others.

In the same book, I argued that differences notwithstanding, Deniz Kandiyoti's (1988) analysis of classic patriarchy in North Africa, the Muslim Middle East, and South and East Asia (particularly India and China) resembled Walby's assessment of British private patriarchy. This resemblance occurs especially in Kandiyoti's discussion of the concentration of women's responsibility in domestic production and men's authority over women. Classic patriarchy is characterized by patrilocally extended households, engaged primarily in rural production. Senior men are the family patriarchs. Married off at a young age, daughters live under the control of their fathers- and mothers-in-law, until they themselves become mothers-in-law and exert authority over subservient daughters-in-law. Women's only access to labor power and to old-age security is through their married sons.

Though excluded from nondomestic production and subject to such discriminatory practices and institutions as purdah and hejâb (the veil), many women tolerate, even revere, these institutions in order to maintain family status. Women opt to maximize their security through manipulation of their sons' and husbands' affection. Through this process of subservience and manipulation—what Kandiyoti calls *traditional patriarchal bargain*—women gain limited security at the expense of economic advantage. This "security" gives the false impression that women fare well under patriarchal relations, though occasionally extreme hardship may befall some women.

Times of crisis in the traditional bargain (e.g., due to capitalist expansion) bring patriarchal coerciveness to the foreground. The classic patriarchal system's "internal contradictions" are revealed and participants in the system are forced "to take up new and seemingly contradictory positions" (Kandiyoti 1991b: 35). Some women, then, could actively participate in conservative movements that aim to enhance men's control over women.

If private patriarchy leads to a traditional bargain, public patriarchy effects a *modern patriarchal bargain*. The transformation of patriarchy from private to public does not necessarily improve women's lives; whether such a transition is beneficial to women requires empirical research and independent appraisal of each case (Walby 1997: 6). Public patriarchy might increase women's chances in certain areas, but it can also impose further limitations on other aspects of their lives. Male dominance is a flexible system; forced to concede to a higher share for women in some arenas, patriarchy can compensate for that loss in other fields. Patriarchy can refashion itself to accord some women a greater role in public life. Then, women participate in the economy and polity, but concentrate in certain areas or are promoted to certain tiers of the organizational hierarchy.

The inclusion of these women in capitalist and patriarchal organizations is certainly an accomplishment of women's struggles. Mary Katzenstein (1998) shows how feminists have continued the protests of the 1960s inside institutions by "their mere presence," or by "claiming specific rights, and by demanding in certain facets the transformation of the institutions of which they are a part" (7). Yet women's inclusion in organizations does not equate altering gender relations. Indeed, Katzenstein remarks about women in the United States armed forces, women's ascent within the Army ranks has fertilized "reformist, interest-group politics," without much need for establishing alliance with those still marginalized and unprivileged (165).

The domination mechanisms of public patriarchy are dangerously elusive. Working through institutionalized mechanisms, male domination can disguise itself more effectively behind a myriad of faceless, apparently nonpersonal organizations. As Bourdieu (1977) discusses, relations of domination and dependence in institutionalized control can secure an uninterrupted reproduction because multiple beneficiaries appropriate the profit produced in such an arrangement. Individuals, even those in command of such mechanisms, can dissociate themselves from the system. With women's expectations growing, with gender identities, relations, even appearance changing, patriarchy is forced to adapt. The patriarch cannot exercise his control in the manner he used to. Overtly coercive control by the patriarch must be modified. He thus cannot claim tyranny: he is now a "benevolent and fair coordinator." No longer can he lay unconditional claim on her: he must take her desires into consideration. Underneath this "gentleness," however, the foundation of his relationship with her remains, uncannily, unchanged. The indisputable patriarch may be a dying breed, but that does not mean the end of patriarchal domination.

Pressured to jettison blatant chauvinist ideas and practices, patriarchal masters the world over now shroud every conceivable misogynist idea in admiration for women. Public patriarchy also curtails the authority of men over women in personal relationships. This change—whether out of a genuine change in how the patriarch views gender relations or merely as a manipulative tactic—can be deceiving for many reasons. It does not openly endorse men's unequivocal rule, condemns brutality, and even enjoins men to be kind. Nor does it denigrate women to a reproductive machine. It claims great respect for women; indeed, cries incompleteness, even total failure in her absence.

Such mechanisms create the impression that male domination is an ugly remnant of the past, that though "some people" may continue to cherish antediluvian values, "society," by and large, is dedicated to eradicating gender inequality. Patriarchy thusly becomes a relic, a free-floating anomaly—as if not reproduced in our daily practices.

To improve women's life chances, the modern patriarchal bargain aims to make women visible and gain recognition of unjust treatment of women. Socio-historical specificities determine the terms of negotiation in individual cases, but overall, modern bargains secure women a qualified presence in public and relative autonomy in personal life. But sexual inequality is reduced in the process to the removal of structural and attitudinal impediments to women's progress within existing structures. Or, weaker yet, "re-reading" gender to afford women a more prestigious status. There are, doubtless, radical potentials in mainstream feminism, potentials that must be cultivated by progressives, as Zillah Eisenstein (1981) has argued. Yet gender reforms through changes in the law or culture, or revisions of the socialization process to accommodate equality of social participation for women, do not alter, or even weaken, the relations of power that exist between men and women.

We need to distinguish here between women's movements that opt to remedy problems within the existing system (e.g., educational limitations for women or custody rights) and those that intend to fundamentally re-organize gender relations. Alberto Melucci (1996a: 22–23) calls the former, "crisis-oriented" movements, the latter, "conflict-oriented."[11] For Melucci, "crises" indicate breakdown of the "functional and integrative mechanisms of a given set of social relations" (22). Crises, in other words, denote lack of integration and imbalances among subsystems. Conflicts, however, arise out of the struggle between social actors, competing to appropriate re-sources that are deemed valuable. From this vantage point, inequity-recognizing strategies, content with integrating women into the existing order, form crisis-oriented movements that aim to alleviate dysfunctions and imbalances of the patriarchal system.

"Practical" and "strategic" interests, or "crisis-" and "conflict-oriented" movements, of course, are not separated by impassable borders; each could undertake struggles that resonate with the other's objectives. What differ-entiates each from the other is their directions, their final objectives. Yet these differences shape the context of political practice in each case. Such human miseries as unemployment, poverty, and hunger are undoubtedly women's issues. But resolving these issues does not eradicate sexual injus-tices *unless* struggle for sexual equality is interwoven into such a resolution from the outset. Movements that aim to resolve "conflict" cannot remain oblivious to problems that cause "crises"—improving women's status in the IRI's family law, or removing barriers to women's education are tasks rightly taken seriously by Iranian feminists, even those who have no interest in seeing the IRI in power. But such demands cannot overlook the funda-mental limits of the existing patriarchal system. Crisis-oriented movements to secure women's "practical interests" do not evolve into conflict-oriented ones that promote women's "gender interests" without the active interven-tion of those who fight for the latter.

Social movements do not always demand deep-rooted changes; even conflict-oriented movements propose some changes that can be achieved in existing circumstances. But, as a political ideology, "reformism" must not be confused with a push for reforms. Reformism deems fundamental change possible through gradual reforms that aim to remedy an existing system's dysfunctions. The objective here is to resolve these imbalances in a manner that leaves the system intact. Islamist reformists, who attribute the barriers to women's social participation in the IRI to misinterpretations of Islam, opt to remedy this problem by offering interpretations favorable to women. Or, these women's recognition of the constantly changing social life prompts them to seek solutions for the practical challenges facing an Islamic system. Realizing interaction between the sexes is unavoidable; for example, these women seek to find the solution to the forbidden act of unrelated men and women looking at each other. Defining the borders of allowable and impermissible *negâh* (looking), then, becomes a challenge for these reformists (Mohammad Soroush 2000).

Conflict-oriented movements deem that problems are rooted not in mis-interpretations, deviations, or the dysfunctions of a system, but in the very nature of the system. Thus, removing blockages to the system is not a viable alternative to these movements. To be sure, not all problems of a social system require fundamental change. Increasing women's participation in some segments of the economy does not require a complete restructuring of gender relations, nor does removing barriers before women's education in certain fields. The question is not whether reformist measures should be taken, but whether such measures are sufficient for resolving conflicts; not whether reforms are good, but how far they can lead us; not whether we should fight for reforms, but whether that fight would be enough. But for reformists, reforms have never been a prelude to fundamental change; they were, rather, mechanisms to contain conflict-oriented movements.

Assessment of the state is at the center of this concern with reformism. Western feminists are divided about the role of the state in the reproduction of patriarchal relations. While liberal feminists regard the state as es-sentially a neutral arbiter, some feminist scholars consider the state to be unequivocally and unconditionally representing men's interests (e.g., MacKinnon 1983). Eisenstein (1981) argues that the state is a condensation of forces, including male domination. Others recognize the state as deeply gendered, but see it as capable of being "both friend and foe" (see Jenson 1987).

As Jacqui Alexander and Chandra Mohanty (1996) aptly point out, fem-inism in the Third World cannot escape state intervention. In societies that experienced nationalist movements, feminists found the state indeed to be both "friend and foe" as the two entities' objectives coincided at a certain stage of state-building (see *Gender Politics*, Chapter 1). In the Middle East, states came to the rescue of women, whom they regarded as a "wasted national resource" (Kandiyoti 1991a: 10). But these states' efforts to reform personal-status laws remained limited in their emancipatory potential for a variety of reasons (12). This weakness stemmed in part from the absence of a democratic political system in which women could establish autono-mous institutions to fight for their gender interests. Sonia Alvarez observes that in Latin America, the politicization and institutionalization of women's demands have resulted in the state co-opting women's movement organi-zations, appropriating their discourse, and turning women's organizations into "auxiliary" societies serving dominant political and economic interests. States acceded to those demands of the women's movement that were "least disruptive" to the status quo. Though in rare cases—for example, Peronist Argentina and socialist Cuba—the incorporation of women's organizations into institutionalized politics bore fruitful results for women, such processes have had limited "desirable outcomes for women and women's movement organizations" (1990: 21).

These comments should not be understood as condemnation of lobbying for women's rights through established political channels. Far from that; even the slightest improvement in women's concrete living conditions must be celebrated. The point, however, is to recognize the limits of such "improvements." More significantly, we must recognize that the state is not a neutral party with "little that is intrinsic to it" (Ray 1999: 14). States have agendas that are shaped by class, gender, race, or ethnic interests; thus, their attention to women's issues—and gender relations in general—must be assessed in the context of state agenda.

The IRI, as I discussed in *Gender Politics*, is not a disinterested party in how gender relations unfold in Iran. Quite the contrary; the patriarchal triad—a union among patriarchy, Islam, and the Islamic state—displays the active role of the Islamic state in the perpetuation of male domination. Even in the Islamist reformists' less strict agenda, co-opting and limiting women's demands poses serious threats to the future of the Iranian women's movement. While (reformist) Islamists had to respond to some demands of Iranian women, what women have gained so far through resistance has been far less considerable than the competing factions of the Islamic regime claim. We must particularly be cautious not to inflate the significance of women's pervasive yet extremely fragile daily resistance, mistaking it for real alteration of gender relations. I so emphasize this caution because, as the experience of hejâb demonstrates (see, for example, Chapter 3), it is the imperatives of Islam and the Islamic state that eventually determine the parameters of the IRI's tolerance of such "deviations." Though it is undoubtedly necessary to demand reforms under the IRI, a women's movement that opts to transcend the limits of the existing gender relations in Iran cannot ignore the Islamic state's gender objectives.

Women's nongovernmental organizations (NGOs) have flourished in past decades. Yet, as I discussed in *Gender Politics*, the tension between such organizations and the state increases considerably when they opt for anything other than outright support of the IRI. NGOs have indeed developed a dual relationship with the Islamic state. Their inclination to be effective in policymaking obliges them to cooperate with the government or (a faction of) the state to devise and implement policies. Yet as soon as they critique state policies, the statesmen deem them oppositional. Khadijeh Moghadam (2000), who heads the Women's Society for Combating Environmental Pollution, reveals this tension. When state policies promote environmental protection, she states, pro-environment NGOs and the government enjoy each other's support, but when these NGOs resist the implementation of policies injurious to the environment, the NGOs are punished. For instance, university students who opposed the destruction of the Sorkheh Hesâr Park were found guilty (see Farhâdpour 2000: 55–62).

The Islamic state's interest in maintaining a certain type of gender relations becomes even more evident when revisions are ideologically defined as subversive and countercultural. The IRI can tolerate women opting to preserve the environment, or even to proposing alternative interpretations of the Islamic family law. But gays and lesbians have to operate clandestinely. Ja'far Bulhâri, the Chairman of Tehran's Psychiatric Institute, has disclosed the existence of an underground movement for transsexuals and transgenders in Iran whose activities revolve around self-help (*Nimrooz*, 2 February 2000). This limited space for autonomous reconstruction of the self and the body, and the life of individuals (see *Gender Politics*, especially Chapter 6) demonstrates that gender politics is so intertwined with the IRI that no fundamental revision can escape the wrath of the Islamist state.

Scholars like Anthony Giddens (1991) argue that new social movements are more concerned with "life politics" than with "emancipatory politics." He considers the former to be concerned with lifestyle choices, that is, with human self-actualization, both on the level of the individual and the collectivity. The latter, holds Giddens, aims to reduce exploitation, inequality, or oppression. Life politics indicates the displacement of oppositional politics from the economic and political spheres toward the expression of new identities. But, as social movement theorists like Verta Taylor (1996) have argued, the distinction between the two politics has been too rigidly drawn. The case of the IRI similarly testifies to the inseparability of life politics from emancipatory politics.

Either life or emancipatory politics could lead to a dulling of a radical women's movement. An emphasis on identity politics in the absence of due notice of redistribution of socioeconomic resources could limit the scope of the feminist movement to reforms that enhance tolerance of revised gender relations among middle- and upper-classes, but that lead to little change in lower classes. Similarly, exclusive attention to socioeconomic justice may improve some concrete aspects of women's lives without necessarily altering patriarchal power relations in society. This tendency, as I will discuss in this book, poses a serious threat to the Iranian women's movement, since sexual discrimination in law, politics, economy, and education is so severe that concerns with individuality, body, and self appear as mere luxury.

The creation of new forms of life politics that will promote self-actualization—what I will discuss as the possibilities of "other forms of being and becoming" in chapter 5—does indeed involve social inequality through what Nancy Fraser, inspired by Habermas, calls the "politics of need interpretation" (Fraser 1989: chapters 7 and 8). Before oppositional demands enter the realm of formal politics, they must be defined as "needs" by "experts" who can influence policymaking. Those most capable of ar-

ticulating women's needs in "expert needs-discourses" are employed: educated women who are connected with "institutions of knowledge production and utilization" (173). These expert discourses, Fraser holds, are generated in academia, judicial institutions and their satellite schools, state
administrations, and social service agencies.

Reformist efforts have a class dimension that cannot be overlooked in
the context of a capitalist system (Fraser 1997; Schild 1998). Gender re-
arrangements benefit some women more than others: educated, employed,
middle- and upper-class, urban, and heterosexual women who belong to
the dominant race, religion, or ethnic group fare better than others. (It is
not necessary to say that this characterization is not exhaustive; it varies
geographically and temporally.) These are the people who bargain with
patriarchy on behalf of *all* women. But not all women bargain with patriarchy—only some do. Those women gain the power to speak for others,
while the "others" must fight their way through with whatever "ammu-
nition" is at their disposal.

Women have not one, but multiple interests. Some of these interests coincide with other women's and men's; others differ. Movements empower
and open new avenues for politicization and action for some women. Attempts to establish, expand, or "democratize" public patriarchy improve
women's status within the family and increase their share of public responsibilities, but fail to eradicate patriarchy. Such movements always uphold the interest of *some* women in the name of *all*. Yet attaining gender
equality requires a complete reorganization of society that aims not to make
dysfunctional parts work, but to resolve deep-rooted gender conflicts that
result from men's appropriation of women's bodies and work. The strategies of conflict-oriented women's movements must respond to the interests
of all women who are denied rights due to their class, race, or ethnicity.
Since social inequalities are interrelated, a conflict-oriented women's movement cannot claim victory until all barriers to women's attainment of equal
rights are removed—or, more significantly, until differentiation on the basis
of gender is rendered obsolete.

In the IRI, as I will discuss in chapters 2 and 3, these "experts" on
women's needs have converged in the Islamist reformist women's movement. They define gender oppression, politicize women's demands, prioritize those demands for equalizing gender relations, and propose legal—that
is to say, shari'ah-based—solutions to the most blatant forms of sexual
discrimination in the Islamic regime. These mechanisms ensure some
women a greater role in public patriarchy, but leave many others unaffected. From the vantage point of "life politics," what is of major concern
here is this reformist trend's claim to define and prioritize "legitimate"
demands. Mindful of proposing demands acceptable within an Islamic
framework, existing gender identities—womanhood, manhood, motherhood, fatherhood, modesty, heterosexuality, etc.—are redefined, but not

subverted. These are defeatist strategies, devised to protect and preserve existing rights, not to gain and transform. Bourdieu (1975) has termed such methods strategies of succession, as opposed to strategies of subversion, aiming not to separate but to adapt to a hostile environment at a time of weakness. Particularly troublesome in this strategy is the future of secularism in this reformist process. What some observers and activists call co-operation of secularists and Islamist reformists—*hamkâri va hamyâri* (see, e.g., Kâzem Kordavâni in Farhâdpour 2000: 161)—I consider dissolution and erosion of the former in the latter's project.

GENDER AND THE POLITICS OF RECOGNITION

In a survey of nineteenth and early twentieth century nationalist and feminist movements, Kumari Jayawardena (1986) found a meeting-ground for the two. Nationalist movements often not only opposed subjugation of colonized societies, but also championed their betterment through modernization (on feminism and nationalism, also see Blom 1995). Such projects proposed a refashioning of patriarchy from private to public. The traditional patriarchal bargain encountered the first signs of a crisis. Revolutionary states called for "modernized," educated women, women who participated in the fight against cultural and economic "backwardness," symbolized their nations' dedication to modernity, and remained dedicated wives and mothers. The emergence of such a womanhood, then, was not tantamount to the abolition of patriarchy. This limitation explains why many male intellectuals and revolutionaries favored the modernization of women. At the same time, women's movements in societies undergoing a nationalist struggle also demanded basic human rights for women—the right to education, to vote, to participate in the formal sector of the economy. The demands of these movements seriously challenged men's exclusive power over their women in family settings. They did not, however, limit men's privileged position in public. The relationship between nationalism and feminism, or more precisely, between attempts toward public patriarchy and the women's rights movement, were coincidental.

Contrary to the trend in the late nineteenth century, most analyses of women in the revolutions of the twentieth century show an incompatibility with, if not outright hostility toward, women's rights.[12] The experience of contemporary revolutions suggests that though revolutionary upheavals can release women's energy, unless there exists a conscious and militant women's movement, there is no guarantee that women will not become the revolution's forgotten veterans. The Algerian revolution of 1954–1962 was the first to operate based on the assumption that participation in the resistance movement enhances women's freedom. Fanon proposes in *A Dying Colonialism* that as the revolution unfolds and women's participation in it increases, men learn to treat them as equals. He was proven overly opti-

mistic. Despite Algerian women's legendary participation in different aspects of struggle against French colonialism, they have benefited little from
the country's independence (Akeb and Abdelaziz 1985; Knauss 1987). Furthermore, the recent rise of Islamism has meant brutal attacks on women's
rights (for a detailed account, see Bennoune 1994). These incursions prove,
as Cherifati-Merabtine (1994) shows, the vulnerable status of women in
post-revolutionary societies, even when they go through heroic episodes of
a nationalist war. Contesting *Moudjahidiat* (heroines of the war) as a mir-
roring image of colonial woman, Islamists have offered the alternative
image of Khadija and Aisha from the early Islamic period. The delegitim-
ization of the representation of women as *Moudjahidiat* is not simply a
match of role models; the heroines of the nationalist movement are rejected
as representing what they had once fought against—neocolonialism. There
does not seem to be a direct line à la Fanon connecting heroic participation
in the revolution to popular acceptance.

In the Vietnamese experience, not only did women actively participate
in armed struggle against the enemies, they also occupied high positions
within the military forces of the independent Vietnam. Nonetheless, both
during the revolution and after its victory, men resisted women's authority
and leadership. The acceptance of women's leadership after the victory of
the Vietnamese Revolution has been so slow that a scholar characterized
it as a frog moving at a snail's pace. "Resistance to women's leadership,"
she writes, "is, perhaps, the most telling barometer of continuing disrespect
for women" (Eisen 1984: 248). Men have been replacing women who had
leadership positions during the war.

China provides yet another example that "priorities" and "more important tasks" led to a considerable neglect of women's strategic rights. In
China, the Communist Party's (CCP) commitment to the eradication of
sexual inequality and family reform has changed over time and has been
tempered with other considerations (Johnson 1983; Stacey 1983). The
Party advocated several feminist goals during the early 1930s. There followed a conservative period. Then in 1950–53, during the land reform, the
"feudal family" was under attack as part of an overall attempt to modernize rural China. During the Great Leap Forward, initiated in 1958, the need
for free female labor introduced measures which eased the grip of the family
on women (Andors 1983). However, the Cultural Revolution of 1965–69
had little impact on the status of Chinese women and their concerns found
no relevance to the CCP's subsequent agenda.

That is, of course, not to say that revolutions do not affect women's
status in any way nor improve any aspects of their life. Since, as Molyneux
argues, women's lives are changed by factors such as class, ethnicity, and
gender, it is essential to specify how socioeconomic measures in post-
revolutionary societies affect women. To realistically evaluate these
changes, Molyneux distinguishes between women's "strategic" and "prac-

tical" interests. She identifies those interests that men or women may develop because of their social position as members of a sex as "gender interests." Gender interests could be strategic, which aim to provide alternative social arrangements: the abolition of the sexual division of labor, collective domestic labor and childcare, recognition of women's reproductive rights, the eradication of institutionalized forms of discrimination, ending male violence (Molyneux 1985: 232–33). Gender interests could also be practical, responding to the immediate needs of women within the existing sexual division of labor. For example, since the traditional sexual division of labor makes women primarily responsible for the household's daily welfare, women develop an interest in domestic provisions and public welfare. While socialist revolutions have shown success in alleviating women's burden in the latter category, they have failed to formulate an adequate response to the former. Thus, though women's practical and strategic interests are intertwined, it is imperative to specify the nature and extent of women's interests in evaluating a state's (or a movement's) advocacy of sexual equality.

Among recent revolutions, the Nicaraguan movement was an exemplary case of integrating women's demands into the revolution's agenda from an early stage. Women participated in the revolution in such various capacities as guerrilla fighters, political commanders, and messengers. In their first program of action in 1969, the Sandinistas recognized women's submission and declared the eradication of sexual inequalities one of their main goals. Though the revolution succeeded in improving women's lives by combating social and economic inequalities, its accomplishment was less striking in response to women's "strategic interests."

These examples, I believe, suggest a profound change in the relationship between women's and revolutionary movements, calling for revolutionary movements dedicated to women's liberation and gender equality. The coincidental relationship between women's and revolutionary movements that once existed in the late nineteenth century has become progressively problematic. It appears that when women's demands go beyond the limits of public patriarchy, revolutionary movements no longer share the enthusiasm of women's movement for changing the gender roles. As women's liberation movements—that is, movements that target sexual inequality and not simply certain unfair practices—replace the women's rights movements, they find themselves increasingly restrained in revolutionary programs that target only class exploitation or national oppression.

Feminist critics have correctly underlined that women are overlooked in these movements, insisting that women's participation and their demands become visible in the revolutionary process. Through persistent demanding, feminists have changed the political discourse so as to recognize women and include women's rights in the political agenda of social movements from the outset. Now, many political movements have learned that they will have limited appeal if they fail to address women's rights.

Mere visibility and recognition do not secure women's rights. For that, we need to delve deeper and investigate the proposed *problem* and offered *solution*. Time and again, women have been "recognized" in history, but history also demonstrates that this recognition can quite easily create opportunities for patriarchy to rejuvenate and reorganize. This is important for the study of women in social movements. Whereas in the past women were simply ignored, and their demands were subsumed under general objectives, oppositional movements, as well as political establishments, can now recognize the "specificity of the woman question," yet remain no less patriarchal by adapting old orders to new demands, or—worse yet—translating old relations into new jargons.

Recognition politics is particularly sensitive in this time of "globalization," with its accelerating inequality and intensifying marginalization. Recognition (or identity) politics has indeed concealed unequal distribution of resources under "cultural relativism." One-sided emphasis on cultural differences has isolated struggling groups around the world. This has negatively impacted women, for it spares oppressive practices under the guise of respecting indigenous cultures (for a discussion, see Shahidian 1999a). This is by no means to deny the significance of collective identities. Yet collective identities must *supplement* struggle for equal distribution of resources, not replace it. Identity politics must deepen the struggle for social justice by underlining the injustices of marginalization, not valorizing difference or, worse, sanctifying oppressive practices (for further discussion, see Fraser 2000).

Gender relations in the Islamic Republic—that is, both the formal state politics and its reformist "Islamic feminist" rendition—is a prime example of a practice that "recognizes" women and gender inequality without much attempt to uproot patriarchal domination. In post-revolutionary Iran, all political players have had to acknowledge "women's issues." But that recognition says very little about how women have fared under Islamists' rule. Equally troublesome is the opposition's token feminism. Despite the strong concern of Iranian activists inside and abroad about the oppression of women, we have yet to see a gender-enlightened oppositional strategy. Feminists are accepted, but feminism is still seen first and foremost as "feminists' concern." The oppression of women is recognized and its blatant forms are condemned, but gender politics has remained limited to fighting manifest injustices. Homosexual rights have gradually received acknowledgement, but critiquing hetero- and homosexualities is deemed "homosexuals' responsibilities." In short, I believe feminists must be extremely cautious in celebrating the "recognition" of women and patriarchal domination in social movements or formal politics. We must, instead, closely scrutinize what such recognition entails.

GENDER AND THE IRANIAN REVOLUTION

Women were the first group who experienced the shock of the Islamists' ascent to power. The revolution was supposed to enhance freedom and equality for people of both sexes. The uprising of 11 and 12 February of 1979 marked the downfall of the Iranian monarchy. A short 24 days later, the first major attack on women's rights was launched by the Ayatollah Khomeini himself, demanding women to put on the veil (Khomeini 1982: 41). The next day, in response to a call by a provisionary committee to celebrate International Women's Day, over ten thousand women filled the streets of Teheran in opposition to Khomeini's decree. After only a few days, continuous demonstrations and sit-ins forced Khomeini to retreat. Ayatollah Tâleqâni, a high-ranking theologian, stated in a press conference that what the Ayatollah said regarding the hejâb (the traditional Muslim dress for women which covers them from head to toe), was merely "an advice of the sort a father gives to his children . . ." (*Kayhan* 11 March 1978: 3). The Islamic regime lost that battle, but it did not give up; the more strength the new regime gained, the more severe became attacks on women's rights.

Demonstrating women's reaction to the evolving situation contains the reflexive quality that I mentioned above. Slogans of the March 1979 demonstrations succinctly expressed the incredulous recognition of a revolution going awry: "In the spring of freedom, there is no freedom for women." "We did not have a revolution to go backward." Or: "We refuse tyranny in all forms. We will destroy reactionary forces in all forms." Could participants of a revolution express their bewilderment more eloquently? Could they express their sorrow about the short life of a raindrop, ominously dropping toward the swamp, more forcefully? These slogans also hinted at the inadequacies of the then-popular notion that deemed fighting against violations of women's rights secondary to the anti-Shah, anti-imperialist struggle. "Our women are toilers; toilers are free!" "Freedom is neither Eastern nor Western. It is universal!"

Both Islamic and leftist discourses defined freedom as conditional. Their arguments could be summarized thus: "Iranians have fought for freedom. Now is an opportunity. But freedom can be guaranteed only when enemies are restrained." Though Islamists and leftists defined "friends" and "foes" differently, they similarly underscored freedom as a *privilege*, to be enjoyed only by certain people—"true believers" in the Islamic doctrine, "toiling masses" in the ideology of the Left. False defense of freedom, then, could prove an effective tool in the hands of the enemies of the revolution. Under the aegis of freedom, monarchists and their imperialist backers could be making seemingly benign demands that in actuality would only jeopardize the revolution. Islamists considered sexual anarchy caused by adherence to Western—that is, non-Islamic—lifestyle a fruitful method of mobilization by counter-revolutionary forces. Though the Left did not concur with that scenario, the participation of upper and upper-middle class women, whom the Left equated with monarchists, cast doubts about the objectives of women's demonstrations. "If affluent women are fighting for 'women's freedom,' does that not mean that the whole problem is a hoax?" "Why should we be concerned whether affluent women have the freedom to indulge in their luxurious lifestyle? And does not concern with something so mundane as clothes indicate that these women are not focusing on serious political matters?" These concerns were frequently voiced among political activists, even those who renounced the IRI from the start. So, when demonstrating women identified all women as toilers and, consequently, free, when they called freedom a *universal* right, they were pointing out the hazards of self-limiting articulations of available revolutionary discourses in Iran.

Gender dynamics of the Iranian revolution cannot be adequately explored unless one understands the gender relations and cultural politics of that society. What made a group of atheist, even anti-Islamic, intellectuals so susceptible to the traditional concepts of gender? Why was the distinction between leftist and Islamic gender ideologies so blurred? More significantly, why was there no organized women's movement in the Iranian revolution prior to the clerical attacks on women's rights? Why were intellectual, militant women so reluctant to articulate a gendered agenda for the revolution? And what accounts for the feeling of shock, for the vexing realization that "we did not get what we fought for?" If women who participated in the Iranian revolution did not all fight for an Islamic revolution, what was their input in the revolutionary struggle? How does that affect our understanding of the dynamics of the revolution in Iran? How are secular, leftist, or at least non-Islamist women to relate to Islam and Islamist women? Clearly, the significance of these issues goes beyond the Iranian border. They are relevant to women and men in struggle all around the world, especially where fundamentalists are also a force to contend with.

More than two decades after the Islamists' ascent to power in Iran, more pressing controversies over Islam and gender have emerged. How have the Islamic gender ideologies changed before and after the revolution? How have actual gender relations and practices shaped the implementation of Islamic gender ideals? Has Islam offered Iranian women a liberating ideology? Are we facing an "Islamic feminism?" How are women activists to deal with Islam? Is a "liberal," "more enlightened," "sexually sensitive" interpretation of Islam possible? Or should Islam be considered an arch-enemy of women's rights? Could Islamic interpretations of "women's rights" be considered in cultural relativist terms—one of many interpretations—in a collective effort to bring about gender equality? How have secular women resisted Islamism? What challenges do these women face to establish and maintain their autonomy? What paths have developed for progressive social movements in Iran after two-plus decades of struggle against the Islamists? What implications does the Iranian case hold for studies of gender and cultural politics?

My intention in *Women in Iran* is to address these issues by investigating how culture, gender, and politics interacted in the 1979 revolution and after. This analysis suggests a multidiscursive, multilayered, contested process of gender politics and cultural production. I argue that the gender and cultural politics in Iran have emerged through lively, often brutally fierce, battles over symbols, meanings, and practices. Studies of women in Iran since the revolution have emphasized the diversity of Iranian women's lives and struggles. Bayat-Philip (1978) and Afary (1989), for instance, reveal women's opposition to suffocating national and patriarchal political processes in the early twentieth century. Sanasarian (1982) chronicles the vicissitude of women's movements in contemporary Iran. Milani (1992) uncovers the long march of women writers to unveil their voice before a public audience. Tabari and Yeganeh (1982) document the multiplicity of discourses on women in the 1979 revolution. Hegland (1986), Bauer (1985a), and Friedl (1991) discuss how rural and migrant working-class women negotiate the borders of gendered definitions of "appropriate social behavior" in ways that at times even contradict the fundamental principles of their environment's gender ideologies. At the same time, a series of studies suggests the variety of personal and political experiences of Iranian women activists (Bauer 1985a; Moghissi 1994; Paidar 1995; Shahidian 1997a). Studies of immigrant and exiled Iranians similarly reveal a strong secular trend among women and men of diverse socioeconomic backgrounds (Bauer 1991, 1993, 1994; Dallalfar 1994; Moallem 1991; Shahidian 1996a, 1999b). Yet the specter of Islam continues to haunt interpretations of women's lives and gender relations in Iran.

I propose that, then, instead of identifying an inclusive Islamic culture in Iran, or even a unitary oppositional discourse, a more accurate approach is to refer to a hegemonic culture, while recognizing multiple cultures and subcultures. In this way, various cultural trends find their appropriate place in the cultural map and genealogy of Iran. This approach will also allow for the dynamics of cultural politics: how a certain cultural trend exerts hegemony over others; how its hegemony is challenged.

I discussed in *Gender Politics* that following the revolution, a "patriarchal triad" has policed gender relations in Iran. The alliance of these elements—patriarchy, Islam, and the state—is by no stretch of the imagination new, but it has found a much higher crystallization in the Islamic state. This alliance has intensified women's oppression, but it has also revealed the interrelatedness of theocracy, state structure, and cultural hegemony. We have reached a point in Iranian history where politics is immersed in Islam. But we are also at a juncture where the cry for a complete separation of state and religion, a progressive secularization of social life, has gathered much momentum. For this reason, I find attempts to modify teleological conceptions of gender insufficient in answering our contemporary demands.

This, as I suggest in Chapter 4, is indicative of a "dual society," one existing publicly in a conventional social form, the other existing behind the safety of closed doors of private life, according to a more relaxed and often contradictory behavioral code. It is a mistake, however, to ignore the unequal power relationship in this arrangement. The dual society reveals not peaceful coexistence, but the subjugation of one way of life to Islamists' plan. Thus, though people's resistance against the IRI has created a space wherein they can enjoy a degree of freedom, that space is constantly exposed to invasion by the state.

The dual society clearly points to the political character of the private, calling for a redefinition of what counts as political. Daily decisions such as the color of one's attire could make a clear political statement. More importantly, many "benign" components of the informal private sphere—that is, family get-togethers or friendship circles—have played a pivotal role in the preservation or emergence of oppositional politics.

To be sure, one should not see here a uniform and comprehensive refutation of the Islamic gender ideology. Though misogynist policies made many women and men more aware of sexual inequality, those policies are also conceptualized and enacted in the context of the hegemonic culture, with its roots in prerevolutionary days. Some aspects of that culture are now challenged in light of the experience of the IRI, some have been modified; yet others have been reinforced. While sex segregation is criticized, for instance, inspired by the hegemonic notions of protection and safety for women, some express a sense of relief that "despite everything else," the Islamic Republic has "at least" curbed sexual harassment of women in public. Furthermore, many men do benefit from the prerogatives offered by the Islamic gender ideology. Whether these men embrace other aspects of the Islamic ideology, they may claim an adherence to Islam to justify their role in the family, in their beliefs, or even in certain actions, such as polygyny or temporary marriage, sanctioned by the Islamic law. Or, they may indeed disavow Islam, but appreciate the control over women. For men (and women) believing in traditional moral standards, IRI undertakes the burden of monitoring male-female interactions and ensures that their women do not appear in public wearing "revealing" clothes.

Besides pro-government women's groups that promote various Islamic gender ideologies, there are tendencies that attempt to open a space for women based on reinterpretations of the Islamic doctrine. These women have access to some channels of self-expression (magazines and publishing houses). For some, articulating an Islamic discourse of women's rights stems from a genuine belief; for others, however, being mindful of Islamic values and beliefs is a pragmatic solution. In either case, reinterpreters must bear ideological constraints of prefabricated ideology. Such conditions are a breeding ground for circumscribed theories and practices that have eventually reaffirmed tenets of the dominant gender ideology.

Here we can observe the role of hegemony by surrender. The emergence of a dual society does not denote only the seeping of Islamic values into segments of society previously skeptical about Islam due to gradual adaptation, or what I discuss in chapter 11 as friction and smoothing. Dual society is also accomplished through surrendering to the dominance of Islamism *and* Islam by some active opponents or passive rejecters of the IRI. Deeming Islam as Iranians' inescapable identity, these individuals propose modification of IRI's gender relations as the only viable alternative. *Iranian women*, with their diversity of lives and beliefs, are categorized as *Islamic women*, content with "indigenous" solutions.

Deprived of resources (more readily) available to reformist women, secular activists voice their opinions primarily in independent magazines and anthologies. They find reformist Islamist women's efforts valuable, yet limited; and propose that women combat not only specific predicaments, but "domination generally." They opt for arrangements that guarantee individual choices and combat gender, class, and ethnic inequalities. Women can attain these goals only through a fundamental change in "lifestyle"— that is, in politics, economy, language, ideas, actions, traditions, and through belief in women's abilities. Women's rights are articulated as human rights, unfettered geographically or by cultural idiosyncrasies.

Quietly but steadily, secular oppositional politics have developed through the cracks of the dual society. Despite economic, social, and political barriers, secular women activists have formed collectivities to pursue practical and theoretical objectives—celebrating International Women's Day, organizing cooperatives, campaigning for reforms in gender policies, forming informal study groups, or running small publications. These efforts have also inspired tendencies to revise leftist political culture and cultural politics. These re-readings have inspired fresh assessments of the Iranian culture, civil society, individual rights, and political priorities. This is not to suggest that these discussions have reached clear articulations; most are ongoing controversies, many in embryonic stages. There are also strong debates and differences of opinion. At the present, a major controversy among secular activists concerns the future of the Islamic Republic: some propose cautious, small steps that strengthen Khatami's position vis-à-vis his opponents, while others adhere to more radical politics that would eventually abolish the Islamic system altogether.

Iranian feminists outside Iran have also discussed the dynamics of the 1979 revolution, the structure of patriarchy in Iran, and what is to be done. Though tendencies similar to those of urban women in Iran can also be found abroad, there is a more pronounced—albeit neither uniform nor exclusive—identification of Islam as a key factor in the persistence of patriarchy in Iran. Many women who formerly sided with leftist organizations in their analysis of the "woman question," have reformulated their position. These women are actively involved in Iranian women's groups abroad. They organize meetings, seminars, and demonstrations. They have radio programs, theater performances, or publish magazines and books on the women's movement. Most emphasize the need for an autonomous women's movement.

The Left remains variegated. The life of the Iranian Left in exile has been marked with disunity and decomposition. Frequent splits within organizations and disillusionment of activists have caused the shrinkage of the organized Left. Limited membership has weakened organizational power in both theory-making and actual intervention in politics. Most organizations live mainly on paper and in memory. This situation is a double-edged sword. On the one hand, the decline of the Left's authority has created a breathing space for unorthodox interpretations of the "woman question." On the other, it means the Left's continued weakness in defending women's rights. Though most organizational declarations criticize the subjugation of women under the Islamic Republic and recognize the need for a women's movement in order to eradicate sexual inequality, not much has been discussed beyond that. It is noteworthy, at any rate, that there are efforts on the part of some organized leftists who call for a profound break from the past. The theoretical endeavor of these activists is still too isolated and too nascent to have real consequences. Yet it does indicate an increasing awareness of the depth of gender inequality.

Chapters 2 and 3 discuss the emergence, meanings, practices, and limitations of Islamist women's reformism. What promised to broaden feminist horizons has in fact limited them by aiming to comprehend gender equality within the strictures of the Koran. Chapter 4 delineates the youth problem and development of secular feminism within "dual society": a contradictory lifestyle of public adherence and private subversion. I will discuss in chapter 5 some key questions of cultural politics, especially in relation to cultural innovation, the dialectics of meaning and structure, and the definitions of power and oppression. Chapter 6 summarizes the book and explores some possibilities for the secular development of leftist feminism and cultural politics. However difficult to implement, such advances are essential—a matter of life or no life.

WRITING COERCION AND RESISTANCE

I would like to conclude my introduction by reflecting on the writing of the companionship of *Gender Politics* and *Emerging Voices*. Both volumes are based on the assumption of multiplicity of cultural and gender experiences in Iran. I discuss articulations of the woman question in the Iranian revolution of 1979 and after in the context of changes in gender relations and identities, as different political actors propose conflicting agendas for reshaping gender roles in both public and private spheres. The theories of every social movement are its "working tools" and it is through a critical evaluation of such theories that a movement can come to terms with its strength and weakness. Thus, the primary source of this study is the literature produced by political forces in Iran. This body of literature consists of books, newspapers, pamphlets, and communiqués published by women, the Islamists, and the Left. I also use articles and commentary published in newspapers and popular magazines. I have also been engaged since 1991 in several research projects among Iranian immigrants and refugees in North America and Western Europe, employing participant observation and in-depth interviews. Though systematic analyses of this data are offered elsewhere (Shahidian 1996a; 1997a; 1999b) and in two forthcoming books, I will refer here to my observations when suitable.

In his concise study of revolution, Calvert (1990) discusses the challenging task of observing and interpreting revolution. An illusive phenomenon, often constructed through complex, secret, and difficult-to-measure mechanisms, revolution is a highly contested concept. "Skilled" observers of revolutions (e.g., social scientists), much like their "unskilled" counterparts (journalists, for instance), are often conditioned in their interpretations by intellectual modalities and by wishful thinking. Revolution, Calvert writes, refers to, among other things, "a political *myth*, a story which describes less how things were than what they ought ideally to have been" (17). My analysis, too, should be read in this context.

Like any other interpretation of gender and cultural politics in the Iranian revolution, my analysis emphasizes certain aspects of the revolutionary praxis. In this respect, in both *Gender Politics* and *Emerging Voices*, I am not writing merely about revolution, culture, gender, modernity, and tradition. I am also writing about a *people* whose experience of the 1979 revolution was profoundly disappointing. I am also writing about a *people* who have experienced a love-hate relationship with their culture. I am also writing about a *people* who have experienced a crisis of gender relations in the very fabric of their lives. I am also writing about a *people* as they find their way out of the maze of tradition and modernity. This also implies that this book is written with the benefit of more than two decades of exchanges, debates, and reassessments to which I have also made an infinitesimal contribution. In other words, I am not casting judgment on others; rather I am assessing the accomplishments and failures of a collectivity. Thus, while being objective, I make no claim to neutrality.

Several Iranians have reflected upon *Gender Politics* and *Emerging Voices*, in their entirety or on chapters or passages. Many have contributed to the forming of my thoughts. Some have read this work in English. Some had to rely on my summaries or renditions in Farsi. Contributors include those I have known from childhood and adolescence—such ties keep my relations with the motherland alive. Other ties developed in post-revolutionary days, through mutual intellectual and political concerns. A few relations have emerged with and as a result of this book, through family and friends, but principally in academe and politics. Several contacts resulted from familiarity with my publications; some merely knew that I was researching "about Iranian women." Some of my readers and informants are secular or leftist, but others are non-secular, even ardent believers in Islam and "Islamic Feminism."

These channels cannot of course foster a sustained study, but through them life flows into these pages. Young people have related to me their problems living in a restrictive system. Older people have similarly conveyed their hopes and despairs, supplying detailed information about education, employment, economy, and politics. Examples of these distant informants include highly influential businessmen with close connections to the IRI; university and schoolteachers; governmental employees; employees in the private sector; women in the workforce; housewives; and the village woman whose couplet about housework appears in chapter 10. Activists and scholars have shared with me insights about their lives and struggles in the Islamic state. They have also provided me with information about secretive, or at least unpublicized, developments, trends, and activities.

Invaluable as their lessons are, we must recall the inherent incompleteness of these accounts. This is an evolving process, a history in the making. So, situations change as they are transferred from my mind to the word-processed document. Some changes are encouraging, since they indicate the victories of Iranian women and men in their struggle for freedom and social justice. Other occurrences, however, leave behind a bitter taste. Mohammad Mokhtâri, whom I quoted at the beginning of this chapter–written initially in spring 1997–is now *the late* Mokhtâri, a victim of the winter 1999 chained assassinations by Islamist "vigilantes." In chapter 2 of the present volume, I noted that attorney Mehrangiz Kar was the target of a nasty media campaign. She was subsequently imprisoned. Examples, unfortunately, are not limited to these.

A second reason for the incompleteness of this account is the fragmented and unsystematic recording of events and developments of the marginalized. Gathering such information is constrained in several ways, including the impossibility of establishing contacts with *all* involved parties. When political and intellectual work is accomplished under the shadow of terror, much is concealed from observers' eyes. Sparks of debates appear publicly. Thus, publications summarize or react to internal debates, whose logic may escape the outsider reader. I have tried to investigate these cases to provide more than their mere reflections in this work. But I have not always succeeded. Thus, passages in some chapters may appear choppy. I have decided to leave them so, because I believe it is important to record these fleeting sparks of an unfolding history. In chapter 4, for instance, I allude to a discussion of "women's nature." In context, my reference sounds cryptic and incomplete—indeed the content of this discourse is not yet fully developed. I am concerned to note the fact that "women's nature" is problematized by secular feminists.

To these difficulties, one must also add the challenges of writing about sensitive topics at a time when *any* information could become a liability for individuals living in adverse conditions. To protect the men and women who supplied me with invaluable information, I made sure that what I wrote they read, with their sensitive eyes, trained through living and struggling in the Islamic Republic. They then not only confirmed that details were reflected accurately—that is, that Such and Such was prepared before, though published after, This and That—but they also "desensitized" the text by modifying narratives that disclosed too much. In one instance, I was asked to replace "activists" with the relatively more benign "authors"; in another, I was instructed that the people I was referring to were activists, not authors. I was struck by these informants' diligence in ensuring an accurate portrayal of their lives.

Their care derives not merely from "security" concerns, nor is a matter of meticulous attention to specifics. It also relates to the politics of representation. Before reading *Gender Politics* and *Emerging Voices*, one person asked me "how" she was to read them: as social and political *analyses*, or as political *essays*. Another reader expressed frustration about secular women's absence in recent scholarship abroad. "Maybe they think all secular, leftist individuals have been eradicated, or have left the country. I suppose those of us still here are not worthy of mention." Someone else was concerned about the treatment of "native" women by academic feminists. Writing about Iranian scholars' "fascination" with such discourses as postmodernism and cultural relativism, popular in Western European and North American academia, she commented in a winter 2000 correspondence:

From a distance, I can realize how determinant a person's concern for career can be. I don't think these writings come out of solicitude for the condition of Iranian women—Muslim or non-Muslim. We have become raw data for research by people who conduct their studies in accordance with mainstream [academic] trends; we have become raw data that boost their careers and legitimacy. Consequently, they can draw mind-boggling conclusions—of the sort you [Hammed Shahidian] have quoted—from things even worse than Islam. I think their "eagerness" (as you mentioned) is inspired by popular discourses over there and career goals, not something found inside our female population here.

Whether such impressions are justified (and in some cases, sadly, they are), they indicate the conflicts that influence sociological endeavor in tense political conditions of revolution and exile. Exile sociology, I have argued elsewhere (Shahidian 2000), is quintessentially political. Tensional loyalties make our works polyphonic in the Bakhtinian sense of "a plurality of independent and unmerged . . . fully valid voices" (Bakhtin 1984: 6). We are at once scholars and participants, observers and observed, outsider and insider, objective and partisan.

Though *Gender Politics* and *Emerging Voices* are neither how-to manuals nor proposals of a program of action, they have developed along with myriad other attempts inside and outside Iran to revive and revitalize feminist and leftist movements. Some ideas in these books can be located squarely at the midpoint of ongoing debates over, for instance, evaluations of the Iranian Left and feminism; assessment of gender relations under the IRI; the relationship between Islam and patriarchy, especially Islam and sexuality; the autonomy of the women's movement; and Islamist women's reformism.

Amidst all concerns that trouble us about the future, flickering hopes appear. One recent example is the gradual recognition of the diversity of sexual orientations as a human rights issue. After over 10 years of struggle by immigrant and exiled Iranian gays and lesbians, the silence about homosexuality is broken. In July 1999, an Iranian feminist scholar criticized my insistence on gay and lesbian oppression as an obsession that had no reflection in Iranian politics. When I submitted an article on "Islamic feminism" to the University of Illinois journal *Social Politics*, the editors regarded me as "the only person . . . —inside Iran or out, male or female, Iranian or foreign—who thinks that this is a relevant and important issue for Iranian feminists (secular or religious)." Now, a burgeoning movement has existed among Iranian homosexuals abroad. Their activities, including the publication of *Homan* and its website, have attracted numerous gays and lesbians inside Iran. Also, in 1998, the Iranian Women's Studies Foundation included on its agenda a section on the rights of Iranian homosexuals. In March 2000, *Arash*, a leading exile monthly review of cultural and social affairs, devoted a section to homosexuality as a part of its annual commemoration of International Women's Day. A few months later, Rah-e-Kargar, a major leftist organization in exile, has revised its bylaws to recognize sexual orientation rights. Colleagues from Iran, too, read my discussion of homosexuality in this book without being surprised. In a matter-of-fact manner, they simply provided additional information and specific examples to strengthen my argument.[13] Two decades ago, such actions would have been political suicide. Two years ago, such bravery would have puzzled many, and have disgusted many more. Today, it is deemed an accomplishment. A reason for hope. But still, much work must be done—*so much.*

NOTES

1. For a social history of Pahlavi Iran, see Abrahamian (1982), Halliday (1979), and Keddie (1981). For a sociological overview of social movements in Iran, see Foran (1994).

2. I use "Islamism" and "Islamists" as alternatives to "fundamentalism" and "fundamentalists" to avoid the ambiguities of these terms. I mean by Islamism a political movement to refashion society on the basis of the model portrayed in the Koran and the tradition of the prophet Mohammad.

3. Shortly after the Revolution, a small religious group called Forghan assassinated several top officials of the Islamic government, including Ayatollah Motahari. Khomeini claimed that the assassinations had been masterminded by the USA. After Motahari's assassination, however, the widely circulating *Âyandegân* published a feature article about Forqân and its role in the recent terrorist incidents. The article implied religious opposition to the clergy's increasing political role—and also showed how deeply Forqân was influenced by Shariati's anticlerical ideas. Furious with the blasphemous paper, Khomeini indirectly ordered its closure. He said that while the people should choose their source of information, he would never again read *Âyandegân*. For hizbullah, Khomeini's proclamation was enough reason to attack the paper's office and close it down. For details of the article, see Akhavi (1980, 177–79).

4. Mehdi Bazargan, the first prime minister of post-revolutionary Iran, referred to the intensity of the February uprising as an unwanted flood. "We wanted rain," he said, "we got a flood instead."

5. According to the Tudeh Party, the clergy represented anti-imperialist, radical petit-bourgeoisie. As the leading force of the 1979 revolution, the clergy had to be supported in its anti-imperialist, anti-big-capital orientation. It was to be goaded to strengthen ties with other anti-imperialist states, especially the socialist camp. The Party expected to lead Iran to socialism through this path. The Tudeh revised its evaluation of the state after the arrest of its leaders in the mid-1980s.

6. For detail, see the six-part article by Bagher Parham (1980a–f) in *Ketâb-e Jom'eh*. See also Khoi (1980).

7. For an overview, see Peter Worsley (1984: especially 41–60) and Lawrence Grossberg and Cary Nelson (1988).

8. For a critical discussion of Gramsci's notion of hegemony, see Anderson (1977).

9. This analysis is developed in the works of Laclau and Mouffe (1987).

10. For a discussion of ideology, see Eagleton (1991) and McLellan (1995).

11. Melucci's division is similar to Molyneux's distinction between women's "strategic" and "practical" interests discussed below.

12. Much has been written especially about the relationship between Marxism and feminism. See Barrett (1988); DuBois (1991); Hartmann (1981); Hartmann and Markusen (1980); Kruks, Rapp, and Young (1989); Rowbotham (1973); Sargent (1981); and Segal (1991).

13. Admittedly, this is not a consensus reaction, as many activists and scholars in Iran still have unresolved concerns regarding homosexuality, as sociologist Nahid Moti' points out in an exchange with me (see Shahidian 1998a; Moti' 1998). I intend, however, to emphasize the receptiveness of some activists and scholars in Iran. Direct observation of individuals harmed by prejudice and discrimination seems to raise doubts about cherished cultural values and to undermine predetermined "political priorities."

2

Modifying Patriarchy: Rescuing Women from Allah's Men

> If this Islamic Republic is defeated, it will not be replaced by another one, to the dismay of the Hidden Imam . . . and you gentlemen. On the contrary, it will be a regime that would please both poles of power. And the deprived people of the world who have turned to Islam and Islamic government will be disappointed and Islam will become isolated *forever*. And you gentlemen will regret what you have done when it is too late and being remorseful can no longer accomplish anything.

This is the Ayatollah's warning to the leaders of the Islamic Republic in his political will and testament (Khomeini 1989: 16, emphasis added). His anxiety signifies the life-or-death situation of Islamic movements in Iran, a situation that, as I have analyzed in *Gender Politics*, has been characteristic of these movements from clerical orthodoxy to the "modernist" attempts like those of Shariati and the Mojahedin, dating back to long before the establishment of the IRI. The same sense of urgency explains, at least in part, the ferocious and merciless tactics of these movements in the political arena. Amidst this desperation, much hope has been invested in Iran's Islamic revolution. The revolution was not supposed to bring only a group of clergymen to power; rather, more importantly, it was to rescue a jeopardized belief and its Allah. Yet though the IRI has been successful in maintaining political power, it has faced a great burden in securing the authority of Islam in the sociocultural domain. Many scholars have convincingly argued the revisionist Islamism of the Islamic socioeconomic projects. Some have commented that the Islamic economy does not differ qualitatively from capitalist economy (Rodinson 1981; Rahnema and Nomani 1990; Behdad 1994). Several authors have astutely observed that the very term *Islamic Republic* is self-negating—a republican state is a Western institution that has no precedent or justification in the shari'ah (Tibi 1991; Chehabi 1996). Others have also commented on the pragmatic and ideological challenges of constructing an Islamic state in Iran (see, for example, various articles in Rahnema and Behdad 1995). After two decades of rule, Islamists are still a marginal group in art, literature, humanities, and social sciences (see, for example, Behdad 1994; Mahdi and Lahsaeizadeh 1992). State protection, of course, offers them a great deal of autonomy and power. They have considerable access to resources for publishing and advertising, attending national and international conferences, running academia, launching defamatory campaigns against opponents in the official media—in all these ways creating an atmosphere of fear and vulnerability for the intelligentsia. Despite such influences, they have yet to enjoy acceptability, let alone legitimacy. They are feared and therefore seldom overtly challenged—but never accepted.

Lacking cultural legitimacy, leaders of the IRI have availed themselves of any and all coercive measures to safeguard the Islamic state and its embodied representatives, the clergy. As the public found overt action against the Islamic state fatal, daily conversation became loaded with antiestablishment remarks. People mocked the clergies and criticized the government, in private family gatherings, at workplaces, or in queues for their basic necessities. The government has conceded—talks, so long as not followed by action, can do little harm. But people's commentary did not stop at affairs of the state; it targeted the legitimacy of religious leaders and Islam. Witty remarks and jokes portrayed the leading figures of the Islamic past and the present clerics as opportunistic, greedy, thickheaded, licentious, and unwanted. This portrayal was so widespread and offensive to the clergy as to prompt them to safeguard Islam and its dead and living protagonists. Insulting or taunting religious personalities of Islamic history, including the *Rahbar*, the leaders (that is, both Khomeini and Khamenehii), is now punishable by up to two years' imprisonment in Iran. A cartoonist was imprisoned for drawing a soccer ball that, according to some authorities, resembled Khomeini. The satirical *Ahangar* became a target of Islamic persecution soon after the revolution for its bitter criticism of the IRI's political, social, cultural, and gender policies. Manouchehr Mahjoobi, *Ahangar*'s editor, went first into hiding, then continued to publish the magazine in exile until shortly before his death in 1989. In sharp contrast to *Ahangar*, nowadays one can go through the entire volumes of the satirical *Gol Agha* and nowhere find the smallest hint that Iranian politics is run by the clergy: commentaries—often neither funny nor forcibly critical—make no reference to clerics; cartoons present no statesmen in clerical clothes. Men of the cloth must not be insulted!

And the officials know well that, as an oft-used cliché in the Islamic Republic puts it, "Islam is in danger" (for an example, see Kadivar 1996: 76). This realization has made some Islamists search for new ways of making Islam appealing to the public. Politically, the so-called moderates have tried to implement more relaxed political and economic policies. On the ideological front, "neo-Islamists" ("religious neo-thinkers" or *noandishân-e dini*), which include individuals like Mohsen Kadivar, Akbar Ganji, 'Emâdudin Bâqi, Saeed Hajjâriân, and Abdolkarim Soroush and his circle in the journal *Kiyan*, have argued for a more lenient interpretation of Islam and a more accepting approach to people's behavior. Soroush was a leading ideologue of the Islamic Republic and a member of the council appointed to implement the Islamization of Iranian universities after the brutal purges of 1979, the "cultural revolution." To counter the decline of Islamic allure for a growing number of the youth, he now distinguishes religious feeling and thinking from established religion, especially a religious state—a clear attempt to distance himself and his version of Islam from the IRI (see Miller 1996; Rajaee 1993; and Vakili 1996). Soroush's criticism has cost him the support of the Islamic Republic; indeed, it has turned him into a target of hizbullah. But some university students have found Soroush appealing. His appeal is understandable, considering that secular critics of the regime or its defected ideologue find limited chance of public debate; in the thick atmosphere of censorship and terror, a moderate vision that is not too remote from the dominant ideology to be perilous, yet distant enough to be independent, is a familiar, attractive, and safe alternative. His followers capitalize on his knowledge of Western philosophers like Kant, Popper, and Fromm to portray him as an open-minded, critical Islamic thinker.

But the Islamists' rescue attempt only partially explains the emerging thoughts in Iran. Giddens' discussion of the changing character of religious belief in conditions of modernity offers us once again an insight into this critical approach to Islam by the believer. We recall Giddens' suggestion that the force of doubt in modern society repels some people from total surrender to religion, while attracting others to an authoritative interpretation of social life. Yet even in the extreme cases of religious submission, Giddens points out, authority is not unquestioned, as religious authorities have to share their "authority" with several other "authorities" in modern society (1991: 195–96).

Moreover, as discussed in the previous chapter (and more fully in *Women in Iran: Gender Politics in the Islamic Republic*), the Islamic Republic has not been successful in keeping women entirely out of the skilled labor market. These women are in a peculiar condition: on the one hand, they are under patriarchal limitations; on the other, they enjoy a certain degree of privilege. Consequently, many of these women have the leverage to negotiate with the Islamic-Iranian patriarchy. With the traditional bargain no longer acceptable, and public patriarchal relations largely contested, these women opt for a modern bargain with patriarchy. They seek a share of the labor market, a controlled patriarch in the house, and regulated and more relaxed surveillance of sexual morality. In return, they curb their gender criticism and offer a mild, nonthreatening "feminist" modification. These women play a vital role in translating women's demands into an Islamic language.

We have seen in *Gender Politics* how the former route has forced some Muslim women into acceptance of Islamic interpretations of gender relations. We have observed that the IRI's gender project has focused to consolidate individual men's authority in family and society by containing the tides of public patriarchy. As I will discuss in the following two chapters, reformist Islamist women's proposed adjustments in patriarchal structure resist this reversal in favor of a public and regulated control of gender relations. In this chapter I will examine how belief in Islam does not preclude a critique of it, inspired by, to borrow from Giddens, the "indefinite pluralism of experience" (195). Drawing upon their experience in the Islamic Republic of Iran, female believers have questioned the very authorities who embody their faith. In this chapter, I will discuss reformist Islamist women's proposals for puncturing holes in the Islamic dam.

Before proceeding with the discussion, however, I need to make a clarification. My treatment of the gender analyses in post-revolutionary Iran under the umbrella of Islamist women's reformism in the next two chapters admittedly gives these attempts a homogeneity that does not always exist. I am well aware that several people who contribute to these discussions do not have Islamic or even religious inclinations, as I discuss in more detail below. Yet I feel obligated to refer to them as reformist Islamist women to highlight a crucial aspect of the cultural politics of gender in the Islamic regime of Iran. As long as gender analyses take shape within the ideological, political, or moral parameters of the Islamic tradition, pivotal concepts such as gender, sex, sexuality, and patriarchy are bound to be distorted. The distortion could be due to a belief in Islam, either as an impervious set of predefined laws and sanctions, or as a system of unsubstantiated assumptions about the general order of being. The distortion may be equally due to the limited parameters of acceptable discourse (e.g., the near impossibility of discussing homosexuality or premarital sexual relationships, especially for women, as legitimate expressions of sexuality). Until the time comes that gender can be articulated free from such limitations, I have to— at least analytically—consider all discourses that are forced, or accept to work within these parameters as Islamic reformism. I do, however, frequently distinguish among various shades of this trend.

GENDER AGONY AND GENDER BLISS

Islamists' triumph over other contenders of the revolution has meant the erection of a patriarchal triad with the primary objective of reversing what women had gained in prerevolutionary Iran. Changes in the Iranian legal system under the IRI have predominantly focused on regaining men's threatened prerogatives in marriage, divorce, and family relationships. The central ideological motif of these changes has been a "naturally constructed" binary opposition of complementary gender identities. According to this gender ideology, men's natural right is to be the "head of the household" and their "natural" duty, to provide for the family. Women, on the other hand, have the "undeniable right of women to be mothers," while enjoying the luxury of being provided for and protected by their men.

Yet both men and women of the Pahlavi society had proved quite inept at dealing with the machination of modernity. Beguiled by Western fascinations, women, ignorant of their rights and duties, abandoned their homes and embraced a licentious life. To ward off the intervention of these untrustworthy subjects, and with the objective of creating ideal Muslim men and women, a paternal Islamic state has intervened since the revolution. The Islamic state compels men and women to abide by the gender laws of the Islamic state, a task that ideally individual men had to undertake in their households.

One role of the Islamic Republic is to guarantee the sanctity of the family and the rule of morality. Examples of this role of the state are abundant in post-revolution Iran. The moral police monitoring women's compliance with mandatory hejâb or controlling members of the opposite sex so they interact under legitimate and morally acceptable conditions are prime instances of such a state function. This role is clearly stipulated in official documents.

But prerevolutionary changes in gender relations have taken root, making the rhetoric of the Islamic state about women's domestic role in a patriarchal family unappealing to several people. The vast participation of women in the revolution and the Islamist leadership's approval of women's public presence—albeit "in the service of Allah"—further raised women's expectations of their role in post-revolution society. But, as discussed in *Gender Politics*, the IRI has failed to meet the expectations of even some of its Islamist advocates. In employment, education, civil and punitive law, culture, and politics the Islamic state cannot offer women the noble status it has promised.

This condition leads to agonizing tensions. Muslim women who have invested a great deal in their Islamic republic find themselves caught between a rock and a hard place. Voicing their Islamic criticism of a state of affairs that claims exclusive Islamic legitimacy, these women anger Islamist male leaders, especially those who adhere to a gender ideology that unabashedly upholds private patriarchy. Reformist Islamist women echo the criticism and resistance of those who over the past two decades have been a sore spot for the IRI.

Gender agony in the IRI, then, results from a confrontation between two resolute opponents. One, having state and religion at its disposal, attempts to bring into reality an ideal gender structure. The other, with minimal official access to power, resists, defies, and revolts against the imposed order. The relationship is agonizing because both parties experience defeat despite their power. In post-revolution Iran, patriarchy enjoys state sanction, religious blessing, and traditional justification. Yet it has been unable to fully implement its ideals. Those undertaking the patriarchal crusade against women realize that their regime is endured, not accepted. Those who resist patriarchal dominance must tailor their lives to dance around the minefield of rules and regulations. That they do not subscribe to the ideal gender is a thorn in the side of the ruling regime and, more importantly, an inspiration for not only women, but also everyone else opposed to the order. One scholar has made the following observation about the veil act in the theater of the Islamic Republic:

Given that the conservative style is the norm in government institutions and in public places generally, those who choose the unorthodox style are accentuating the role of silent dissident that they are playing. Moreover, when these same women switch to the orthodox style out of expediency, they are putting on even more of an "act" since they are assuming a role they do not usually play. Once they leave the "theater" of the government office, however, and they are not being watched by the audience of the Komiteh [revolutionary guards], they no longer have to play in that particular act. They can leave that assumed identity and resume their usual roles and their preferred attire for different audiences (their families, for example). (Shirazi-Mahajan 1995: 50)

But there are also many women who support the IRI, and still many more who, regardless of their assessment of the government, adhere to (some version of) Islamic gender ideology. The Islamic regime has enhanced the economic power of the bazaar to which Khomeini referred frequently as the "pillar of the Islamic Revolution." The purchasing power of women from merchant families has consequently improved. The IRI has also nurtured a new class of Muslim rich. These improvements become particularly significant when compared to the diminishing financial status of the modern middle and working classes. The younger generation of these women has been mobilized to fill various positions—sometimes even without proper qualifications. Others have been mobilized in the various governmental organs responsible for upholding public morality. They not only are no longer the "backward" members of the Pahlavi society, but also can determine how others should behave. It also means that they no longer have to be confined within the four walls of the house; as devout Muslim women, they can participate in social life as long as it is within the boundaries of an Islamic society.

Not unlike other revolutionary states (Skocpol 1994), the Islamic Republic has mobilized women believers to promote its political agenda, especially in displaying support for the Iran-Iraq war. Nonetheless, coming to terms with Islamic gender ideology is not easy even for Islamist women. These women are elated by a rhetoric that claims acceptance of women's capabilities and promises to elevate their status in society. Numerous women have taken part in the implementation of the misogynous policies of the Islamic Republic regime, belying the conviction of some feminists about the moral superiority of women.

In practice, however, these believers face the limitations of a gender ideology that rests on fundamentally patriarchal premises. Some of these women face the contradictions of IRI's egalitarian claims and its practice. Although the government maintains that Islam grants women equal opportunity and encourages them to participate in the affairs of the society, there are numerous obstacles before those women who desire a more active life. These constraints have generated criticisms even among women closely affiliated with the government (see, for example, Sciolino 1997). Among the rural or urban poor, this conflict becomes more pronounced for younger women as their access to education and new social experiences increases their expectations. This contradictory process of mobilizing women under the aegis of Islam, and at the same time casting doubt about how women are treated in (Islam and) an Islamic state, reveals another aspect of the gender agony. The bliss of gender creates tensions in the loyalty of the blessed. In other words, as Giddens puts it, in modern times, even religious authority "is no longer an alternative to doubt" (1991: 195).

THE EMERGENCE OF ISLAMIST WOMEN'S REFORMISM

The discrepancy between the promises of better life for women and the realities of the Islamization project is especially troublesome for those women who have turned to Islam in search of sexual equality. Now a system that was to liberate them, praises on the one hand, and discriminates against them on the other. Melucci qualifies the conditions under which discrepancy between expectation and reward could lead to collective action:

Without an actor able to define its own identity, without a relation of opposition in which the actor is located as one of the poles, and without a field from which is derived the meaning of what the actor fights for or feels it has been deprived of—without an adequate account of these, establishing a link between expectations and rewards and, especially, explaining why collective actors mobilize themselves is impossible. (Melucci 1996a: 59)

To be sure, the "generic and abstract" discrepancy between expectations and rewards, as Melucci (1996a: 59–60) points out, could not by itself account for any collective action. After all, a great number of men have also reacted to their portrayal in the IRI gender ideology, especially in the reduction of all contacts between them and women to a sexual one (see, for example, Mousavi 1994). Yet male believers who have acknowledged the gap dividing IRI's gender promises from realities, do not necessarily consider it discriminatory. ʿAbbâs ʿAbdi of the newspaper *Salâm*, for example, believes that women's legal and social dilemma in post-revolutionary Iran is due to a "backwardness" of Iran's legal system—a system that wants to remain loyal to the edicts of the days of the Prophet, yet faces the challenges of a modern day state. "Our legal system," he proposes, "is not discriminatory, it is 'backward' " (*Zanân* 1997a: 15).

But a number of factors have turned women's discontent into a concerted effort. Disenchanted female believers and the IRI share a common belief system, thus these women's grievances regarding what they consider un-Islamic treatment of women under IRI are defined in terms that are rooted in their shared frame of reference (Kadivar 1996, see especially the intro-duction and 69–78). Besides, this different treatment is experienced at the time of a strong public discussion around women's rights (see, for example, *Zanân* 1997a). Furthermore, interaction with outside societies and the chal-lenges and criticisms of the international community and immigrant and exiled Iranians regarding women's status in the Islamic Republic have made the issue ever more sensitive. Kadivar, for instance, reflects on her experi-ence at the 1995 Beijing Conference that "the wave of women's awakening has shaken up the world" (Kadivar 1996: 99). She then poses a crucial question:

Why should women have such a misfortune, or better put, why were they put in this position? To the extent that we need to have international conferences to im-prove their living condition—where [*sic*] we, as Muslims claiming to have the best and the most complete religion in regards to valuing and respecting women, voice a similar concern about the unjust treatment of women and propose plans for ameliorating this situation? (100)[1]

Mindful of the precarious status of women in the Islamic Republic of Iran, a group of individuals have called in recent years for some changes in gender policies. To guarantee its leading role until the day of resurrec-tion, Islam, they contend, must be compatible with contemporary social and cultural developments (Kermânshâhi 1993a: 56).[2] They seek a gender ideology, purportedly on the basis of a reinterpretation, or a "correct in-terpretation," of the Koran and the Islamic shariʿah, that opts to increase women's access to social, cultural, economic, and political resources (Ka-divar 1996: 11–16). This trend has emerged around a few journals such as *Zan-e Rouz*, *Farzaneh*, *Zanân*, and *Hoquq-e Zanân*. Of these, *Zan-e Rouz* and *Farzaneh* show more explicit support for the Islamic Republic. *Zan-e Rouz* originally appeared in the mid-sixties and was considered a women's weekly in a tradition similar to *Cosmopolitan* and *Mademoiselle*, publishing fashion tips, social gossips, cooking tips, self-help guides, personal and legal advice, and literature. After the revolution, *Zan-e Rouz* gained an Islamicized form. Since its rebirth, *Zan-e Rouz* has remained loyal to the IRI (Eskandari 1988: 7–8), and its criticism of the Islamic government has been directed at specific agencies or practices. One example of this orientation is the discussion about a bill that limited women's education abroad only to married women who are accompanied by their husbands. *Zan-e Rouz*'s editorial criticized the bill for limiting opportunities for higher education for the unmarried, divorcées, widows, and barren women "who do not have the opportunity to remarry" (*Zan-e Rouz*: 1985). On another occasion, the editorial of the magazine criticizes IRI's Sound and Vision (radio and TV) for portraying a negative picture of women and presenting them as the source of all social ills (*Zan-e Rouz*: 1989). *Farzaneh* is published by the Center for Women's Studies and Research, comprising women like Massoumeh Ebtekar, Mahboobeh Abbas-Gholizadeh (Ommi), and Moneer Gorgi who have been prominent figures in the IRI politics and cultural scene. Mahboobeh Abbas-Gholizadeh, the editor of *Farzaneh*, initially wrote in *Zan-e Rouz*. *Zanân* has no official tie to the Islamic government; it is, however, supportive of Soroush. Its editor, Shahlâ Sherkat, also initially worked with *Zan-e Rouz*, but later broke alliance with that journal and published *Zanân*. Directed initially to "students and professional, employed women," the magazine now intends to bridge the gap between "the middle stratum of the society and the more enlightened, educated group" of women (Sherkat 1991b: 3). Shahin Gerami, the editor of *Hoquq-e Zanân*, also worked for several years with *Zan-e Rouz*.

Islamist women's reformism must also be viewed in the larger context of controversies among Islamists regarding how to rule. Islamists have subscribed to divergent paths on dealing with a society that nears the boiling point from the heat of suppression. The conservative ideologues—characterized in the Iranian press as the "traditionalist right," "monopolists," and "power-seekers"—backed by the Supreme Leader Ayatollah Khamenehii, see the solution in harsher control, closing even the tiniest open space. Another orientation, led by the President Khatami and broadly known as the *jebheh-ye dovum-e khordâd* (the May 23rd Front),[3] proposes to protect the rule of Islam by allowing a wider range of tolerance. Hoping to gain the initially desired cultural and moral leadership of a considerable majority, Khatami seeks to gain legitimacy for the Islamic system through "giving freedom" in his proposed "Islamic civil society." In December 1997, in his opening address to the Islamic Leaders' Conference in Tehran, Khatami states:

In the civil society we envision, though the axis and circle of thought and culture is Islamic, there would be no sign of individual or group tyranny, or even the dictatorship of majority in an effort to dissolve the minority. In that society, human beings are revered and honored as human beings and their rights are respected. The citizens of the Islamic civil society will have the power to determine their destiny (haqq-e ta'iin-e sarnevesht) and control over the management of their affairs and hold authorities accountable. The government in such a society is the people's servant, not their master and must answer to the people whom God has given sovereignty over their lives. (Kayhan Havâ'i 17 December 1997 [vizhehnâmeh]: 3)

The promise of less control by Khatami and his supporters has attracted the support of reformist Islamist women (see Zanân, 43). To overcome the limits of the Islamic law, some reformist ideologues like Sa'idzâdeh have argued that Islam merely defines the general borders of social life. Far from constituting social practices, fiqh, or the Islamic law, merely "reflects" popular beliefs and practices. Fiqh, he argues, can then easily accommodate social change if they do not contradict the broad precepts of Islam. "Since women's presence and participation [in society] is an entirely social issue, it is up to their discretion. If women step forward on their own volition (and men welcome them too), fiqh cannot bar their presence" (Sa'idzâdeh 1998: 10). Such a distinction leads Sa'idzâdeh to deny any disharmony between Islam and civil society:

There is no conflict between civil society and Islamic society. Because, when we talk about Islamic society, we mean a society in which people's individual and religious (fardi-'ebâdi) life is organized based on Islam. And by civil society is meant a community of people who manage their public life on the basis of collective responsibilities and rights. (63)

It is difficult to assess the influence of reformist Islamist women in the Iranian politics in the absence of empirical evidence. But reformist Islamist women and the "moderates" or "reformists" faction of the IRI have been mutually supportive. Such a relationship has undermined the autonomy of reformist Islamist women, making women's gains contingent upon the regime's internal conflicts. For example, after the election of President Khatami in 1997, the "conservative" Majlis representatives passed laws to segregate hospital services, forbid using pictures of women on magazines' front pages, and curtail discussions of women's rights outside the shari'ah. Some women activists, like Shirin Ebadi and Mehrangiz Kar, have received death threats; Kar and Lâhiji were imprisoned in spring 2000; and Mohsen Sa'idzâdeh has been defrocked.

Though authors associated with this trend have not yet explicitly identified themselves as "Islamic feminists," several scholars inside and outside Iran have referred to them as such. As I have discussed elsewhere (Shahidian 1993a), I consider this term an oxymoron. Though in earlier works I used the term, in this book I will refer to this trend as Islamist women's reformism. I do so because a reformist Islamist trend has emerged in Iranian politics with the explicit intention of reforming the Islamic state and modifying the extremism that prevailed since its inception. Reformist Islamist women have been a part of this movement. In addition to this political congruency, the term "Islamic feminism" has been used with great reluctance by these activists. In fact, Shahlâ Sherkat, the editor of *Zanân*, has doubted the clarity of such a mixture (see Sherkat's interview with *Avaye Zan* no. 40, Summer 2000: 42). By "Islamist women's reformism" I mean attempts, in government, the academy, or the media to articulate women's demands for sexual justice in Islamic ideological or institutional frameworks.

Like other movements, Islamist women's reformism unites a number of convergent streams. Some are led by token women in the higher echelons of the Islamic government, including relatives of prominent political figures. Despite their few-and-far-between (though always mild) criticisms of Iran's laws and culture, they basically promote the IRI and its gender policies, attributing the problem to some "inauthentic" interpretations of Islam by "traditional, backward" individuals. Others have adopted a more critical approach, growing careworn about the future of Islam's claim to liberate women of the "Islamic world." Offering new interpretations of Islam, these authors have attempted to save Islam from masculinist "misconceptions." And there are others still, nonreligious thinkers trapped in the confinements of an Islamic state, who seek a space for their criticisms. To avoid censorship and censure, they shroud their ideas in an Islamic discourse, or at least a discourse that does not overtly and fundamentally challenge Islam. Thus the term "Islamic feminism," even if legitimate, remains problematic because it applies to a heterogeneous group with diverse objectives—hence I place the term in quotation marks. I will reflect further on this issue in the following chapter. These women seek an "indigenous" feminism and, emphasizing the heavy weight of the Islamic culture, propose that changes in gender relations could be achieved through modernizing Islamic discourses on gender. In effect, as I will argue in chapters 2 and 3, this reformist trend proposes a new bargain with the Islamic triad whereby, in exchange for curtailing private patriarchy and a guarantee of (some) public roles for women, the pillars of Islam are left secured and women fulfill their familial tasks and moral obligations.

REINTERPRETING ISLAM

If, as reformist Islamist women contend, Islam is the answer for sexual oppression, the immediate challenge before them is to explain why an overwhelming majority of Muslim women have little freedom and equality in Muslim societies. If an Islamic system could guarantee women sexual equality and human dignity, why are women in the IRI treated as inferiors, deprived of some fundamental human rights? Answers to these paradoxes should be sought, according to reformist Islamist women, in the *incorrect interpretations* of the Koran and other Islamic teachings. The argument could be so summed up: as the rule of the Islamic world fell into the hands of hypocrites—which, according to Shiites, happened immediately following the death of the Prophet and the usurpation of power by Abu Bakr, the first caliph—Islamic states became the home of corrupt men who enslaved women in the name of religion. In order to guarantee women's rights in the contemporary world, we must reinterpret Islamic scripts and laws and put aside the discriminatory interpretations of earlier jurists and religious scholars.

The fundamental task of the reformist Islamist women, then, is to offer a new interpretation of the Koran and other Islamic scripts and to revise those aspects of Islamic fiqh[4] that explicitly speak against women.

Much of the discussion on gender relations in Islam revolves around verse 34 of the sura *Women*:

Men have authority over women because Allah has made the one superior to the other, and because they spend their wealth to maintain them. Good women are obedient. They guard their unseen parts because Allah has guarded them. As for those from whom you fear disobedience, admonish them and send them to beds apart and beat them. Then if they obey, you take no further action against them. (Koran 1988: 370)

According to reformist interpretation, this verse is descriptive, not normative: "This verse by no means refers to men's superiority over women, but reminds of the status of married men and husbands, and reveals a social reality and men's position in marital life. Besides, this verse does not refer to single or widowed women and men" (Yâdgâr-Âzâdi 1992a: 20).

If we read the verse in the context of a marital relationship, husbands will have authority over their wives, but not all men over all women. "The verse refers to married women and calls them to fulfill their familial task" (21). The author dismisses a similar argument on the basis of verse 228 of the sura *Cow*: "Women shall with justice have rights similar to those exercised against them, although men have a status above women" (Koran 1988: 456). If we assume that managing the family is an innate characteristic of men, then current practices of divorce, wife battery, men's reluctance to do household chores all will be nothing but logical results.

Hojjatulislam Hassan Yousefi Eshkevari argues that in verse 34 of the sura *Women*, men should be treated as women's "keepers," *negahdâran-deh*, not superiors. And "men-as-keepers," he contends, is different from "men-as-bosses:" though women need a protector; they do not need a boss or guardian (see his interview in *Avaye Zan* Summer 2000: 52).

In a manner similar to Yâdgâr-Âzâdi and Eshkevari, Mohsen Qâ'eni refutes the argument that men are chiefs of the home. That notion of family, he emphasizes, treats men as royalties and reflects traditions of pre-Islamic Arabia. Thus, what is reflected in the said verse is merely a description of social customs. Early Islam accepted that custom without substantially modifying it since social conditions were not ready. But Islam did propose certain regulations and conditions for punishing wives. Qâ'eni (1994a: 56) cites a number of hadiths (narratives about the lives of the Prophet and Shiite leaders of rthe early Islam) in which the Prophet frowns on physical abuse: "Do you not embrace your wives with love? Then why beating?" "Keep your whip visible in the house; it will be more effective for chastisement." "The Prophet prohibited men to beat their wives. When the men complained, the Prophet said: 'The good ones will not.' " Based on these evidences, Qâ'eni makes the following conclusion:

Islam tries to solve disputes through advice and logic. It then suggests indirect means, like *qahr*, refusal to talk. Finally, it employs threats. In marital discords, the attempt is to achieve a resolution through advice and *qahr*. Then, in accordance with the common interpretation, it has offered the option of beating to men, not as a means that should be used, but as a threat. If even that does not prove fruitful, one should resort to beating. (57–58)

Islam's recommendation about beating is merely guidance, not dogma one must obey (58). In part 2 of the article, Qâ'eni discusses interpretations of different Islamic authorities on how and under what conditions men should punish their wives. All these, however, are unacceptable to Qâ'eni, because they rest on a mistaken definition of the Arabic word, *zaraba*. According to Qâ'eni, *zaraba* in Arabic has several meanings: to turn away, to prohibit, to stay in the house, to change, and to have sex. On the basis of these options, he proposes that the real meaning of verse 34 of the sura *Women* should be as follows: "There are three kinds of disobedient wives. One group will mend their ways by advice. The second will realize their wrongdoing through *qahr*, the husband's refusal to talk or sleep with them. The third should be caressed and made love to, to change their ways" (Qâ'eni 1994b: 72). *Zaraba*, then, really means to caress and make love to, not to beat. Another reading of the same verse recommends that by *zaraba*, the Koran meant modifying the woman's action with the hope of her return to normal, peaceful behavior.

The objective is not at all to frighten her or to rough her up to intimidation [*sic*], as the idea that a man would be able to beat up his wife in any way he desires in order to chastise her, that he would act as [judge and] executioner of the law is principally in conflict with Islam's humanitarian goals and its value for women. (Shokri and Labriz 1991: 63)

When sexual equality is recognized, then there is no reason to deny women decision-making roles in society. Women are argued to qualify to issue *ijtihâd*,[5] as there is nothing in the Koran or the hadiths that forbids women from playing such a role (Yâdgâr-Âzâdi 1992c). Against those who oppose such a role for women on the basis of women's household responsibilities, Yâdgâr-Âzâdi comments that "hejâb and household chores are admirable duties" (26), but these do not preclude women from performing in society. "A woman's work outside the house and deprivation of husband and children from their rights [of benefiting from her services] are not interdependent. This is in case she is married; single and elderly women [divorcées and widowed?] should not be barred on this basis" (26). At any rate, he argues, *ijtihâd* and *iftâ'* (issuing *fatwa* or religious decrees) should be distinguished from judging, because women can issue *fatwa* even from the privacy of their home. Furthermore, it is preferable that women turn to women for answers, which precludes issues of propriety. "Why ought a woman learn about regulations regarding menstruation and ablution from a man? What could be the problem if another woman teaches her on these issues?" So, if men and women are equal, there is no need to turn down a woman for the position of *marja'-e taqlid* (leader of the believing community)—except, of course, for "certain interests" (*masâleh*):

If a woman, with beautiful face and beautiful voice, wants to lead a man in the public prayer (*namâz-e jamâ'at*), and if that intervenes with the objective of prayer . . . [complete devotion and closeness to God], that woman may not be permitted to perform. But in all other cases, she may. (26)

Can women be judges? Minâ Yâdgâr-Âzâdi responds in the affirmative. Those Muslim jurists and scholars who deny women's ability for judgeship—that is, the majority of Islamic jurists throughout history—misinterpret the Koran. They interpret, Yâdgâr-Âzâdi argues, verse 34 of the sura *Women* to mean that all men are by nature superior to all women. As such, Yâdgâr-Âzâdi goes on, they deny that a woman could judge the actions of those superior to her (1992a: 20). But this verse, according to Yâdgâr-Âzâdi, is descriptive, not normative, and cannot support a categorical claim that women cannot be judges.

Another hurdle before accepting women as judges is guidance by Imam Ali:

O People! Women suffer from three deficiencies, of faith, of mind and of share in heritage. Their deficiency in religion is apparent from the fact that at certain times they keep away from prayers and fastings, deficiency of mind could be gauged from the circumstance that two female witnesses are considered equal to one male, and deficiency in shares of heritage is plain from the incident that their share is equal to half of the share of male members.

Keep yourself away from the wiles of wicked women and do not indulge too much even in good ones, do not blindly follow their advices even in good deeds so that they may not be tempted to lead you towards bad ones. (Ali ibn Abi Talib 1971: 173)

Islamic Jurists have conventionally interpreted this as Imam Ali's testimony to women's inadequate intellect (*kherad*). The author once again relies on semantic reasoning to argue in favor of women's judgeship:

By intellect ('*aql*) is meant thought (*andisheh*) because women are not tolerant in "enduring" their testimony and they are probably more forgetful than men. They also lack forceful thinking to analyze events and emotions, and feelings make them change their mind. (Yâdgâr-Âzâdi 1992b: 23)

Regarding the notorious Law of Retribution,[6] the author favors equal punishment for both men and women on the basis of their equality. This approach, the author contends, could prove pragmatically sound: "If the payment of blood money is abolished, several difficulties for female victims' families will be resolved and numerous murderers who are currently in prison because their victims' families do not have the resources to pay for their blood money will be punished according to the law of Retribution" (Kermânshâhi 1993b: 43).

One of my theoretical underpinnings in this book is that failure to rupture with the Islamic discourse has played a pivotal role in the failure of the leftist and women's movements in Iran to articulate alternative sociopolitical agendas—that the use of value-laden concepts has created an ambiguous theoretical terrain for social movements, giving rise to ideological confusions and practical ineffectiveness. In the following chapter, I will argue that far from presenting a liberating alternative for women, reformist reinterpretations of Islam diminish the rigor of feminist theory and praxis.

WOMEN IN SOCIETY AND FAMILY

Top on the reformist Islamist women's agenda has been provision of legal protection for women in social and familial spheres. In the social arena, reformist Islamist women have demanded primarily the power to occupy judgeships—though in fact, they have rejected all limitations on women's employment. One article in the first issue of *Zanân*, for instance, points out that though women's numbers in educational and health-related fields have increased after the revolution, they have had drastic losses in the private sector (Bâqeriân 1991: 6). The majority of women, Mitrâ Bâqeriân points out, are employed in unskilled labor or professions that rely on women's traditional roles in the family. A minuscule portion of women workers occupies managerial positions. Sherkat points out the findings of a study on women's employment in governmental offices (see Sharifi 1991) that between 1976 and 1986, women comprised only 12% of the governmental employees. Of these, only 18% have higher education and a meager three percent have managerial positions. Such a condition, she emphasizes, is adversarial to any progress in women's social status:

Education and employment, especially in important and distinguished managerial positions, provide the main context for women's intellectual and social progress, since if she finds no place to manifest and prove her capabilities, she will remain the same weak, incomplete creature in the public eye that now appears in our media. (Sherkat 1991b: 3)

Reformist Islamist women also criticize the unequal access of women to education. Though the literacy campaign has reduced the number of illiterate women across the board, Zhâleh Shâditalab emphasizes that since some 15% of girls between the ages of six and nine in rural Iran do not attend schools, Iran will have at least one more generation of uneducated mothers (Shâditalab 1995: 7). She also points out that the educational system does not prepare rural girls to enter the economic sector as skilled labor. Women are underrepresented in higher education as both students and personnel. Shâditalab points out that women's presence in technical and engineering fields is markedly low (8). Research conducted by Shamsussâdât Zâhedi at three major universities in Tehran (University of Tehran, Shahid Beheshti University, and ʿAllâmeh Tabâtabâʾi University) concluded that women professors constantly face discriminations in various aspects of their work (Zâhedi 1995). Related work at the Institute for Cultural Studies and Research–Social Science Group (1993) shows that women's presence in primary-level textbooks is limited; that as children read more advanced books, the representation therein of women as skillful professionals declines. Shâditalab considers the lack of portrayal of women in textbooks harmful to the development of mothers who should encourage their children to learn and advance. When women are excluded from textbooks as professionals, they are not taken seriously and they in turn will not value professional development in their children (Shâditalab 1995: 8).

Along with calling for changes in educational and employment policies, reformist Islamist women have demanded a greater share of political life. Rosâ Eftekhâri provides a picture of women's presence in the parliaments of various nations. Throughout the world, she reports, women occupy, on the average, some 11.6% of seats in the parliament. However, in Iran women have constituted less than 4% of the parliament since the revolution—1.5% in the first three Majlises and 3.5% in the Fourth Majlis (Eftekhâri 1995). In the spring of 1996, members of the Fifth Majlis were elected. Ten out of 231 representatives are women (for biographies of female representatives, see *Zanân* 1996c). Fâezeh Hashemi, daughter of for-

mer President Hashemi Rafsanjani, founder and director of the Coordinating Council of Women's Sport in Islamic Countries and head of
Iran's Olympic Committee, earned over 852,000 votes, the highest number
among Tehran candidates, except the Speaker of Majlis, Nâteq Nouri.[7]
Reformist Islamist women also call for an official recognition of women's
eligibility to become presidents, arguing that the qualification of *rejâl* in
the IRI's Constitution should be understood as an experienced and well-
known political figure, not as "man" (see various interviews and commentaries in *Zanân* 34 and 35). A recent poll by the Group to Assess Future
Ideas indicates that over 62% of respondents supported the notion of a
woman becoming president, the majority of supporters being female and
young (1997). None of the women candidates for presidency, however, was
considered eligible by the Council of Guardians.

But even the most liberal policy toward women's education, employment,
and political involvement immediately proves inadequate if familial relationships do not undergo a similar revision. We recall that Article 1105 of
the IRI's Civic Code grants men the position of head of household. This
provision has been a sour point between scores of Iranian women and the
Islamic government. Such a monopoly will render women's other legal
gains meaningless. Were a woman elected president, she would still need
her husband's permission to go to her office. She might occupy a high
position in the country's politics, but the head of her household will be her
husband. Women have vehemently opposed these blatant violations of their
human rights. Reformist Islamist women have voiced these concerns for
restoring women's rights in the family. This project entails a twofold effort:
a long-term goal that requires educating new generations and forming new
cultural patterns; and a short-term and more easily achievable goal of legal
reforms in family relations (Zâhedi 1993: 5). Kar also emphasizes the crucial implication of the ideological orientation of the ruling clergy in this
process:

Even if the Constitution has regarded women and men as equal, as long as political
leaders do not believe that women and men are equally qualified and able to run
the country, or that they have similar abilities in the context of family life, they
will interpret the Constitution in a way that will not benefit women's rights. (*Zanân*
1997a: 13–14)

The contemporary Iranian family is evolving. Modernization, cultural
interaction with the West, state interventions, migration from rural to urban areas, the development of a middle class, all have profoundly changed
Iranian families. Family is ever more incorporated into the public sphere.
Individuals derive their identities first and foremost from belonging to a
nation, instead of identifying themselves exclusively with their families. Interpersonal relations in families have also changed. Men have lost their

monopoly of power; husbands and wives have a more personalized relationship; relatives and family members have become less influential in their
affairs; and parents have to contend with rebellious teenagers (Farid 1992).
Women are educated about family law and instructed that they could stip-
ulate some of their marital rights, such as their ability to divorce or being
permitted to leave the house or continue with their education, at the time
of signing the marriage contract. (See, for example, five short volumes on
this subject by the Research Group on Women's Issues 1996.) To bring the
law into agreement with these real social changes, once again reformist
Islamist women rely on alternative interpretations of the Koran. A case is
made for the equality of men and women based on verse 13 of the sura
Chambers: "The noblest of you in Allah's sight is he who fears Him most"
(Koran 1988: 275). Allah considers both men and women equally human.
The only distinction among human beings is between the pious and the
impious. "In understanding the generalities of existence and comprehension
of religion, men and women are equal and each could gain over the other"
(Shokri and Labriz 1992: 27). In the same tradition as Motahari, Shokri
and Labriz point out that "the differences between women and men, without pointing to the superiority of one over the other, is due to the propor-
tional relationship of creation" (27).

As to verse 34 of the sura *Women*, the authors favor defining *qavâm* not
as "to be superior," but as "to stand." Thus, they suggest, the verse should
be translated as "men are standing to serve women," instead of "men are
superior to, or in charge of, women" (28). As heads of household, that is,
as people who provide for the family, men actually serve the family. In
other words, their economic ability is a source of obligation and burden,
not power. "A boss is not master or superior. . . . The chief of a group is
their servant" (28). Authors clarify that they see no need to speak of family
in terms of boss (*re'is*) and employee (*mar'us*), and that Article 1105 should
be limited to economic provision for the family. In other areas of family
life, such as childrearing, which require a woman's input, the notion of
men as sole decision-makers should be abandoned. They also oppose regarding men's role as heads of the household as their innate characteristic
(31). Qâ'eni goes so far to view men's rule over the family as contingent—
as men's and women's familial and social roles change, men's rule must
also alter (1994a: 55).

In a review of Âzari-Qomi's *Women's Visage in the Islamic System*,
Mousavi cites the following hadith from Mohammad to refute the idea of
men's role as the high commander of the family:

The man is the protector of the interests and the guardian of his and his wife's
family members and is accountable (*mass'ul*) for this responsibility. And the
woman, too, is the protector of the interests and the guardian of her husband's

home and (in charge) of his children and is accountable for that. (Quoted in Mousavi 1994: 39)

Mousavi then stipulates the following from this hadith:

1. The husband is accountable and can be prosecuted accordingly. "He cannot be a self-centered tyrant. He ought to consider the interests of his wife" (39).
2. "The subject[s] (ra'iyat) of the man, that is, family members, are insured through the husband or children through the wife" (39). Thus any insult or mistreatment is punishable.
3. The woman's responsibility for protecting the house and the children means that her husband cannot interfere with her decisions (40).

In another instance, a reader, aged 28, married, employed, mother of one, inquires whether her husband can force her to obtain his permission to go to work every day. The reply is that there are two interpretations of this situation among Islamic jurists. One interpretation is that women should ask for their husband's permission to leave the house. The other holds that as long as the husband does not specifically forbid his wife to leave the house, there is no reason for the wife to ask for his permission. The author favors the second argument, since after all, marriage is all about cooperation. A woman is a free being who is her husband's partner, not his slave. In effect, both partners should be content about their mate leaving the house: "on several occasions, the husband should seek his wife's permission to leave the house" (Kermânshâhi 1993c). Can a husband threaten his wife that in return for her defiance, that is, leaving the house without his permission, he will refuse to provide for her? The answer once again is that marriage is about cooperation. A man's responsibility to provide for his wife is not supposed to be in exchange for her obedience. If a woman defies her husband, his response should aim to rectify her behavior, not withdraw his economic support, since such an act will break the chain of affection (mavaddat) and mercy (rahmat). "When the wife defies, the husband advises her; then stops talking to her; and when that does not work either . . ." (Kermânshâhi 1993c). The author leaves the sentence unfinished; we recall the Koranic guideline: ". . . admonish them and send them to beds apart and beat them."

The guardianship of children has been another contested issue in Islamic law. A guardian should have several characteristics. He should be of sound mind, mature, religious, just, knowledgeable, concerned primarily with the welfare of the child, and male. The last qualification is accepted by virtually all Islamic jurists, saving a group of jurists known as Hanafi, who accept the guardianship of the mother or a female relative. The question of guardianship becomes particularly sensitive for daughters, for whereas sons can marry at their own discretion, daughters who marry for the first time ought to have their father's (or another paternal male relative's) permission. This requirement is based on the assumption that young women may not have the discretion necessary to protect their welfare. The question facing women in the Islamic Republic is whether guardianship of children should belong exclusively to fathers. An article in *Zanân* disputes this monopoly (Qâ'eni 1997). After juxtaposing different hadiths and arguments in Islamic law, the article concludes that there is no conclusive evidence that Islam regarded guardianship a monopoly of men (21).

I will explore in the next chapter the primary outcome of these revisions in family relations to regulate individual men's control over women. In accordance with the new patriarchal bargain, reformist Islamist women's proposals for alteration of family relations eases women's confinement to domestic life and facilitates their incorporation into public patriarchy.

THE HEJÂB

On rare occasions when women's appearance is concerned, the emphasis is on curbing the extremists'—that is, hizbullahis', Pâsdârs', or vigilantes'—transgression against women (Khâni 1997). Here, again, the discussion revolves around different interpretations of Islamic scripts. A case in point appears in a review of Âzari-Qomi's *Women in the Islamic System*. Âzari-Qomi favors strict rules regarding hejâb. The proper hejâb prevents recognition of even the outline of a woman's body. But this form of hejâb, he concedes, is too debilitating and even the leading women of Islam could not observe it. Yet the least women could do is to wear the chador that covers them from head to toe. Âzari-Qomi offers a hadith according to which Imam Ali suggested that his daughter refrain from interacting with—"knowing"—people. Reviewing Âzari-Qomi's book, Mousavi (1994) rejects this idea on several grounds. First, on the basis of religious scholars such as Ayatollah Kho'i, Mousavi rejects the narrative for having weak and unreliable sources. He rejects the narrative because the source of narrative never clarifies if Imam Ali was addressing Fatima, or his son Mohammad. Furthermore, according to Mousavi, "not knowing" (*la-yafar'n* in Arabic) should be understood here as close intimacy and deep knowledge of someone, that which can only be achieved through constant contact, not mere visual contact. The objective of Imam Ali's saying, Mousavi advises, was that a woman should only get to know her husband and no one else, not to be "a blind, deaf, and dumb person, isolated from society, confined to the four walls of the house" (38). Finally, Mousavi comments, if Âzari-Qomi finds even Fatima's hejâb inadequate, then no form of hejâb in our society could find his approval, short of literally dividing the country into two zones, one for men, the other for women.

A report on why women wear only black advises against extremism (Pourzand 1994). The report relays that the majority of people interviewed do not necessarily equate dark colors with women's dignity and purity; that constant exposure to only dark colors is depressive; that there is no prohibition regarding colors in Islam. The report offers three explanations as to why black *seems* the preferred color of hejâb:

1. There is a prevailing perception of religion that is mixed with an admiration of sadness. This notion of religion has made people reluctant to wear colorful dresses that suggest happiness (7–8).

2. Nobody likes to wear only black, but society has a mind of its own. Though society is made up of individuals, it cannot be reduced to a mechanical amalgamation of them. Society has a life of its own and, like any other living organism, acts independently of the parts that make it (14).

3. Women make a rational choice by weighing the odds and deciding to comply. Based on a "cost-benefit analysis," Pourzand suggests that many women see the cost of not wearing dark clothes dearer than its benefit (15). These include both social costs and financial expenses associated with brighter clothes that reveal dirt faster (see also Shah-Rokni 2000).

As I will discuss in the next chapter, Islamist reformists' concession on hejâb reflects much more than advocacy of the veil or even an understandable attempt to avoid ostracism in the Islamic state. I contend that the failure of Islamist women's reformism to address hejâb stems from articulating key issues such as gender, sexuality, and the relationship between the individual and the collective within the framework of Islam and the Islamic government (see Jamileh Kadivar's interview in *Avaye Zan* Summer 2000: 51). This failure, I will further argue, alienates Islamist women's reformism from a great number of women, especially among the younger generation, who have to constantly experience the constraint of mandatory veiling.

THE CULTURAL POLITICS OF GENDER

Islamic gender ideologies in Iran have been founded on a natural difference between the sexes. As women and men are created differently, their roles and rights are dissimilar. Reformist Islamist women question the justification of discriminatory treatment of women on the basis of physiological difference:

How do you define equality? Does equality mean likeness? Women and men are undoubtedly different in physiology. They are also different in their bone structures, muscles, and hormones. They are also different in their moods and psychological characteristics. Women have gentler emotions, are more dutiful, more easygoing, and more precise. Men follow logic more than they rely on emotions. They are less disciplined, less flexible, and more daring. (Zâhedi 1993: 4)

But do these differences justify inequality? The answer is negative, as both are equally important in life. "The beauty of a man is in his manhood; of a woman, in her womanhood" (4).

Inspired by Western sociology and women's studies' distinctions between sex and gender[8], reformist Islamist women's literature suggests a social basis for sexual inequality. Gender is argued to be shaped by socialization and therefore gender roles could be revised. In the review of a book that endorses conservative attitudes toward women, Giti Shâmbayâti criticizes the author for the notion that motherhood is women's most important "talent" (Shâmbayâti 1994). She points out the existence of "so numerous women, educated and uneducated, who without a husband or in his absence, take care of themselves and their families both in and outside the house" (25). Shâmbayâti argues that because of the changes in family life, a number of responsibilities that used to fall on the shoulders of the family are now taken up by institutions like schools. She refers to some measures in Sweden that make it possible for women to both fulfill their quest for a professional life and to remain attentive to their family responsibilities (26). Nahid Moti' (1996) similarly argues that traditional socialization creates subservient women and domineering men. This, she concludes, is detrimental to developmental strategies and harms both women and society.

Though emphasizing social roots of gender formation, Moti' criticizes Western feminists for considering "complete similarity between women and men" (1997a: 23). This approach, she argues, has caused women and men to become similar, but, due to the dominance of masculine culture, it has been mainly women who have become like men. "The growing likeness of women to men implies a grand revolution in values that has led to such developments as homosexuality, bisexuality, and the destruction of family" (24). Instead of this dangerous path, Moti' recommends, an Iranian women's movement should look back toward prehistoric times when men and women were different and performed complementary roles, yet both sets of roles were deemed valuable.

In the modern age, though the egalitarian system is replacing the patriarchal one (primarily in the West), the resultant equality is at the cost of "femininity;" it is at the cost of devaluing and overlooking women's reproductive power. In other words, Western women have been able to compete with men only by becoming like them and devaluing their biological capacity. (24)

Neither complete likeness nor complete complementarity of the sexes is an appropriate response to women's oppression, Moti' contends. The answer is a combination of likeness and complementarity such that neither "masculinity" nor "femininity" will be sacrificed. This complementarity, she holds, differs from the patriarchal notion of the complementarity of the sex roles, as here we are dealing with the complementarity of *equal* roles. "Equal complementarity means that women's and men's different and distinct roles, both in their familial and social roles, have equal weight" (24).

In her discussion of gender, Nayereh Tohidi rejects the idea that male and female are the opposite of one another. Relying on the ideas of Carl Jung and Sandra Bem, she states that each man has a feminine side (anima), just as each woman has a masculine side (animus).

A balanced person is one who is both feminine and masculine (androgynous). Social and cultural conditions—how we are raised—encourage and reinforce "masculine" characteristics in men and prevent the emergence and development of the so-called feminine characteristics. (Tohidi 1997a: 20)

Every "balanced individual," according to Tohidi, should behave, when occasion rises, as an emotional, sensitive, delicate, and tender person, or as a rational, logical, or decisive one. Though throughout the article, masculine and feminine are problematized by being placed in quotation marks or qualified by "so-called," the former set of characteristics are labeled masculine, the latter, feminine.

In the following chapter, my discussion will focus more closely on how the seemingly liberating discussion of gender as a social product in effect will end up glorifying fundamentally essentialist notions of womanhood and manhood. Far from rupturing from other Islamic interpretations of gender, Islamist reformist women reinforce this notion by arguing that sociocultural usurpation of the natural capabilities of men and women, especially the feminine reproductive capacity, has caused deviation from the natural, harmonious complementarity of the sexes.

FAMILY LIFE

Reformist Islamist women attempt to improve women's legal position in family life is paralleled by their effort to improve relationships in the family. Here, the reformist Islamist women's project focuses on empowering the woman while curbing men's unbounded power (see, for example, Kar 1995). These measures are understandably proposed mainly on the familial level, though every now and then discussions emerge on long-term social changes that influence women's status in the family. One such discussion concerns the age of marriage. An article in one of the early issues of *Zanân* addresses this issue. The author holds that though there is no hard rule on this, if the basis of decision for marriage is physical, emotional, intellectual, social, and economic maturity, then most people are not ready for marriage before the age of 20 (Shahâbi 1993: 26). The author also argues against late marriage for its negative consequences, such as childbearing complications, increased risk of cancer, a shortened reproductive period, and disparity in age between man and woman. Though its significance is not specified in the article, concern about higher age at the time of marriage corresponds with the push for legal revisions that affect women's lives. Considering that the legal age of marriage under the IRI has been reduced to 9 for girls and 15 for boys and close to 50 percent of Iranian women marry before the age of 19 (Shâditalab 1995: 9), this is an important discussion to further women's power in the family. Mehrangiz Kar also addresses the legal aspects of early marriage in a later issue of *Zanân* (Kar 1997b).

Men's tyrannical rule in the family is opposed as a breeding source for social problems. In a commentary in *Jâme'eh-ye Sâlem* (Healthy Society) magazine, for instance, Sa'idzâdeh reflects about the news of a 28-year-old woman's attempt to leave her husband and child behind and cross the border to the Republic of Azerbaijan (1997). Trapped in a marriage with an abusive husband, she tried several times to legally leave the country and join her mother in the Azerbaijan. When those attempts failed, she made arrangements with a woman merchant. She was hidden in a sack of rice in order to be smuggled out of the country, but was found by the authorities. Sa'idzâdeh argues that her action is caused by men's monopoly over decision-making. What could she do? She was not tempted by the luxury of the West; all she wanted was to rid herself of the unfair treatment of her husband. The injustice she suffered at home is augmented by the prerogatives that the Iranian legal system offers men. "The child belongs to the father and after seven years of raising him, she has to give him up to his father. She cannot open a bank account for her son, or register him in the school." All these are denied her in the law that considers the father the guardian of the child. "She is not entitled to freedom. She is a slave to her husband. Any time he desires, he can let her go. She does not have the right to [legally] leave the country." Thus, women in her situation are forced to abdicate homeland and family. And they will do so as long as men have exclusive decision-making power. The solution is to "humanize" decision-making: it should be neither masculine nor feminine. And, Sa'idzâdeh contends, that is exactly what Islam prescribed. Any law that makes people disappointed about their God-given rights is incompatible with Islam. Since Islam claims to be opposed to injustice, any law that upholds injustice is anti-Islamic—and if a law is anti-Islamic, it must change.

Reformist Islamist women have also proposed to modify the issue of *tamkin*. We recall that according to the IRI's Civic Law, *tamkin* is a woman's obligation to live under her husband's roof and to surrender herself to him when he desires sexual intimacy. *Noshooz*, refusal to *tamkin*, can cost her his economic provision. The controversy surrounding *tamkin* concerns what constitutes women's defiance and violation of this principle and under what circumstances a husband can refuse to pay *nafaqeh* (daily expenses) to his wife. Shokoh Shokri and Sâhereh Labriz offer a modified understanding. They reject, for instance, that refusal to do household chores makes a woman disobedient. They also hold that sexual relations should be subject to the wife's physical and emotional readiness. What constitutes violation in regard to sexual relationship is not rejecting sexual intimacy in some incidents. The authors rely on Khomeini's specification that *noshooz* is an act that conflicts with a man's obtaining of sexual pleasure from his wife. On that basis, they propose the following:

The specific *tamkin* concerns not just the incident [i.e., a woman's refusal to have sex], but her failure to eradicate problems that interfere with his sexual pleasure. For example, if a woman's cleanliness and made-up appearance indicate her inclination toward her marital life and an effort on her part to attract her husband, and if a woman is so careless regarding these measures that she does not distinguish between her husband and other people [in other words, appears equally unappealing before her husband as she does before others], she has acted in a manner contradictory to principles of marital life and marriage philosophy. The same is customarily true about the man, for no man can be oblivious to these measures and at the same time expect his wife to be attentive. (Shokri and Labriz 1991: 61)

On the whole, authors argue, a man can demand from his wife only that to which shari'ah has entitled him. The husband is obligated to meet his wife's needs, including *nafaqeh*. A woman is entitled to *nafaqeh* not because she provides sexual services, but *because she is his wife*. The authors also reject polygyny on the ground that a polygynous man cannot treat all wives fairly. "A woman has the right to have sexual relationship with her husband once every four nights, for deprivation from this relationship would lead to her deviation [from the right, moral path]" (62).

A report on wife battery criticizes a "notion among some men" that a woman is to give services and to think and do as her husband wants, otherwise she should be punished (Ardalân and Kâkhsâz 1994: 7). Ordinary men interviewed for the report explain why they do or do not beat their wives. These explanations include: "why beat a weak creature?" "she disobeys and beating brings her to her senses"; "beating is a learned behavior"; "he is insane"; and "he is unemployed." The report criticizes the legal system for its reluctance to intervene to protect woman against "ignorant men" (9). It also recommends better psychiatric care for people under stress (13). Men are reminded that they should regard their wives as their ally in life, even at times of hardship (14). The report reveals that even educated, independent women can be abused in the hands of their educated, well-to-do husbands (17). Fortunately, younger women are more aware of this problem and are more resistant to entering into bad marriages:

Because of the increased awareness and an accurate understanding of their mothers' lives and marriage, most young women will live aware and empowered. They have learned from their mothers' lives that victims breed perpetrators. Reports like this, however, will make them fearful of marriage. (19)

Conceptualizing gender as a set of masculine and feminine social roles, the reformist Islamist women's literature has not yet drastically challenged the existing sexual division of labor in the family. Instead, the emphasis has been on revering women's familial role.

In peaceful houses, the woman is the axis; acceptance and patience are what softens all the sharp edges of hardship and bitterness. . . . Whatever is true in practice, it is traditional that everybody expects patience and acceptance from women. . . . Total self-sacrifice is the essence of the most beautiful feminine and maternal roles. When objects arrive at this household land of peace and the domain of the mother's monarchy, all the values of the dominator and the dominated trade places. It now is the tyrannical monarchy [of the mother] that . . . employs all its power to avail her children and [their] father of all these—from food to clothing to sweets to medicine to fresh air. It is the woman who stands last in taking advantage of benefiting from these. (Mazdâpour 1996: 32–33)

That role of sacrificing and standing last to take pleasure from material and mental riches, Mazdâpour contends, "is an enthusiastic choice that befits the lofty status of this household commander." At the time of destitution, it is "a mother's emotional wealth, her magnanimity (*'olovv-e tab'*), that guarantees her oblivion[9] to securing for herself the minimum of content and health" (33).

It is patriarchal culture, Mazdâpour acknowledges, that sets no limit as a mother's sacrifice. But she quickly adds that this "beautiful" expectation is accepted by the whole society, including "all the women who have enjoyed a healthy upbringing in this culture." This selflessness, nonetheless, is only one side of the coin; the other is children's appreciation of their mother's efforts. And children should make a gift of their appreciation not just at the turning of the year, but every day.

Moti' (1997a) rejects the notion that household chores are not work and convincingly points out that Iranian women's participation in the nation's economy, both in rural and urban areas, is far more than an official statistics project. She argues that housewives do more than take care of cleaning and cooking; they contribute to the economy of their family and society. On that basis, she calls for a reassessment of traditional female roles so that these can be granted their due worth. She argues that contrary to a widely held misconception, the contemporary Iranian housewife does much more than before (Moti' 1997b). Though technological advances in home appliances have made some work easier for her, more is expected of her now. She is supposed to mediate between the rational, programmed, and formal modern life and the spontaneous and emotional world of family relationship. She is expected to supervise her children's education, yet she is also required to entertain unexpected guests. At the same time, she is responsible for protecting her family's honor and social image at all times. Changing roles and role conflicts, according to Moti', have augmented the pressure of domestic life for women. Thus, she concludes, women's role as housewives should be appreciated as complementary to men's role, not inferior to it.

Changing gender relations have created new concerns for women. Numerous popular magazines—for example, *Zan-e Rouz*, *Fazilat-e Khânevâdeh* (Family Virtue), and *Khânevâdeh* (Family)—have published numerous articles on such issues as pop psychology, dietary regimes, and midlife crises. These problems are also addressed at some length in various issues of *Zanân*. Issues like assertiveness, health and diet tips, depression, PMS, communication in marriage, working mothers' feeling of guilt, and summer vacations are regularly discussed.

The prevalent approach to family relationship is mutual understanding, compromise, and communication. Asqar Keyhânniâ (1996), in his marriage manual, emphasizes the significance of good communication and attentiveness to each other's needs and preferences in matrimonial relationship. *Today's Woman, Yesterday's Man* alarms men that fundamental social changes in gender relations create perplexing conditions for which neither partner has ready-made answers. Thus, men could easily recede to their old habits and react hostilely toward women—in short, become "yesterday's men." In his discussions, Keyhânniâ relies on his experience as an attorney and family counselor and provides case histories to illuminate his points. In one example, he relates the case of a woman who holds a Ph.D. and teaches at the university, whereas her husband has a B.S. in engineering. The husband makes disparaging remarks about his wife in front of others. Keyhânniâ is supportive of the woman and instructs the man to value his wife's accomplishment and search for his own self-worth:

If you are an educated man, but have less education than your wife, you should pay attention to your valuable personal traits. You should keep in mind your own accomplishments and even be proud of your wife's capabilities and creativity. You should remember that though your wife has a higher degree, she has no problem with your educational background. Her decision to become your wife was conscious and free. In effect, good emotional rapport with you makes the difference in your degrees insignificant. Then, when she is content and does not blame you, why do you unjustly belittle her? If you are interested in your marriage, you ought to stop this irrational behavior. Otherwise, expect unhappy consequences. There is a limit to your wife's patience and eventually she will choose a different path. (59)

This approach differs markedly from that of sociologist Qolâm'abbâs Tavassoli, who in one of the round table discussions of *Zanân* expresses concern about women behaving superior to men if they have higher education than their husbands (*Zanân* 1997c: 33).

A happy marriage without a healthy sex life is inconceivable, thus learning about sexual relationships is an essential step in renovating family life. In a society like Iran where "even educated men and women do not value sexual education and consider it beneath their dignity," experts need to teach men that sex is a relationship between two people, thus that he ought to be attentive to the needs of his wife (Keyhânniâ 1996: 154). Women should similarly be encouraged to become active partners in bed. Frigidity in women results more from men's ignorance about female sexuality than from women themselves. A healthy sexual relationship does not just happen; a couple must plan for it. They must pay close attention to such factors as emotional and physical readiness, time, and ambience. Intimacy both before and after sex is vital, as is each partner's concern about the other person's gratification (159–60).

I will return to reformist approaches to family relations in the following chapter. I will discuss, among others, that the reformist renovation of family life eases the burden of many women; but that far from doing away with patriarchal family relations, Islamist women's reformism vies to synchronize the patriarchal family with the realities of women's participation in the labor force while saving institutionalized domesticity.

FEMINISM, NATIONALLY AND INTERNATIONALLY

A major obstacle before Iranian women has been the lack of a consciousness about feminism and women's movements around the world. In her assessment of the first year of the publication of *Zanân*, Sherkat comments about ignorant hostility toward feminism among some segments of the society. They refer to feminism as "a deviation from women's nature." She writes that the long domination of patriarchy has led to a lack of awareness about feminism. "And if there is any reference or analysis to feminism, it is mixed with negative convictions" (Sherkat 1993: 2). Feminism, she goes on, is mistakenly identified in Iran as endorsing a shunning of responsibility toward men and family members, and carelessly seeking occupation and social life. The same people, she points out, deny the depth of "the well of ignorance and darkness they have created for women" (2). This denial, she concludes, serves as a basis for these men to refute the legitimacy of women's actions to gain their rights. Citing a few examples of the deprivation of Iranian women, Sherkat questions rhetorically:

Can we still consider the awakening of Iranian woman and her struggle a deviation, an imitation of the decadent (!) Western woman? Is it not true that until there is injustice, there will be struggle? Struggle against inequality, not against men. As men, too, have been raised by unaware mothers who accepted injustice. That is why we believe the real solution is in enlightening women. (2–3)

In effect, there is a constant effort to convince women not to formulate their demands in feminist frameworks. Most male discussants in *Zanân*'s round table discussions about the most pressing problems of Iranian women, contend that women's issues result from some general deficiencies of Iran's legal or cultural systems. Alireza 'Alavytabâr, for example, guides women to avoid extremism:

Another very important point is that . . . we must avoid looking at the Iranian women's problem from the perspective of feminist ideologies. In other words . . . explanation of difficulties of women's lives must be distanced from feminist ideologies, especially those strands of feminism that are radical. There is a reason for that. You see, feminism is an ideology and like any other ideology, it is reductionist and [operates on the basis of] making an enemy. It is more useful for the destructive phase than for the constructive one. (*Zanân* 1997b: 15)

Shirin Ebadi, a woman attorney discussant, replies that her "concerns are not feminist, they are based on a quest for justice ('edâlatkhâhi)" (16). Moti' goes yet further and rejects 'Alavytabâr's entire claim. Feminism, she says, "is more a scientific theory than an ideology" (16). In the literature about civil society, mostly developed by the neo-Islamists, there is a tendency that civil society precludes the need for any gender-based movement, thus rendering feminism obsolete except in the familial sphere (see Mohammadi 1999: 54–75. Also see several interviews with the intellectuals of this trend in *Zanân* 57 and later).

In her first editorial in *Zanân*, Sherkat identifies four major sources for the subjugation of women: religion, culture, law, and education (Sherkat 1991a). In March 1997 (33), *Zanân* initiated a series of round table discussions around the following questions: What are the most important problems of women in Iran? Are these exclusively women's issues or are they consequential for the entire society? Do Iranian women have common problems? What are the national and international dimensions of these problems? And, finally, what are the root causes of women's problems? Most discussants have offered some combination of the areas identified by Sherkat as the source of women's subordinate position in Iran.

Though reformist Islamist women have not yet explored their definition of feminism, some discussions about the term "feminism" and women's movements in the West have been translated. These include a few pages from Mary Wollstonecraft's *A Vindication of the Rights of Women*; Jill Stephenson's entry on "Feminism" in the *Dictionary of Modern Political Ideologies*; and short excerpts from Allison Jaggar's *Feminist Politics and Human Nature*. Articles also cite the works of Western feminist scholars.

Yet much of this endeavor has been undertaken by secular feminists co-operating with *Zanân* with the intention of attracting and educating university students and other interested readers.

Some authors believe there is a need to transcend national boundaries and to establish a dialogue with other cultures. Several articles in *Zanân* deal with women's access to legal rights, education, employment, and politics in industrial and underdeveloped societies. Regular news items about women across the world in *Zanân* and other publications also keep women up to date about developments in women's lives cross-nationally. Interaction with women's movements around the world performs several functions for women activists. It provides moral support; helps to create continuity between Iranian women's efforts and their sisters across the globe; the intellectual exchange offers them a context for formulating their ideas and demands; and it strengthens their position in the face of adversaries by locating their grievances in the context of a worldwide cry for justice. Thus, Iranians are warned that in order to survive in the "global village," it is vital to rethink assumptions governing gender dynamics in the Islamic Republic, including adopting a more relaxed attitude toward interaction between the sexes (see Shâmbayâti 1993a). Another author emphasizes the need to pay more attention to gender and cultural issues of neighboring societies, instead of being exclusively focused on women in Western societies (Shahshahani 1991).

Shafi'i (1996) argues for an international solidarity among women on the basis of their common problems, while acknowledging the problematic nature of building that solidarity in light of powerful nationalist, religious, and racist movements in the contemporary world. Issue-oriented coalition among women of different countries, she proposes, could provide an opportunity for women to bridge the gaps that separate them, without falling prey to governmental international politics. Yet she cautiously warns that "what separate women/sisters are so complex and broad that without a comprehensive understanding of them, it is possible that women would not achieve broad solidarity" (28).

Interface is not limited to the levels of ideology and action; daily experiences of women and men in the West are also scrutinized toward formulating solutions to the challenges of daily life amidst changing gender relations. Articles from popular Western magazines (sources are mostly unidentified, but authors' names are included) on topics like blended families, childrearing, dealing with stress, being a working mother, and how to deal with marital disputes, appear in translation in issues of *Zanân* or among the lists of self-improvement publications. *Today's Woman, Yesterday's Man*, for instance, suggests that when husbands are late, instead of greeting them with fury, women should avoid unnecessary tension by showing concern for their well-being:

Westerners have a pleasant custom for situations like this and we could benefit from following them here. If her husband is late, a Western woman does not confront him by "I am so angry that you're late." She would ask "Something wrong?" or "What happened to you?" This way, she shows to her husband that she was worried for him. (Keyhânniâ 1996: 71)

In the discussion that will follow this chapter, I will raise several problems regarding this "indigenous" approach to feminism. I will argue, for instance, that the "indigenous" definition of feminism is indeed an attempt to void its vigor, to turn it into something harmless in the eyes of Iranian men. I will also problematize the identification of Iranian women with Islamic women not only for the detrimental effect of such an equation on feminist and leftist politics, but also because that equation is simply anti-democratic.

REACTIONS AGAINST ISLAMIST WOMEN'S REFORMISM

Not surprisingly, reformist Islamist women have been subject to controversy from the outset. Sherkat (1993: 2) writes in her editorial celebrating the anniversary of *Zanân*'s publication that some opponents of the magazine have tried to discredit the efforts of the magazine by proclaiming that feminism promotes a debonair attitude toward family and society. Bâd-âmchiân, advisor on social affairs to the Chief of the Judicial Branch, criticizes *Zanân* for "constantly writing about violence." He even finds the titles of articles offensive: "nutritional deficiencies among women," "painful stitches after labor," "wife battery"—"almost entirely negative and bitter titles" (1994: 11).

Obviously, fistfights are unpleasant and bad under any circumstance. . . . But why do you overlook this warm family environment, filled with kindness and respect between wives and husbands and children, and go after a handful of cases of which even a small number is too many, and generalize this to all corners of this honorable land? You could have written 10–12 pages about the warm family life with nice and pleasant photos, then write a few pages about families that after bitter experiences achieved sweet compromises. Of course at the end, you could have also written a few pages about this unpleasant act which goes contrary to morality, etiquette, and sincerity. In this way, your magazine would have served to increase kindness and console couples. You would have made people optimistic about establishing families. In that way, you would have pleased the God, prophets, and the honorable martyrs of this revolution, and the people of this land who have suffered in the hands of kings, lords, and colonizers and now, thanks to the Islamic Revolution, enjoy independence and freedom. (10)

A more serious opposition is to the Islamist women's revisionist interpretation of Islamic law. In a commentary on Kar's critique of IRI's laws

regarding women, Mozhgân Kiâni Sâbet points out that the IRI's laws are
based on the Islamic fiqh as stipulated by the Koran, the hadiths, *ijmâ'* or
the consensus of the jurists, and *ijtihâd* or the reasoning of religious experts
(see note 4). "These regulations and edicts," she contends, "are purely 'to
imitate and obey.' " Since the sources of the laws of the Islamic Republic
of Iran are divine revelations and the purity of Imams and other saints,
"any criticism of Islamic laws is tantamount to a blow against the faith
and belief in Islam" (Kiâni Sâbet 1993: 42). If there are discrepancies between what Islam offers to men and women, it is only due to the natural
differences that exist between the two. No wonder then that Islam does
not offer judgeship to women—they are emotional. But that only men can
become judges is not "a virtue or an honor" for them; it is merely a task
that men should perform. Neither men's rationality nor women's emotion-
ality denies equality between men and women.

What is at stake is that a Muslim woman should clearly understand her real value,
that is, her worth and human honor according to Islam, and fulfill her humanitarian
task and remain aloof to the disrespect and babbling of the imbeciles—for if the
whole world refuses to accept the truth, she cannot change the truth that the glo-
rious God has designed. (Kiâni Sâbet 1993: 44)

The efforts of reformist Islamist women to curb some of the extremist
anti-women measures of Islamists is an essential part of the Iranian
women's struggle to gain their rights. For that reason, the defeat of Islamist
women's reformism in their rivalry with extremists could cause a setback
in the women's movement. Yet the imperatives of the feminist project in
Iran will expand far beyond the horizons of reforming the Islamist state. It
is thus crucial to both support reformist women in their struggle, and remain critical *and* independent of them. The effectiveness of radical social
movement in Iran is integrally related to the continued vigilance of specific
crises of daily life, while simultaneously—uncompromisingly—pushing for
the resolution of the deeper social conflicts. I will expound on this issue in
the following chapters.

RECAPITULATION

I discussed in this chapter that the Islamic regime's gender policies have
led many women to question and revise some prevalent principles of the
IRI's gender ideology. Based on Giddens' observation about the contested
nature of religious authority in the uncertain age of modernity, and deriving
from Melucci's qualifications of how discrepancy between expectation and
reward could lead to collective action, I explained the emergence of reformist Islamist women as resulting from diverse factors such as common
beliefs with the policymakers of the IRI, continuous concern about

women's status in post-revolutionary Iran, and the influence of developments in women's lives around the world. I pointed out that terms like "Islamic feminism" and Islamist women's reformism are imprecise because they refer to a group of heterogeneous activists and theorists with diverse orientations. This ambiguity is intensified by the fact that some nonbelievers also use public channels available to reformist Islamist women (such as the magazine *Zanân*) to express their views.

Providing women with legal protection in family and society is the most pressing goal of the reformist Islamist women. At the center of this endeavor is reinterpretation of Islamic texts regarding women and criticizing IRI's laws on that basis. Reformist Islamist women call for women's increased participation in social, economic, and political arenas. Reformist Islamist women reject the prevalent Islamic notion of the natural basis of Islam's differential treatment of the sexes. Most reformist authors acknowledge differences between the sexes, but argue that gender superiority is rooted in society and culture. Thus, biological justifications for the superiority of one sex over another are not acceptable. Improvements in women's social status, reformist Islamist women argue, can be meaningful only if accompanied by changes in family laws. Acknowledging changing gender relations in contemporary society, couples are encouraged to base their relationship on communication, self-esteem, and respect for each other's rights.

Reformist Islamist women have faced the opposition of conservative Islamists. They are accused of portraying a bleak picture of family life and threatening the peace of family life. On the whole, reformist Islamist women have an unstable position in the Iranian political scene. Their emergence has also stirred controversies among Iranian scholars and activists outside Iran. In the following chapter, I discuss the strengths and weaknesses of Islamist women's reformism.

NOTES

1. For a similar concern, see Tâleqani (1995: 4).

2. Zeynabussâdât Kermânshâhi is a pseudonym for Mohsen Saʿidzâdeh. He first published his works in *Zanân* under women's names—Minâ Yâdgâr-Âzâdi, Zeynabussâdât Kermânshâhi—as well as the masculine name Kâzem Musavi (see bibliography). When his use of women's names was revealed in the program information of the 1995 Conference of the Iranian Women's Studies Foundation (Toronto), many participants objected both to the fact that a member of the clergy was invited to participate in a conference of exiled and immigrant Iranian women; and to his concealment of his gender identity.

3. The May 23rd Front refers to the day President Khatami was elected. The "front" is a loose community of religious and secular individuals whose shared desire to limit hard-liners' power brought them together.

4. Both shari'ah and fiqh can be translated as "law." The shari'ah refers to the law of Allah; fiqh is Muslim jurists' interpretation of the law of God.

5. *Fiqh* is the interpretation of the Islamic law. Since not all circumstances are covered in the Koran or the *sunna* (the tradition of the Prophet), Muslim jurists introduced several categories of jurisprudence: *qiyas* (argument by analogy), *ijmâ'* (argument from the consensus of the Muslim community), and *ijtihâd* (independent argument in the absence of consensus). Despite sharing many aspects of Islamic law with the Sunni tradition, Shiite jurisprudence is different in inheritance law, rejection of *qiyâs*, and free use of *ijtihâd*, which the Sunni tradition strictly regulated after the thirteenth century.

6. The Law of Retribution (*qesâs*) specifies that if a Muslim man murders a Muslim woman, the woman's guardian must pay the murderer one half of a man's blood-money before he receives *qesâs*.

7. There are allegations of wrongdoing against Nâtiq Nouri that he moved his numbers up to the first place. In an interview with *Zanân*, Fâezeh Hashemi was asked to comment about that; she refrained.

Fâezeh Hashemi is not a member of the Sixth Majlis. She decided to drop out of the race and encouraged her supporters to vote for her father, the former President Hashemi Rafsanjani—who also voluntarily dropped out after a scandalous controversy surrounding the first round of elections. Having wavered in her support for women's causes, even *Zanân* (February 2000: 4) grew critical of Fâezeh Hashemi's performance in the Majlis.

8. Examples include the works of Janet Saltzman Chafetz, Juliet Mitchell, and summarization of these ideas in such textbooks as Anthony Giddens' *Sociology*.

3

Feminism or Islamism?: Challenges of Feminism in Post-Revolutionary Iran

It was a wintry day. I was passing by the university's cafeteria on the way to the library, when I saw an announcement posted on the windows of the cafeteria. Oblivious to the content of the announcement, I continued ahead. When I reached the library, I saw the same announcement. That was unusual, since due to a paper shortage, university authorities would make a few copies and post them only in different departments. So we were not used to seeing the same announcements posted so close to each other. That was why I became curious to find out what it said. Well, the announcement was in regard to the suspension of six [female] students for disobeying standards of morality (a'mâl-e monâfy-e 'effat). I found my friend's name among them. I was concerned for her. Later that evening I called her to inquire about the situation. Indifferent, she said: "Nothing, I was smoking in the university yard. . . . But don't worry, I got my visa to go to Italy. . . . will leave this place soon." I talked to her recently again. She's in Italy now, married to an Italian artist. They both paint for a living and for fun. She told me that she was kicked out of the university because she was labeled as a Tudeh sympathizer because during the first months of the revolution, she went to listen to Beh Âzin, a Tudehi author. . . . Several years after the revolution, she had a gallery of her artworks . . . and Nâmehy-e Mardom, the Tudehi paper, published her name and the Islamic Government was alarmed. When I asked if she really was with them she said: "When everybody was with somebody, I was with the Fedaiin, not with the Tudeh."

A young Iranian woman, now living in Canada, narrated this story for me. Though the "incident" happened to her friend, her own life story in the IRI included similar incidents in which she had to protect herself against persecution for her use of makeup, choice of color, and deportment. In the summer of 1992, a young woman was shot to death in a phone booth by a Pâsdâr, revolutionary guard, after an argument about her appearance. On a similar occasion, according to a communiqué issued by the Pooyâ Center for Art and Culture in Europe (24 November 1995), five actors were barred from work by the authorities. Of them, Akbar ʿAbdi was guilty of criticizing censorship in the media; Reza Shafiʿi-Jam, Arzhang Mirfazli, and Nosratullâh Radish of being popular among high school girls—the Minister of Education complained that girls collected their photos. Mâhâyâ Petrosiân, the only woman in the group, was guilty of smoking and laughing on the scene (See *Zan dar Mobarezeh* December 1995: 7). In the summer of 1997, a university student was incarcerated and whipped for allegedly dancing and not obeying the dress code in the designated women's zone on the Salmânshahr beach of the Caspian Sea. Male soldiers raided the women's zone, grabbed and kicked her, called her "filth," tore her shirt, and dragged her to their patrol car. As one agent tells *Zanân*'s reporter: "She was naked and dancing in a group. And it is obvious that we won't let anybody dance naked." "Was she really naked, or just not careful in her hejâb?" the reporter wonders. "She was wearing a shirt and a pair of pants. She did not even have a scarf" (Khâni 1997: 13). Many Iranians—from different social classes or regional backgrounds, women more than men, of course—have similar experiences. People learn how to tiptoe around the ever-present surveillance.

I see a common theme in these "incidents": people's vulnerability to everyday violence in the IRI. After years of learning about events of this nature, I still cannot but feel something surreal about these stories: something that defies human reason—not to mention human rights. The late Iranian playwright Gholamhossein Saʿedi (Saidi) portrayed this aspect of post-revolutionary Iran in one of his last plays. *Othello in Wonderland* is an artistic testimony of the censoring of art and life (Saidi 1996). A theatrical group has to obtain permission to produce Othello in the Islamic regime. And Saʿedi masterfully pictures the human tragedy of that process in a most befitting style—satire. Shakespeare and his play, along with actors, undergo scrutiny, revision, and forced metamorphosis before they can be granted permission to come to life . . . or to survive. What Saʿedi wrote about theatrical production in the IRI is at the same time an allegory for life under the Islamic regime, as he himself pointed out in an essay on performance art in a performing state (Saʿedi 1984). How vulnerable people become to the whims of individuals who, under the aegis of that moral system, with the now tacit, now explicit support of a government (or a faction of it), see themselves heaven's gatekeepers. And how vulnerable women are when even the sanctity of a male/state-defined "women's zone" on a sex-segregated beach—physically divided by a curtain in the sea—is not respected. And how vulnerable could women be when the moral rules of a few define wearing pants and a blouse as "naked"? And how vulnerable could life be when smoking and laughing could be punishable, not just—just?—for a curious, talented Muslim university student, but also for an Armenian-Iranian actress forced to comply with the rules of an Islamic state in her own homeland?

I think of these issues and ponder about reformist Islamist women's piecemeal and painstaking efforts to create a "safe" space for women when they are constantly reminded of their lower status, but revered for their grand mission in life—mothering and being wives. It is against this backdrop that one can appreciate the efforts of women to secure for themselves a position in the labor force, courts, politics, and the family. And it is against the constant surveillance that one can appreciate the perilous attempts of some reformist Islamist women to strip women of the symbolic function they occupy in current political discourse, so that issues affecting women's lives may be discussed *in their own rights*, free from the fear of moralistic judgments and political orthodoxy (see Jalali Naeini 1997: 22–23).

Yet against this very background I find Islamist women's reformism both limited and limiting. Limited, because as long as it is articulated within the political and ideological confines of Islam, it cannot afford a radical rupture from the patriarchal assumptions of Islam. It leaves women vulnerable to the limitations of predefined legal precepts and moral codes, limitations that deny women (and men) the chance to be autonomous individuals. Limiting, because the enthusiasm that it has generated among some activists could disarm Iranian feminism. The enthusiasm has been especially high among some Iranian scholars in the West. Najmabadi joyously considers Islamist women's reformism a positive contribution to the polyphonization of the Iranian women's movement (1995). Haeri commends *Zanân* for "reinterpreting the scripture within an Islamic feminist framework" (1995: 140) and goes so far as to credit *Zan-e Rouz*, an overtly pro-government publication, with taking up "feminist issues while paying lip service to the Islamic regime" (Haeri 1995: 141). Mir-Hosseini argues that the "new tendency within the centre of the religio-political establishment" proposes "a brand of feminism which takes Islam, not the West, as its source of legitimacy" (1996: 315). Tohidi (1996) in a tearful letter to *Zanân*, writes that Sherkat's editorial about the political and personal hurdles of an "Islamic feminist" made her feel beside herself. On another occasion, in a lengthy tribute to "Islamic feminism," she attributes a "sensitive and historical" role to "veiled or turbaned idol-breakers" in the political developments of Iran (Tohidi 1997b: 97). Afary introduces *Zanân* as "a literary and cultural magazine with an explicitly feminist agenda" (Afary 1997: 104). She calls upon Iranian women activists and other "progressive movements" to encourage "the work of individuals and institutions that are dedicated to developing an indigenous expression of Muslim feminism" (110).

In this chapter I will discuss the limited and limiting aspects of Islamist women's reformism. I will argue that confinement to an Islamic framework deflects the development of some crucial theoretical and practical dilemmas facing the Iranian women's movement. I will show, for example, the difficulties and limits of reinterpreting Islamic texts on gender relations. This limitation, I believe, makes reformist women particularly inefficient in an area that they themselves consider crucial in the struggle for sexual equality—cultural politics. I will argue that despite their advocacy for women, Islamist reformists promote the interest of a selected group of Iranian women, leaving many others vulnerable to the transgressions of patriarchy. Their narrow interpretations of gender, patriarchy, and individual freedom leave many women vulnerable to patriarchal intrusions and aversions.

At the risk of sounding repetitive, I will discuss in detail the myriad titles that appear in Islamist women's reformist publications. I do so because other analyses of this trend—often more favorable than mine—have drawn conclusions on the basis of seemingly novel concepts and theoretical approaches adapted in the "Islamic feminist" literature. Though reformist women articulate some of their ideas through terms (e.g., *gender*, *sex roles*, *patriarchy*) seldom used by earlier Islamic authors, I believe that the "novelty" of their approach is limited. Details will help us recognize the similarity of reformists' arguments with those of other Islamic authors. After mapping the contours of Islamist women's reformism in the previous chapter, I will analyze in this chapter the implications of Islamist women's reformism for the cultural politics of the feminist movement in Iran. I do not intend to promote a single definition of feminist theory and practice. Rather, I aim to show the discrepancies between the "Islamic Feminist" reading of "Western" feminism and what Western proponents of Islamist women's reformism contend.

THE ISLAMIC IMPERATIVE

Reformist Islamists discuss women's rights in the context of an Islamic framework not necessarily due to a heart-felt belief, as I discussed in the previous chapter. But regardless of the authors' intent, the Islamic context shapes their discursive boundaries. The prime *objective* of *believer* reformists is maintaining their Islamic identity; *nonbelievers* must abide by the restriction of not violating an Islamic frame of analysis.[1] Without taking this Islamic imperative into consideration, no analysis of Islamist women's reformism could be complete. Islam's presence is felt both through an overall worldview and through the ideological and legal systems within which reformists must operate. The fundamental premise of Islamist women's reformism is that women can attain equal status only in the context of Islam. Zahrâ Rahnavard (1995), for example, argues that only when Islam replaces patriarchy will women and men be truly free. Mahboobeh Abbas-Gholizadeh (Ommi) writes similarly:

The main objective of religions is the establishment of social justice and in this quest, they set mandates and basic examples for future generations to follow. These mandates today override the progressive resolutions of women's coalitions and conferences at local or global levels in terms of efficiency, flexibility, and universality. Even though the principles of religious scripture have found deep roots in the cultural foundations of mankind, they have seldom been officially referred to as resources for legislature and policymaking, particularly at the global level. (Abbas-Gholizadeh 1994b: 64)

The Ayatollah Khomeini's authority continues to be strong. For some, he remains the true leader of a Muslim women's movement; for others, he becomes a shadowy yet ever present figure who could be cited here and there in support of one's argument. Jamileh Kadivar (1996: 63), for instance, argues that Khomeini "has qualitatively changed" our understanding of women (also see Sa'idzâdeh 1993: 53). Some hypocrites, Kadivar contends, had secluded women under the name of Islam for centuries. The Ayatollah, however, rejected women's objectification, promoted an active social presence for them, highlighted their role as educating mothers, emphasized the centrality of Islam in guiding women to liberation, and granted women election rights (55–68; also see Abbas-Gholizadeh 1994b: 65).[2]

Sherkat, in her first editorial in *Zanân*, expresses similarly:

It is time now that the sage and the intellectuals caring for religion, in their contemplation of *fiqh* and its edicts, think a bit more seriously on issues related to women so that after centuries of the decline of Islam, the Muslim woman can rid herself from disorientation, distraction, and multiplicity of orientation (*chandgu-negi*) toward her religion and, at times, even her own God. So that to uncover the kind, rational, and progressive vision of religion, in the tired souls of women, therefore substitute love for force, respect for fear, prayer for hypocrisy, and tranquillity for anxiety. (3)

Ziâ Mortazavi, editor of *Payâm-e Zan*, argues that without a comprehensive understanding of Islam, one cannot comprehend Islam's treatment of women. Without such an understanding, he fears, Islamic laws regarding divorce, custody, or retribution will seem mere cases of unjust treatment of women; with that understanding, on the other hand, these laws make sense and relieve our concerns (*Zanân* 1997e: 52). According to the Islamic interpretation, women's quest for an improvement of their social status is guaranteed in religion, and, more specifically, in Islam. Historically, the denigration of women in the Islamic world paralleled a distortion of reli-

gious teachings. According to one article in *Zanân*, prior to Islam, all religions enhanced sexual oppression. Gradually, women were reduced to
objects, adorning palaces and satisfying powerful men's lust. Islam, however, offered women their lost dignity. Inspired by Shariati, the author regards Fatima as the model of "the liberated woman in the history of Islam"
('Ellini 1991: 6). But Islam's intention to liberate women was derailed after
Mohammad's death. Hypocrite men who advocated a "false" Islam made
women victims of their ignorance and greed (7). Denigrated and deprived,
Muslim women found a false refuge in the West, until finally the reawak-
ening of the East enabled them to break the chain and set on their journey
of liberation.

An English article in *Farzaneh* on the Koran's portrayal of the Virgin
Mary (Mariam) considers Mary *à la* Koran a relevant contemporary model
to offset the "models of indecency [that] prevail today" (Gorgi and Ebtekar
1994: 69). The conclusion of the article summarizes the qualities of an ideal
woman in the eyes of Islam:

Mariam has been depicted by the Quran as a woman possessing a strong personality
with attractive and charismatic attributes, namely, decision-making power, perse-
verance, and the capacity to accept responsibility, among other attributes that constitute a strong character. She ultimately gives birth to a child who is the savior
and thus she lays the foundations for the new faith in a society severely oppressed
by Roman hegemony. Mariam is depicted as a personality honored with a mission
with strong political, social, and economic implications. (79–80)

Islamist women's reformism is, to repeat, a bird of many feathers. Thus
one cannot consider ideas expressed by any one author as representing
other reformist women. My intention here, however, is to show the borders
of this trend. Despite the suggestion of some scholars, reference to Islam is
not mere lip service. *Whether authors believe in Islam, they are compelled
to show that they remain within the Islamic framework.* Articulation of
the problem in the dominant religious discourse, using words whose "prosthetic function" is entrenched in their current definitions, leads to maintaining the integrity of that discourse. Daily life is constructed in a narrative
fashion to suit the dominant discourse. This means that the hegemonic
culture is reinforced even when possibility for change exists. Working
within the framework of the hegemonic gender ideology, proposals for revising gender relations ought not to contradict Islamic assumptions about
the complementarity of roles. That explains the sparse treatment of hejâb,
or avoidance of such pivotal issues as morality, sexuality, zena (adultery),
or stoning of adulterers.

Islamist women's reformism does not offer women the opportunity to
form an independent identity; it aims to (re)construct the ideal "Muslim
woman." To "Islamic feminists," the historical models for this woman al-

ready exist in the history of early Islam in women like Khadija, Fatima, and Zeynab (or other exceptional women like Mary as portrayed in Islam); interpretations then revolve around what their characteristics are and what constructing such a woman entails. "Modernizing" Islamic gender ideology comes to mean figuring out how Fatima or Zeynab would act if they lived in today's society (*Zanân* 1997e).

The Islamic imperative also points to another problem in the development of the Islamist reformist discourse: censorship. I have discussed in *Gender Politics* the emergence of a "patriarchal triad" in post-revolutionary Iran, where Islam, patriarchy, and the IRI collectively perpetuate male domination. Censorship is an example of the convergence of these forces: sanctification of patriarchal relations under the aegis of the Islamic state. Working in the political and ideological framework of Islam *and* the Islamic government means that any fundamental undermining of that framework is suppressed. Farideh Farrahi points out in a *Zanân* round table discussion that in today's Iran, the woman's body and the relationships that affect her life are seen as signifying "something that transcends women's daily lives." Women have thus become a bargaining chip in the political game (*Zanân* 1997a: 13). Discussing even minor problems subjects women to such accusations as being imperialist agents (17).[3] The "politicization of woman" along with the conviction that women's issues are subcategories of other problems, considerably limits discussions of women's rights. This prevents even those among the clergy who are qualified to propose fundamental changes in the Islamic law.

Direct and indirect forms of censorship do curb the sharpness of reformist analysis, something that even some readers of the magazine have also pointed out. One such reader writes from Tehran that *Zanân*'s coverage of women in Afghanistan was disturbing,

but when I read the other articles in *Zanân* concerning Family Laws and learned of your weak confrontation with the injustices [of the Family Law] . . . , I was even more disturbed. If you, the responsible and intellectual people, had the courage to discuss women's problems, in other words, if you were loyal to your responsibility toward oppressed women of Iran, you would have no doubt left aside your considerations (*molâhezât*). (*Zanân*, March 1997: 56)

In response, *Zanân* asks rhetorically: Do you think it is possible to write about any issue "unconditionally"? "If the magazine is to be published, its first constraints are the law, custom (*'urf*), and market. . . . In other words, there will always be 'consideration' and one neither can, nor is it correct to defend something unconditionally."

Najmabadi (1995: 205) and Tohidi (1997b: 133) commend *Zanân* for creating, in Tohidi's words, "an atmosphere of friendship, single-heartedness, and cooperation" among Iranian women activists from diverse ideological persuasions, "without anybody's autonomy of language and vision being sacrificed for this cooperation." In the face of the limitations that *any form of censorship*, regardless of its degree, imposes on the development of feminist theory and praxis, crediting any journal for granting its contributors such vast latitude is at least wishful expectation, something that, as the editor of *Zanân* admits, defies the reality of cultural production in the IRI. Secular women who worked with *Zanân* state that an atmosphere of mistrust ruled over their interaction with the editor Shahla Sherkat, that she was suspicious of these authors' hidden agenda. To be sure, the feeling was mutual. Many leftists in Iran have been categorically against any cooperation with *Zanân* from the outset. Of those who deemed limited collaboration possible, some were never accepted by *Zanân* and several others found its restrictions too much to bear.

GOING HEAD-TO-HEAD WITH ALLAH?

We have seen in the previous chapter that a major preoccupation of Muslim reformists is the reinterpretation of Islamic texts. Such an endeavor often requires them to promote certain interpretations of Arabic words over others, question the authenticity of certain hadiths, or contextualize narratives in history and thereby refute their universality.

There is nothing novel about this procedure. It has been standard practice throughout Islamic history. Muslim authors in contemporary Iran, from Khomeini to Motahari to Shariati to precursors of Islamist women's reformism like Rahnavard, have preceded reformist women in this practice. These ideologues have all argued that "true Islam" should not be blamed for the lot of women in the Muslim world. During the Pahlavis' reign, even the government joined the show. Many attempts to modify the laws affecting women or family have been cloaked in a "liberal interpretation" of Islam. A number of authors elsewhere in the Islamic world have made the same argument (for a review, see Afshari 1994). The fundamental common assumption of these authors is that Islam, as the final and most complete religion, cannot but be egalitarian toward women. In the words of a scholar of theology:

God, who speaks through the Qur'an, is characterized by justice, and it is stated clearly in the Qur'an that God never can be guilty of *zulm* (unfairness, tyranny, oppression, or wrongdoing). Hence, the Qur'an, as God's word, cannot be made the source of human injustice, and the injustice to which Muslim women have been subjected cannot be regarded as God-derived. (Hassan 1996: 62)

Indeed, dismissal of some hadiths seems the easiest strategy, since unlike the Koran, which is considered to be the word of Allah, hadiths are merely stories from the Prophet and the Imams, narrated by mortal human beings.

The reliability of such stories can be disputed. Yet, though this is a legitimate practice in the Islamic shariʿah, we have to keep in mind that even here women are at a disadvantage: they are going against some highly orthodox stories. There is little discrepancy between the inclination of Islamist reformist women and some members of the clerical community to dismiss those stories that have a weak sequence of narratives. But this is not always the case. If they question highly accepted narratives, they will be competing against scholars whose reliability has been accepted for centuries.

In her assessment of "Islamic feminism," Tohidi justifies underemphasizing the role of Islam on the ground that Islam is a historical phenomenon, constantly undergoing modification. Thus, she argues, like any other religion, Islam is an evolving social theory, not a fixed religious dogma (1997b: 117). Though there is no question that religions undergo profound changes over time, they are not empty vessels that believers can haphazardly fill. In addition to being responsive to sociohistorical conditions, religions consist of metahistorical teachings that cannot be altered. For this reason, the problem before "Islamic feminists" is much more serious than the authenticity of some hadiths or mistranslation of Arabic terms. The real hurdle is that Islam's "authoritative" discourse leaves little room for foundational changes. Here, Bakhtin's distinction between the "internally persuasive" and "authoritative" words can be helpful. According to him, the "internally persuasive word" is shared between parties holding a dialogue, whereas "authoritative" words limit creative interpretation. While the internally persuasive word encourages creativity because it "awakens new and independent words" (Bakhtin 1981: 345), the authoritative word demands allegiance:

The authoritative word demands that we acknowledge it, that we make it our own; it binds us quite independently of any power to persuade us internally; we encounter it with its authority fused to it. The authoritative word is located in a distanced zone, organically connected with a past that is felt to be hierarchically higher. (342)

Islam teaches that the Prophet is the seal of all prophets and his religion is the most complete, not just one religion among many. The Koran is deemed the word of God. In the words of a contemporary scholar, Islam is a "strict, uncompromising monotheism" (Tibi 1991: 38). Herein lies the limit of any reinterpretation of Islam on woman-centered or "feminist" bases.

Alternative constructions of the Koran, for instance, can cite a verse that considers equality for all pious people in Allah's eye. But what about those verses that specifically refer to men as superior to women, grant men a higher share of inheritance, or present women as the land that men till? In these cases, there are no recourses except playing with the semantics. As we have examined in the previous chapter, the range of reinterpreting Islamic scripts is limited. Reinterpretations end up leaving women in their starting position: vulnerable. Worse yet, this time women's vulnerability is intensified because it is purportedly a position created by women, for women. Reformist women's central cultural project, therefore, fails. That after over a decade of concerted efforts, "Islamic feminists" have not been able to produce a "feminist theology" is due in large part to the impossibility of revising Islamic precepts.

Furthermore, reinterpretation of Islamic texts has the grave danger of reading the present into the past. Concepts like sexual equality, emancipation, gender, and patriarchy are meaningful only in the context of contemporary history. Imposition of these ideas on old writings obfuscates the differences in political economy, society, and culture of twentieth and twenty-first century Iran and the Arabia of fourteen centuries ago.

The enthusiastic reception of the Islamist women's reformist reinterpretation project by Iranian feminist scholars in the West is unwarranted. What Najmabadi calls *zabânbâzi* (1995: 201)—"linguistic" or "word" games—indeed goes far beyond simple playing; it involves masterful acrobatic reading of texts. To argue that when men are put in charge of women and the family, this really means that men are demoted to the position of servants, requires ingenious innovation. To interpret the verse regarding battery as making love to women goes far beyond reinterpreting the text—it is rewriting the text. Though these acrobatic interpretations may demonstrate an active imagination, they hardly secure safety for women.

Najmabadi proposes that "Islamic feminists" take the novel approach of calling for independent reasoning, or *ijtihâd*, instead of citing certain narratives or interpretations against others. In fact, as we have observed, the basis of "Islamic feminist" arguments is exactly to pose one set of narratives against another. The reference to *ijtihâd* is marginal in their work, appearing only in passing in a few cases cited by Najmabadi. Still, we should keep in mind the limitation of *ijtihâd*; it is not a remaking of Islam. It has to stay within the confines of Islam. Furthermore, *ijtihâd*, which literally means "striving," is forming an opinion in a case of law by applying analogy (*qiyâs*) to the Koran and the sunna. Though *ijtihâd* was initially understood as each Muslim's ability to form his opinion, it gradually became the task of those with expertise whose judgment should be followed by others.

Dismissals of historical narratives, reinterpretations of the Koran, or independent reasoning—whatever the tactic, the result is the same: leaving women's rights contingent upon interpretations, making women vulnerable.

GENDER AS SOCIOCULTURAL ENCROACHMENT UPON NATURE

Though Islamist reformist women condemn patriarchy, there is no analysis of who benefits from patriarchy and perpetuates it—patriarchy in the "Islamic feminist" interpretation is without patriarch. Fâezeh Hashemi Rafsanjani points out emphatically: "I don't intend to say at all that men are to blame. I don't intend at all to put the blame on anyone. I want to say that it is the traditions and the culture that have created this condition" (quoted in *Zanân* 31 1996: 51). Ebadi attributes the "roots" of sexual inequality to the dominant sexist ideas and convictions (*Zanân* 1997b: 19). Moti' (1997a) points out that unequal valuing of the complementary masculine and feminine roles is to blame. Some neo-Islamists (*noandishân-e dini*) even deny any fundamental sexual discrimination in the IRI Constitution, save for some exceptions in family and punitive laws (Nouroozi 2000).

One could argue that reluctance to identify men as individual and collective beneficiaries of patriarchy avoids public indignation. Yet I believe the problem goes deeper. As I have elsewhere discussed (Shahidian 1995), most social scientific literature in Iran treats patriarchy and sexual oppression as essentially a "mistake," not a systematic sexual inequality governing access to economic, political, social, and cultural resources. Women's oppression is attributed to ambiguous factors such as "ignorance" or "corruption." Thus, the women's movement fights against a "social problem" that affects all. This approach makes women's quest for equal rights contingent upon the satisfactory solution of "cultural problems." Sociologist Qolâm'abbâs Tavassoli argues that our "cultural problems" force us to have men who earn more or are more educated than their wives. Otherwise, "the pillar of the family will collapse" (*Zanân* 1997c: 31). As soon as she has a higher degree than he, as soon as she earns more than he, she will act superior to him. So, before we call for women's employment, we should first work to soften these role conflicts. Political scientist Nasrin Mosaffa concurs: "It is my contention that changes ought not to be in a fashion that would upset family and social structure. Many women tell me that premature discussions of women's rights have made their lives unstable. I wonder again whether it is worth creating tension in families when there are not yet adequate possibilities for realizing many goals. What should the extent of change be? At what cost?" (35) She proposes that before any fundamental change can take place, men must be changed. And of course it is up to mothers to raise enlightened sons.

The reduction of patriarchy to a "cultural problem," to a misunderstanding, leads to an emphasis on "improving understanding" between men and women as fundamental to the women's movement, as if the development and perpetuation of patriarchy has resulted from a wrong turn men have taken in the labyrinth of logic. That also explains why romantic wooing of wives is so emphasized in the Islamic Republic—oppression is romanticized and gains a humane appearance.

The peril of this approach is that improvements in women's legal and social status, moderation in cultural extremes, *could easily be mistaken for sexual equality*. That is why, for example, sociologist Moti' argues the central task of the Iranian women's movement to be teaching people to value women's domestic responsibility. This agenda coincides with the neo-Islamists' emphasis on the root cause of sexual inequality being differences in valuing male and female roles, not the role differentiation itself (see *Zanân*'s interview with Mostafâ Malekiân, May-June 2000: 34).

Furthermore, as cultural beliefs are transmitted through socialization, sexism is seen to be reproduced through socialization. This approach displaces the IRI from the center of the problem. The political foundation of the "patriarchal triad" is thus obfuscated in the reformist women's rendition of patriarchy. No wonder social and political pressures on women are attributed in "Islamic feminist" literature to some unspecified force, to *extremists whom the Islamic government is supposed to control*.

We recall from the previous chapter that, based on contemporary Western sociological discussions on gender, Muslim reformist women argue that the basis of sexual discrimination is social, rather than natural. This recognition has stirred much optimism among some scholars. Najmabadi considers this recognition positive and believes the refutation by these authors of the equation between natural difference and men's superiority could open the door to new possibilities for equality (Najmabadi 1995: 186–87). But there is little justification for this optimism since, unlike the ideas of their Western teachers, the reformists' discussions on this issue do not rid gender of its a priori nature. Gender always appears as the social cause of turning women's biology against them. There constantly exists an essential womanhood or manhood to which members of the two sexes must aspire. In Moti''s analysis, Western feminism is criticized for achieving sexual equality by sacrificing an unspecified womanhood (1997a). In Tohidi (1997a), the Jungian anima and animus dichotomize human beings. This tension is even more vivid among Islamist reformers. Abdolkarim Soroush, for instance, emphatically points out that a foundational value in male-female relationships is to ensure that "woman is woman, man is man." In fact, he holds, that is what "chastity" ('*effat*) is all about (See *Zanân*'s interview with Soroush, December 1999–January 2000: 32, 34). Kadivar identifies four structures that, "according to sociologists," enslave women: production, reproduction, gender, and socialization.[4] This approach, Kadivar disapprovingly reflects, eventually leads to the conclusion that women have become the "second sex" because of their role as mothers and caregivers. This analysis, she goes on, makes biology women's destiny. Opposing this view, Kadivar argues that "as she is a woman, as she is a mother or reproducer, a woman can traverse through different phases of evolution" (Kadivar 1996: 16). In other words, gender, according to Kadivar, does not create womanhood, mothering, and caregiving; gender creates what comes next: turning womanhood and motherhood—i.e., biology—into a trap for women.

Androgyny and likeness of men and women have been criticized in social sciences (Heilbrun 1973; Treblicot 1982; Jaggar 1983). But in the reformist approach, a rejection of androgyny becomes an occasion to celebrate existing gender roles, as long as both masculine and feminine roles are equally valued. For instance, though Moti' encourages men to value women's child-rearing, she does not discuss how men assigned childrearing responsibility to women because it did not enhance men's power in society. Her analysis obfuscates the role of unequal distribution of social resources that has given men the power to *both* define masculine and feminine roles *and* value them differently. *Recognition* of feminine roles takes the place of *redistribution* of resources (see Sacks 1974; Sanday 1974). The "different but equal" argument falls within an Islamic paradigm. But traditional Islamists follow this assumption to a conclusion that is not entirely illogical. If men and women have different essential gender identities, laws that equally pertain to them do not treat them equitably. They are different and the law should treat them differently.

Posing gender against sex is more vivid in the writings of reformists with a more pronounced belief in Islam. Ebtekar expresses in her first editorial to *Farzaneh* that women's identity is "defined by a particular set of traits and qualities unique to her womanhood as well as human attributes which are common to both sexes" (Ebtekar 1993a: 1). Due to a "conceptual misunderstanding," women have been victimized everywhere around the world. In order for women to regain their denied rights, they have to avoid "encountering women's issues with a biased inclination toward women as a particular social stratum."

Instead of isolating women's issues from the mainstream of human life and societies, and dealing with her from a prejudiced, woman-centered, woman-oriented, viewpoint, Feminism could have chosen to consider the woman in the context of her natural identity and role, to lay emphasis on the rapidly disintegrating family and her central part in that institution and finally to balance her dynamic relationship with her society both male and female. (2. Also see Ebtekar 1995–1996a: 133–34)

Mohammad Hâshemi (1997) and Ahmad Âkouchakiân (1997) clearly distinguish between "sex roles" and "gender roles"—while the former refer to innate physio-psychological differences, the latter refers to social arrangements of roles. Adapting the "wrong" sex role is unacceptable:

From a psychological perspective, the secret of creation has made women and men with irreversibly different psyches and characteristics. False manifestation of feminine or masculine characteristics, in other words, men acting like women (*zan-namâ'i*) or vice versa (*mardnamâ'i*), without needing any scientific explanation, is innately repulsive. (Hâshemi 1997: 34)

These differences merely testify to divergent characteristics, not privileges. "Mistakenly," however, these differences were taken by "ancient traditions" to mean men's superiority over women. Now, on the other hand, "extremist" reaction to sexual discriminations has caused women to "ignore the principle of sexual differences" (35).

Islamist reformists' acceptance of motherhood as a natural attribute of womanhood leaves women in an uncertain position. Let us consider an exchange among the participants of one of *Zanân*'s round table discussions. Nasrin Mosaffa poses a dilemma she faced one day. Her baby was sick, she had to give a lecture, and her husband was not around to take care of the baby. What was she supposed to do? Should she cancel the lecture to take care of her sick child? Her social responsibility pushed her in one direction, her "maternal instinct" in another. (Interestingly, day care does not appear as an alternative.) Commenting on Mosaffa's experience, Tavassoli deduces that in discussing women's rights, we ought not to ignore "nature." We should not be oblivious to women's role conflict. "On the one hand, she has to give a talk. On the other, her baby is sick. I think the woman will choose the baby" (*Zanân* 1997c: 31). Sociologist Homâ Zanjânizâdeh objects. Not only does Tavassoli place too much emphasis on traditional roles, she forcibly argues, but under the aegis of saving the family, he also tends to quiet women's cry for changes in gender roles. Tavassoli concedes, justifying his position that he merely speaks about what exists today. Men should certainly "help and do their share of the housework" (33).

Gender distinguishes women from men, but it also distinguishes false and fabricated (*ja'li*) woman from the authentic (Kadivar 1996: 80). There is an authentic womanhood toward which women must aspire. In the reformists' rendition of gender, the concept of authentic woman is ambiguous. They seem to have uncritically borrowed "authenticity" from the discourse of secular social critics about cultural imperialism. The notion of "inauthentic" or "rootless" woman refers in that discourse predominantly to the "modern woman" of the Pahlavi era, but in post-revolutionary discourse, these categories have been applied to any woman who has opposed Islamic gender ideologies or to urban women critical of traditional lifestyles. It is in the latter context that Shahshahani judges urban women: "Urban woman, especially the urban woman of the past few decades, has become 'rootless' and has looked down upon every urban, rural or tribal tradition.

She has made the Western woman her role model" (Shahshahani 1987: 21). These secular critiques never clarify what exactly constitutes an "authentic woman." On the basis of discussions in *Zanân* and other sources of this trend, one could only venture that an "authentic" woman would be both a good wife and mother and an active member of society.

For the Islamists reformists, authentic womanhood is essentially a divine creature. For believers, the authentic womanhood is embodied in religious figures like Fatima or Mariam (the Koranic rendition of the Virgin Mary). The social construction of gender, then, primarily refers to the developments of conditions that prohibited (Muslim) women from following in those women's footsteps. (On Maryam, see Gorgi and Ebtekar 1994; on Fatima and other Muslim figures, see Kadivar 1996; Gorgi and Ebtekar 1997). As symbols of Islamic establishment, women of early Islam become personae whose actions reflect not their own will, but the intention of Allah. Consider the example of a hadith in which the Prophet, after hearing that a woman ruled the neighboring Iran, proclaimed that people who are led by a woman would never find the path to salvation. Juxtaposing this supposition with the vision of Fatima as a political woman could indeed raise some concern: one has either to question the validity of the Prophet's judgment or reject the Shiite portrayal of Fatima as a shrewd politician. To resolve the paradox, Kadivar approvingly quotes Ayatollah Sâlehi Najafâbâdi's comment about the hadith: "The important point here is to know if the Prophet's objective was that even if leadership were in the hand of a woman like Fatima, the nation would be ruined. Can anybody make such a claim?" (Kadivar 1996: 88). A social-historical approach, in my opinion, would suggest that Fatima's leadership is the deed of a specific individual in specific historical circumstances. Her action suggests that contrary to what the Prophet assumed, women could also lead people toward a moral order. Cases are not rare in the history of early Islam when women did in fact reproach holy leaders for their androcentric ideology (for some examples and their treatment by Islamists, see Shahidian 1995: 119–21). The acrobatic religious reader, however, jumps from one interpretation to another, from one qualification to another, to highlight the message of Islam—and in the process usurps the individuality of "chosen women" in the history of Islam.

CULTURAL ACCOMMODATION OF DOMESTICITY

The dominant belief in Islamist women's reformism is that housework is women's work; the husband should, under special circumstances and for certain types of work, assist his wife, and should always be appreciative. Keyhânniâ instructs Iranian husbands that a woman who has an outside job usually returns home tired. In this case, the husband should learn to do some housework, especially heavy tasks that might be tiring for her (1996: 300–303). In his interviews with a number of social and cultural personalities, he asks who is to take care of the house when a woman returns tired from her job. All but two interviewees answer that perhaps the family needs to hire a maid; but if they cannot afford that, he should help—they agree unanimously, however, that it is really her responsibility. Shirin Ebadi, to whose discussions on law I have referred in the previous chapter, responds as follows:

If the family can afford it, they'd better hire a maid. If not, the husband and children must cooperate with the woman, or at least not be too demanding. But the woman should know in any case that she has the prime responsibility. A woman's most important responsibility is at home, and if a woman is skillful enough, she will be successful both outside and inside the house. (Interview with Shirin Ebadi in Keyhânniâ 1996: 354)

Keyhânniâ instructs women in how to balance outside and inside jobs. First, she should find the right job. That is, she should make sure that her job is compatible with her personality and the family's economic condition. She should also beware not to bring home her job-related frustrations and fatigue. Most importantly, her outside employment must not adversely affect her chores around the house (109). If she wants him to help with the housework, she should pamper him. And who better than a male family counselor to advise women on how to accomplish that? Here are Keyhânniâ's recommendations:

1. Give the man the opportunity to do the tasks he likes.
2. Instead of nagging and complaining, encourage your husband to do a chore.
3. Do not blame him for his mistakes, otherwise he might get offended and refuse to do anything. Commend him on everything he does right; that will encourage him to do more.
4. Help your husband to gradually understand that you need his help and that it is his duty to help you.
5. Do not assign tasks to men. Men do not like to feel restricted. Let him do the work on his own accord. (Keyhânniâ 1996: 302–3)

Housewives are instructed to do something in addition to their household duties to enrich their lives. Even so, they should "know that household chores have certain attractions in their own right," says Ashraf Gerâmizâdegân, the then-editor of *Zan-e Rouz* in an interview with Keyhânniâ (1996: 382).

But a man is not automatically entitled to the support of his great wife; he should earn it. As Keyhânniâ put it:

A kind, hard-working woman will put her family in the domain of her love's gravity. The warmth of her kindness will affect all members of the family and turn them
into outstanding beings. If a man does not appreciate the productive role of this
woman, he has undoubtedly done injustice to *himself*. Woe to a man who is under
the mistaken impression that if he appreciates this woman, he will diminish his
worth and grandness. (281, emphasis added)

And a pampered husband must not forget to be appreciative. "Appreciation" is essential to the gender relations à la Islamist gender reformism.
Sociologist Moti' (1997a) proposes that a nativist women's movement in
Iran must encourage men and women to appreciate traditional female duties. Keyhânniâ explains this even more effectively: "If he does not show
his appreciation for her work, she will shrug and say in protest: 'I'm not
a maid!' And she is right," he emphasizes, "since nothing in the shari'ah
compels her to do housework. But what a man is not entitled to according
to the shari'ah, a man can obtain through love, respect, and appreciation"
(1996: 286–88).

THE CULTURAL CONSTRUCTION OF SEXUALITY

The essential womanhood and manhood of Islamist reformism are embodied in essentially sexed bodies. Just like other Islamists, sexuality in
Islamist gender reformism is a fixed identity into which women and men
are born. Allah has defined (verse 1, sura *Women* of the Koran) the proper
relationship between these sexed bodies: "Men, have fear of your Lord,
who created you from a single soul. From that soul He created its mate,
and through them He bestrewed the earth with countless men and women"
(Koran 1988: 366).

Nothing in the Islamist reformist women's literature questions this fixed
sexual identity. Quite to the contrary, reformist gender analysis rests on the
notion that people are born either male or female, and that society then assigns them distinct gender identity (see the discussion on gender in the previous chapter and above). The teleological assumption of the Islamic gender
ideology and the fixity of sexuality in this predefined system are not questioned. That physiological differences lead to two, *and only two*, clearly dis-
tinguishable sexes is taken for granted in this reformist trend. Yet,
especially in the context of policing gender and sexuality in the IRI, it appears quite important to question the very social and cultural assumptions
that define not just gender, but also sexuality. We recall, for instance, men
who do not appear or act "manly" (e.g., in their voice, facial construction
and expressions, gestures, or "non-masculine" dress) risk suspicion of homosexuality. Only by questioning predefined sex can we countervail such
restrictions. Islamist women's reformism cannot undertake this project, not
only because such an endeavor in the conservative atmosphere of the Is-

lamic Republic subjects them to accusations of perversion (the spread of corruption on earth, or *efsâd-e fel arz*, is severely punished) and going against Allah's creation, but also because fixed sexuality is central to the Islamic *and* "Islamic feminist" worldviews.[5]

In light of the complex relationship between body and culture, the notion of sexual desire as a natural phenomenon is equally suspect. Sexuality may be defined as socioculturally accepted responses to bodily desires (Weeks 1986). "Natural" or "unnatural" sex, "normal" or "abnormal" sex, "legitimate" or "illegitimate" sex, and "licit" or "illicit" sex are all understandable only in their sociocultural contexts. The Islamic definition of sexual desire and sexual relationship exclusively in the context of matrimonial relationship both denies the individual's control over one's body and limits sexuality to heterosexuality. Reformists' quiet acceptance of the Islamic approach reinforces heterosexuality within the bounds of matrimony as the only natural, normal, legitimate, and licit form of sexual expression. Thus, Islamist women's reformism fails to accommodate women (and men) who do not define sexuality only in the context of procreation. It leaves out individuals seeking sexual life outside marriage. Quite possibly in the Islamic Republic, where deviation from the marital bed is severely punished, some activists have chosen silence due to political exigencies. Yet state policing of individuals' relationships and failing to recognize sexual freedom cannot be easily dismissed. What does Islamist women's reformism offer people who wish to experience sex outside marriage? What alternatives does it provide women who desire neither marriage nor mothering? What does it propose for those who wish to cohabit? Limited to ideological and legal constraints, Islamist women's reformism proves ill-equipped for these issues.

Fâtemeh Safari reflected on sexuality in a four-part article in *Payâm-e Zan*. In Iran, writes Safari (1999a), morality and sexual education are intertwined with Islam, though Western influences in all societal aspects have caused confusions in these realms as well. Consequently, we find two conflicting approaches. At one extreme, people adhere to unrealistic dogmas and harsh controls; at the other, individuals cheer for lax sexual morality, similar to that in the West. Safari believes that the rejection of free liaison between males and females in Iran, which stems from the religious nature of this people, forces us to ponder the perimeters of acceptable interaction between the sexes. Neither the prohibition of interaction nor the free pursuit of lustful instincts that ruin the family are satisfactory. Instead, she recommends the creation of a moral-rational sexual actor who has internalized (Islamic) sexual morality and can discern good and bad in the sexual field:

The middle-of-the-road approach means a rational interaction [between the sexes] based on mutual knowledge and respect, observance of social and religious laws, and concern for the health of society in such milieus as the workplace, the university, or the house. This framework is vital for appropriate and healthy interactions between boys and girls, and adherence to morality in this age when women work shoulder to shoulder with men in universities, offices, factories, and hospitals. . . . The realization of this approach depends on individuals' [moral] development and understanding as well as their internalizing social values. (41)

Just as sexual anarchy threatens the health of a society, too many restrictions bear no fruit but trouble. It is not that authorities should let young people do as they please, Safari insists; but Muslims should beware of the dangers of violent suppression of the Iranian youth. "The point is that the adolescent crisis and sexual instincts cannot be directed to the right path merely with incarcerations, trials, lashes, beatings, advice, prayers, or discussions of death and Judgment Day" (Safari 1999b: 42). Some cases, to be sure, cannot escape physical punishment, especially in matters of *hodud*, offenses such as zena whose punishments are stipulated in the shariʿah. "It is clear that the *hodud* stipulated by God must be implemented. In cases when criminal acts are proven in accordance with the shariʿah, we cannot easily ignore *hodud* and Islamic edicts" (43).

But, she wonders, are not divine laws to guard the health of the society? Then can lashes alone make healthy societal foundations? Even when, according to the shariʿah, a crime is committed, Safari suggests, we must rely on psychologists and sociologists to determine the best recourse. "The enforcement of the law and punishment must be reserved only for malice (*sharârat*), when society is threatened" (43).

Safari is critical of the "irrationality and impracticality" of the Plan for the Spread of Chastity, *tarh-e towseʿeh-ye ʿefâf* (Safari 1999d: 46).[6] The Plan divides men's and women's spaces and stipulates details of their interactions. Yet it is impossible to tackle social interactions between different sexes merely with outdated clichés and laws. The Plan recommends marriage for those who feel sexually pressured, but fails to provide practical solutions for problems young people face concerning marriage. Most importantly, Safari points out, restraint is a personal decision; it cannot be forced on the individual (45–46).

To combat sexual immorality, Safari suggests that young people must participate in sports and arts, develop a plan for the future, and nourish a love for science (38). Early marriage offers no solution unless based on clear objectives and reasonable understanding of marital life. Officials must take seriously the negative moral consequences of unemployment: social frustrations make sexual pleasure an appealing alternative. The authorities must control external stimuli: films with sex scenes, articles that excite and promote sexual anarchy (*biband-o-bâri*), not to mention the way some women dress and behave (Safari 1999d: 42–43). At the same time, young people must strengthen their faiths and resist temptations. In particular, it is necessary to dismiss what Safari calls the "feminization of chastity" (*zan-âneh shodan-e 'effat*)—the notion that women alone corrupt a society. Men must learn that they are responsible for upholding social morality as much as women are (42).

Developing personal strength against sexual temptation, according to Safari, must be at the core of Islamic sexual socialization. "Girls must be reared to be proud of their femininity and of their efforts to preserve their honor" (Safari 1999c: 39). They must control (*meydândâri*) their interaction with men; they must be circumspect and alert (*noktehbin va houshyâr*) so that their "feminine pride" (*qorur-e dokhtarâneh*), their "strictness and prudence, shall protect them against potential slippage and [boys'] deceit and connivance" (39–40). Boys must learn that chastity and purity are not only for girls (40). They must be prohibited from using foul language so that "despicable behavior" does not take root in them (41). They must become aware of the biological changes at puberty; they must learn not to play with girls' emotions (41).

In the confines of the marital bed, proposals have been made to spruce up the sexual field. Numerous Islamic texts address this issue, though Islamist reformist writings have not directly taken up this issue. Instead, the writings of marriage counselor Asqar Keyhânniâ on marital relationships have been discussed in *Zanân*. Keyhânniâ, we recall, instructs couples that a healthy sexual relationship does not just happen; couples have to work on it. Emotional and physical condition, ambiance, and mood are key ingredients of a successful sexual encounter. Both parties are taught to be attentive to the needs of their partners. Once again, however, assumptions of a fixed sexual nature come into play. Keyhânniâ repeatedly refers to the lower intensity of sexual desire in women. Her sexual urges come to the fore only in the marital bed; while she should be a prude outside marriage, she is supposed to be a fireball for her husband:

Being demure (*hayâ*) is an admirable trait. Perhaps it is one of the positive points of the Iranian woman. But it is a mistake to be a prude when having sex with one's legal husband. The reason is that coyness will becloud a marital relationship instead of promoting better understanding. (Keyhânniâ 1996: 157)

Keyhânniâ then disarms women in the sexual field by threatening them with husbands' infidelity. Women are warned that if they fail to attend to their husband's sexual needs, he might become "aloof and violent" (158). Women, too, could traverse the forbidden path, but temptation is never nearly as immanent as for men "for sexual pleasure for a woman has only secondary place" to her obligations as mother and wife (158). Women particularly should remember not to "misuse" (*su'-e-estefâdeh*) sexual relationship. A woman who uses sex as a weapon in settling marital quarrels should beware that in the long run, *she* is the real loser: her action could push him toward infidelity. He concludes the chapter on sex with a stern warning and fatherly advice: "No wife should deprive her husband of sex for feeling hurt (*ranjesh*). It is even possible that her accommodating response to his demand will lead to the dissolution of hurts or his reciprocal attempt to heal her wounds" (169).

An outstanding omission from the discussion of sexuality is homosexuality. In Islamist gender reformism, as in other Islamic interpretations, heterosexuality is sexuality proper. Homosexuality is only a deviation, a pathological tendency. That is why the issue is raised only to highlight the decadence of the West and the mistake, or even the false path, of Western feminism. Moti' refers in passing to "homosexuality, bisexuality, and the destruction of family," and implicitly considers these negative consequences of Western feminists' oblivion toward the distinctiveness of femininity and masculinity (Moti' 1997a: 24. For further discussion, see the previous chapter). I raised this issue in my private correspondence with some reformists. None, however, were willing to discuss the issue. Islamist reformists' stand is quite clear. Ebtekar, for instance, opposes considering homosexuality as "normal":

The realm of sexual roles is, according to all divine religions, confined to the biological and physiological framework of the individual and any contradiction in this aspect is considered pathological. Psychiatry and sociology as pure science [*sic*], also originally considered any contradictory sexual behavior such as homosexuality to be among sociopathic personality disturbances. (Ebtekar 1995–1996b: 96–97)

She specifically criticizes the 1990 edition of the *Diagnostic and Statistical Manual* for removing homosexuality from the list of personality disorders. "Later," she continues, "in order to comply with the decadent social trends of their societies, homosexuality was removed from the sociopathic list, only to provide a scientific pretext for the normalization of homosexuality" (97). It was with the same orientation that the IRI joined other Islamic states and the Vatican to oppose feminists' concerns with sexual orientation rights. Ebtekar quotes approvingly a Yemeni representative in Beijing that Western countries' support for sexual orientation rights stems only from their unburdened lives (*bidardi*) and lack of understanding of the real problems of the women of the world (Ebtekar 1995–1996a: 136).

A pivotal task of any feminist project in Iran, I believe, is to critically reassess familiar social assumptions of sexual beliefs and values. Only through such rigor can the Iranian women's movement rid itself and Iranian culture of patriarchal sexual ideologies. Only through such rigor can the Iranian women's movement promote sexual pluralism. The urgency of this endeavor can be understood if we consider that more than any other period in contemporary Iran, the IRI has foregrounded sexual oppression in such forms as compulsory veiling, strict sexual morality, valuing virginity, shaming homosexuality, and violent punishment of "sexual deviance."

IN THE NAME OF THE COLLECTIVE; IN THE SERVICE OF ALLAH

I have emphasized above that Islamist women's reformism fails to offer a liberating alternative to the dominant Islamic understanding of sexuality. The key to this failure should be sought in positioning the individual and the collective at opposite poles. My proposal may sound far fetched, considering that the objective of Islamist women's reformism is to achieve happiness for women and men in family and society. But we have to consider that happiness is defined here exclusively in the context of the "collective good"—the individual cannot expect anything that the "collective" does not approve. At the center of the Islamic universe stands Allah who owns the universe. In verse 66, sura *Jonah*, we read: "To Allah belong all who dwell on earth and in heaven. Those that worship false gods follow nothing but idle fancies and preach nothing but falsehood" (Koran 1988: 69).

As creations of Allah, our divine nature compels us to follow divine rules for the well-being of the individual and society. Human beings neither own their bodies nor can they defy the will of God, that is, if they opt for salvation and happiness. Any assertion of individuality, therefore, questions Allah's rights of property and thereby threatens the health of the collective (for further discussion see Sabbah 1984).

Islamist women reformists distinguish themselves from Western feminism particularly on the basis of their orientations toward God. Whereas Western feminism, according to the Islamist observer, is essentially a struggle to guarantee women's personal choice, Muslim women fight to guarantee the central slogan of Islam—There is no God but Allah. The objective of Muslim women's movement is "the denial of any enslavement and surrender (*'uboodiyat va bandegi*) to history, tradition, and false ideas, and the deepening of enslavement and surrender to God alone, the quest for human freedom from anything but God." Such a "revolutionary-believing woman will sacrifice even her husband and children" toward that goal (Abbas-Gholizadeh 1995–1996a: 113).

This adversarial approach to individuality also marks a criticism by Islamist reformists of Western feminism. According to this assessment, human rights are relevant for the political, not social, sphere. Western feminism, however, has subjected social life to human rights. People justify everything on the basis of human rights. Consequently, Western feminism has weakened collective life, most notably, the family.

Imaginations (*tasavvorât*) that do not consider the human rights confined only to political rights, are the cause of discussions in the West that include individual freedom in choosing the form and content of one's life, especially in the realm of the identity of the mate, divorce right, number of children, and prevention from pregnancy. (Abbas-Gholizadeh 1994a: 160)

The women's movement, according to Abbas-Gholizadeh, is not solely culpable, as Western feminism is itself influenced by humanism, dominant in Western philosophy since ancient Greece. Due to this philosophical disposition, Abbas-Gholizadeh contends, Western women have sought individualism in reaction to their denigration during the Middle Ages:

Western women's search for freedom borrows its premises from "individualism" and on the basis of it develops schools like "liberal feminism," "conservative feminism," "radical feminism." This itself shows the astonishment of Western woman when it comes to defining "freedom." (Abbas-Gholizadeh 1994a: 160)

The logical outcome of this emphasis on individualism is the emergence of single-parent families in the West. "Children are deprived of the natural right of having both father and mother and the woman loses her irreplaceable capital of mothering" (161).

Moti''s discussion of Western feminism echoes a similar concern. For her, Western feminism's emphasis on similarity of the sexes has caused a "grand revolution in values that has resulted in such phenomena as homosexuality, bisexuality, increasing divorce, and domineering tendencies in women" (Moti' 1997a: 24). In her analysis, however, a prefabricated, sexed body replaces divine human nature. Individual women or men are subsumed under collective femininity or masculinity.

These approaches to individualism and collectivity, however, do not sufficiently address the complexity of present social life. The problem facing contemporary Iranian women and men, as it does their fellow humans elsewhere, is not a dichotomy of collective and individual good. At stake is the individuation process that had been launched at the turn of the century and hastened after the reforms of the 1960s. This process has provided members of that society with increasing autonomy and self-realization. As we have observed in *Gender Politics*, a combination of changes in employment, education, and law has enhanced women's capacity to define who they are. These self-definitions call for revisions in personal and social living arrangements. Mothers who used to sacrifice their lives for children can now lay more emphasis on their own life projects. Wives who used to stay in rotten marriages can now feel justified to ignore the "sanctity of family life." Women who used to stand behind successful men in the family or in the boardroom can now claim a share for themselves. All these new stances appear from the vantage point of hegemonic gender relations, as if women were caught in a selfish attempt at promoting their interests at the cost of collectivity. Yet as long as we continue to frame the problem in the context of a dichotomy between the individual and the collective, we are bound to endorse the same solution: sacrifice the individual to protect the collective from the evils of individualism. The woman will end up compromising herself to maintain the sanctity of a patriarchal order. To avoid that, we need to shift attention from the dangerous dichotomy to consider individuation. Whereas an individualist could not bring together the interests of both her self and her collective, an individuated person can accomplish that. If the "collective" does not threaten her individuation, she does not need to view the collective as a threat or competitor. After all, it is not the "collective" that suffers from a rearrangement of social power—individuals do, specifically individual men. Were this distinction made clear, collectivity would then be deconstructed. We would have to redefine "collectivity" so as to afford individuals the ability to construct themselves as they envision. Such a project would by nature be a temporal one, as we constantly revise ourselves in relation to new external and internal challenges. The Islamic outlook cannot accommodate these nuances. For one thing, a predefined notion of gender defies constant reinvention of the self. Besides, the individual needs to own oneself, to have control over oneself, to be individuated—whereas Allah's property may roam around all it wants, but must eventually remain in his territory (for more on this, see chapter 5).

THE CULTURAL POLITICS OF "SHROUDING FREEDOM"

As Iranian women marched the streets of Tehran in March 1979, they called the mandatory veil "the shroud of freedom." Ironically, however, Islamist reformist women are at their weakest when encountering the veil. Here, too, the problem is that many leading figures in the reformist movement are devout Muslims (Haeri 1995). Having played such a central role in the Islamic revolution, hejâb has become the prime symbol of Muslim womanhood. Islamists do not tolerate any modification of the Islamic Republic if it does not include some form of modesty in dress. This could explain, at least in part, why there is no serious discussion about the veil in reformist women's literature. Not only that, Islamist reformist women have recognized a need to clarify from the outset that any critique of hejâb is inconceivable. The editorial of the first issue of Zanân attributes "opposition to hejâb" to "nonbelievers and adversaries of Islam" (Sherkat 1991a). Worse yet, in line with the official ideology, the long struggle of Iranian women against hejâb is either attributed to the Westernization efforts of the Pahlavis (Zahir-Nezhâd Ershâdi 1995) or simply overlooked. In a round table discussion of Zanân, historian Mansureh Ettehâdiyeh lists the grievances of Iranian women at the turn of the century. Ettehâdiyeh's list includes inequality in the law, employment, political participation, and education; lack of economic independence; and lack of social security and welfare (Zanân 1997d: 26). She conveniently leaves out, however, women's strong opposition toward the veil. Oddly enough, one eloquent critic of hejâb in early twentieth century was Tajussaltaneh, a Qajar princess, who left behind memoirs edited by Ettehâdiyeh (Tajussaltaneh Qajar 1983).[7]

Hejâb simply cannot be questioned. Hojjatulislam Mohsen Kadivar, a prominent neo-Islamist figure, clearly states this in an interview about the religious meaning of a civil society (*Khordâd* 7 December 1998). The difference between a religious republic and a democratic republic, he explains, is that the former relies on religion and popular vote counts *only if* it does not contradict religious edicts.

In the Islamic Republic, for example, if all people vote to abolish the hejâb, we would say this edict is obligatory (*elzâmi*) and does not depend on majority vote. Hejâb is like Einstein's theory of relativity. Can we subject Einstein's relativity to popular vote? Definitely not. Thus, the people's vote is not binding in areas of exact science or religious obligations. In what areas are people's votes legitimate? In the areas of scientific exactitude or obligations of the Shar'.

On those rare occasions authors address the veil (Kar 1993; Saʿidzâdeh 1993), they merely point out the inequality in making the veil mandatory for women but not having similar regulations for men. There are also criticisms and complaints about *how* hejâb is implemented, but nothing about the institution of hejâb itself. Jamileh Kadivar, for instance, states in an interview with *Avaye Zan* (Summer 2000: 51) that hejâb is an Islamic principle, but it should not be imposed:

Hejâb is an Islamic principle; our country, as a religious country, and our people, as Muslims, have accepted this principle. It is natural that a minority would have problems with the very principle of hejâb and would oppose it, but then since the majority is Muslim and the Constitution is Islamic, it is natural that Islamic laws rule. There is no doubt about the principle of hejâb, but so far as its form, color, and design, our women must be free to choose.

Though the report about people's preference for dark colors, discussed in the previous chapter, rejects any conflict between colorfulness and Islamic teachings, there is no discussion of whence the reportedly widespread practice of wearing only dark colors in the Islamic Republic stems. Another report by Nâzanin Shah-Rokni (2000) on dark colors distorts the history of the imposition of the veil in the IRI. Quoting Fatemeh Tondgooyân (Advisor to the Minister of Education on Women's Issues), the report claims that women chose the hejâb at the time of the revolution and freely wore the black chador to state that "the blackness of women's chador is stronger than the redness of martyrs' blood" (2). If by "we women" Shah-Rokni or Tondgooyân means *Islamist women*, they are substituting this subgroup of Iranian women for the whole. If they mean *Iranian women*, their assertion that women voluntarily donned the black chador or the hejâb is a blatant misrepresentation of the history.

The veil, an issue political to its core, is depoliticized in this manner. The persistence of dark colors in the mosaic of the Islamic Republic is attributed to the vague category of "our culture." A similar approach is evident in an account of Iranian women in France by Shahshahani (1997). She treats hejâb as an unproblematic "choice" of an Iranian woman, a choice that causes internal conflict for such a woman once in a society unfamiliar with this phenomenon, a society that regards hejâb as a sign of backwardness. She unveils merely to accommodate her environment. Though undoubtedly this is true about some Iranian women, the majority of immigrant and exiled Iranian women do not just abandon the veil for one reason or another; *they oppose it.* Similarly, in Iran, the persisting problem of mal-veiling and the brutal presence of the moral police indicate a defiance of hejâb, of at least *imposed* hejâb. Any account of hejâb that denies, overlooks, or downplays mechanisms of coercion and resistance in relation to this symbol, makes the problem appear benign.

Tohidi's passing remark about hejâb also minimizes its significance. She observes that in the observing eyes of Westerners and Iranian secularists, hejâb has come to signify oppression. The presence of veiled Muslim women in social scenes refutes this assumption. She writes about the Iranian women delegation to the Beijing conference: "The presence of women wearing manteau and headscarf in colors other than black and alongside women wearing the châdor indicated that other clothes are acceptable in Iran" (Tohidi 1995: 6).

Tohidi's depiction distorts the problem in several ways. First, the manteau and headscarf ensemble are *tolerated, not accepted*, as substitutes for châdor by many officials of the Islamic Republic. Besides, "colors other than black" include dark gray, dark brown, and dark blue. Some authorities of the Islamic state have even come to accept diversity of colors in clothes. According to a report about the government-sponsored Second Conference on Hejâb held in Tehran in the fall of 1995, for instance, a professor from Azzahra (Al-Zahra) University proposes that colors have psychological consequences and therefore people should not be limited in their choice of color (quoted in Shah-Rokni 1995: 8). But considering this as a sign of improvement, as Tohidi alludes, is self-deception, to say the least. Had this tolerance even included a wider spectrum of colors, it would hardly constitute an *alternative*, simply because it continued to be compulsory. Finally, the objection of Iranian women to hejâb has been against the *imposition of a dress code*. The opposition is not against those who want to wear the veil, but to the mandatory veiling of those who do not wish to wear the veil. Nor has the opposition been exclusively to the châdor or limited color selection.

Alongside efforts to curb pressure on women to comply with the dress code, some Muslim women activists also try to make the châdor appealing by presenting it as a national dress. In other words, they propose the châdor that covers from head to toe, to be worn over the headscarf and manteau. Nâhid Shid donned the châdor after her candidacy for the Majlis was approved by the Council of Guardians. The reporter of *Zanân* asked her for an explanation. She replied: "The Council of Guardians accepted me with the *maqna'eh*, the veil. But since public opinion has chosen the châdor as our national dress, I did not want to defy it" (*Zanân* 1996b: 19). "The châdor is the superior form of hejâb (*hejâb-e bartar*)," Fâezeh Hashemi comments, "it has been a part of our tradition and indeed, other than its religious-traditional significance, it is also a national symbol" (*Zanân* 1996a: 17). Massoumeh Ebtekar similarly started to wear the "national symbol and the superior form of hejâb" after being assigned to head the Organization for Environmental Protection in President Khatami's cabinet, in most likelihood following a "recommendation" by the president (*Zanân* 1997f: 4).

The châdor as an all-enveloping dress is favored by conservative Islamists. Why would women who favor relaxation of gender policies adhere to that? To understand this paradox, we should keep in mind that this argument has been predominantly put forth by women who are part of the Islamic state apparatus. Figures like Kadivar, Shid, Hashemi, and Ebtekar, as well as the men who assign them to offices, are under constant scrutiny by the conservative Islamists. For Nâhid Shid this surveillance is perhaps considerably tight because of her reported beauty, to which some even attribute her success in politics, as the report in *Zanân* suggests. Fâezeh Hashemi's proposals for more relaxed laws concerning women's participation in sport and overall presence in society have caused quite a stir among the hizbullah. These women are forced to prove their allegiance to Islam by constantly guarding their reputation. Their opponents question their moral standing; they in turn have to protect themselves by giving their opponents no reason to justify their mudslinging.

In much writing about women in the Islamic world, the significance of hejâb is underestimated on the basis that women choose the veil, that it is a symbol whose meaning women negotiate (see for example, Hoodfar 1993; Watson 1994; Khan 1995; Karam 1996). This argument overlooks the fact that regardless of the actor's intention, the veil has a defined function in Islamic ideology. The veil ensures that God-made moral order is not defied. However the veil is worn, whatever the style of the veil, whether a woman actually wears a veil, the deportment dictated by the Islamic gender ideology veils her soul; hence, the restrictions implicit in veiling remain. *The veil is an institutionalized practice of Islamic patriarchy.* Thus, though it is true that many women wear the veil voluntarily, it is questionable whether that exonerates the veil from its role in maintaining patriarchal gender relations. As I commented on this point on another occasion:

coercion consists not simply in forcing someone to do something; a coercive act does not simply result from the use of direct, overt force. When certain values or goals are offered by a dominant social power (men, political establishment, religious beliefs, ideologies, etc.) as *the only* legitimate "options," choosing from among them is no sign of freedom. Undoubtedly, those subjected to this oppressive rule use whatever means available to negotiate social distribution of power. And the significance and courageousness of their actions should be neither overlooked nor understated. Yet in recognizing such actions, one should not lose sight of the fact that they occur *in spite* of an oppressive system. These actions are loci of resistance against, of oppositions to, and of compromises with the dominant oppressive system—but they are not signs of freedom *from* or *within* that system. (Shahidian 1997b: 331)

The irony of "free choice" becomes particularly poignant when we keep in mind that in the Islamic Republic every means is utilized to promote compulsory veiling (see also Shahidian 1993: 41–44).

TOWARD AN "INDIGENOUS FEMINISM"?

Reformist women have a push-pull relationship with native and foreign non-Muslims. On the one hand, they distinguish themselves from nonbelievers (or "bad Muslims"—see Chapter 6 of *Gender Politics*) in order to justify their claim for authenticity. On the other, they are attracted to nonbelievers for support and intellectual inspiration. In effect, they need to establish their legitimacy on two grounds: both for the believing defenders of the IRI and those critical of the regime. On both grounds, they have to smooth the tension that currently exists between Iran and Islam. This measure conceals the role of both Islam and the Islamic state as constitutive elements of the patriarchal triad. We recall, for instance, that some Islamist reformist women promote the châdor as a national dress, oblivious to the compulsory nature of hejâb in the IRI or to the fact that the châdor in ancient Iran and in Islam has different philosophies and functions. In a similar vein, Fâezeh Hashemi comments in an interview with *Zanân* that she considers the Shah's cultural policies his worst sin:

The fabric of our society is traditional-religious, aside from that minute percentage who probably liked things like unveiling of women and following Western models, or considered such acts as women's liberation. I do not agree with that since to me, freedom is rendered meaningful in the context of culture. That freedom was only for a few people. (*Zanân* 1996a: 13)

She thusly delegitimizes opponents of Iran's "traditional-religious" fabric as non-Iranian in essence. Also, by qualifying freedom with culture, by limiting freedom to specific sociocultural contexts, she immunizes Islam against criticism on grounds of cultural relativism.[8] In *Zanân*'s interview with Hashemi, the reporter refers to the hizbullahis' opposition to women's attempt to attend a soccer match. She inquires what the Coordinating Council of Women's Sport did in response. Nothing, Hashemi replies, since soccer is not a concern of the Coordinating Council. "Why not?" "Well, because women do not play soccer," she answers laughingly. The reporter asks why women shouldn't play soccer? There is no problem if women play soccer, she responds, "but why should we concern ourselves with men's soccer? Let us first solve women's problems, then take up men's."[9] "Why do you not let women decide for themselves?" "I believe limitations imposed on women are cultural problems of centuries and we cannot solve them overnight" (14). A reasonable argument, indeed—cultural problems cannot be solved overnight. There is, however, this difficulty. She refers to "centuries of cultural problems" denying women their rights as if Islam has not been a major source of the problem, as if Islam has not been a chief guardian of Iranian patriarchy in law and culture. Some believers' fierce opposition to women attending a sporting event *is* a "cultural problem" nurtured in the Islamic Republic.

"Islamic feminists" propose that critiques of Islam as a patriarchal ideology are only relevant to a particular, albeit dominant, interpretation of Islam. Rejecting a monolithic interpretation of Islam, "Islamic feminists" set out to provide an alternative to the oppression of women in a cultural context with which Iranian women and men are familiar. Foreign and native observers alike are instructed that Islamist women's reformism may not appease *their* notions of feminism, but it is congruent with Iranian women's cultural background. Non-Muslim critics are charged with inadequate familiarity with Middle Eastern cultures, Orientalist orientations, lack of respect for cultural diversity, or, more seriously, outright racism.

This analysis is also reflected in the writings of some Iranian and other Muslim feminist scholars in Western academia. Homa Hoodfar (1993) sees a link between Western racism and criticism of the veil. Riffat Hassan, the Pakistani scholar of theology, similarly expresses astonishment about "the outpouring of so much sympathy in, and by, the West toward Muslim women" appearing in the midst of Western hatred toward the World of Islam. "Few of us," she emphasizes, "can forget the brutal burning of Turkish Muslim girls by German gangsters or the ruthless rape of Bosnian Muslim women by Serbian soldiers" (1996: 64).

No one could condone such inhumane behavior; racism must be condemned in all forms. Yet I wonder if by the same token one could dismiss Islam and the Islamic approach to women because of the Islamists' abhorrent treatment of women, non-Muslims like Bahaiis, and secularists in Iran,

Turkey, Pakistan, Bangladesh, Afghanistan, Egypt, and Algeria. Moreover, clearly not everyone who criticizes Islam and its treatment of women is a racist, nor are they necessarily culpable for the crimes committed against Muslims around the world.

Similarly, that Islam is not the only misogynist religion (Tohidi 1997b: 107) is hardly a reason not to critically address Islam—after all, *Islam, more than any other religion*, is relevant to the case of women in Iran and many other places in the Middle East. "Islamic feminists' " defensiveness toward critics of their Islamic solutions resembles the perilous rejection of criticism by conservative Islamists on the ground that Islam had already offered the best guideline for women's lifetime happiness (for a discussion, see Shahidian 1993).

Both Islamist reformist women in Iran (as elsewhere in the Middle East) and their defenders in the West have founded their arguments on cultural relativism. The fundamental assumption of cultural relativism, championed nowadays by postmodernists, is that different cultures provide indigenous answers to their social problems that should be judged in the context of their own environment. On the basis of this argument, Islamists and "Islamic feminists" propose that any universal criterion for assessing sexual oppression is invalid. Kia Tabatabaie, a senior political officer in the IRI's Ministry of Foreign Affairs, writes:

The effective enjoyment of human rights for men and women alike requires that these rights be defined and explained in the context of the basic cultural and religious mores of each society. Particularly since religious values in themselves constitute a system of rights which apply to individuals, family and social spheres of life [*sic*].(Tabatabaie 1995–1996: 87)

Parvin Ma'rufi, author of the IRI's report on Iranian women to the UN for the preparation of the Fourth World Conference on Women (FWCW), states in an interview that such factors as literacy and health are not good indicators of women's well-being:

There are other things that are more determining of a woman's happiness. We consider, for instance, the stability of the family an indicator of development. We say in societies where the family has a strong foundation, women are happier. Where the family is unstable, women feel more unprotected and miserable. These issues are not among the indicators suggested by the UN. (Abbas-Gholizadeh 1995–1996b: 143)

On the same basis, defenders of Islamist women's reformism question the validity of the argument that Islam's treatment of women is unjust. To them, if women themselves define Islamic edicts such as hejâb and hetero-marital sexuality as liberating, there is really little for others to critique.

This approach has led some scholars such as Patricia Higgins to refrain from supporting women's anti-hejâb demonstrations in March 1979 (Higgins 1983; 1987). Nearly two decades later, the cultural relativist stance is embracing a patriarchal ideology on a similar ground (see Shahidian 1993; 1997b; 1999a).

Many natives, firmly rooted in their culture and society, have also adopted a critical approach to Islam. Islamists—reformist and not reformist alike—claim monopoly over Iran's cultural history. They delegitimize secular trends in Iranian culture to show that they are *the* legitimate representatives of Iranian society. It is unfortunate that even some secular critics accede to this offensive. Since the turn of the twentieth century, a strong intellectual and political trend in Iran has called for progressive reforms in virtually all aspect of society, including the social status of women. Save for some exceptions, these movements have systematically confronted religious oppositions. The opposition of the clerical establishment to social reforms in women's status has been particularly fierce (see *Gender Politics*). Now, however, some apologists argue that feminism and Islamism are not only compatible, but at least for believers, they are in fact complementary (Najmabadi 1995: 201; Tohidi 1997b: 118 and 129).

ISLAMIST WOMEN'S REFORMISM AND "WESTERN FEMINISM"

Optimism for the development of an "indigenous feminism" has prompted Iranian feminist scholars in the West to applaud "Islamic feminists" for their treatment of Western feminism. Najmabadi (1995: 178) considers the openness of "Islamic feminists" toward Western feminism an indication of accepting feminism, *instead of Islam*, as a viable alternative for women, at least for women of some societies. Najmabadi cites Massoumeh Ebtekar questioning the validity of the Old Testament for the twentieth century woman (Ebtekar 1993c). Contemporary societies, Ebtekar argues, yearn for a revolution to wipe clean the dust of centuries of corruption, degradation, and injustice. At the end of the article, she leaves the reader with an unanswered question: "Which Book can shoulder this grand task?" Najmabadi comments that perhaps the answer to this question is all too obvious: the Koran. "But," she wonders, "in leaving the question unanswered, has Massoumeh Ebtekar not given her readers the opportunity to generalize upon the logic of rejecting the applicability of the Bible and the Old Testament to include the Koran and to reply: no Book?" (180). But in the context of the article, and in reference to a religion that considers itself the last and the most complete answer, what is surprising is not Ebtekar's analysis that neither the Bible nor the Old Testament can liberate women. Nor is her rhetorical question in need of an answer in the context of the Islamic tradition—the Koran is the Book that can liberate all. What is surprising is that a feminist intellectual so familiar with Islam could entertain the possibility that a devout Muslim such as Massoumeh Ebtekar could consider that the Koran is anything but perfect. In fact, not only in her Persian and English editorials to the same issue of *Farzaneh* (Ebtekar 1993a; 1993b), but also in all other issues of the journal, Ebtekar explicitly criticizes Western feminism for its limited, secular vision and promotes Islam as an alternative. Najmabadi, reflecting upon her own earlier unyielding approach to the possibility of a feminization of Islam, wonders if that rejection was not due to the limitations of her thoughts, her unwillingness to accept that possibility (204–5). It seems, however, that the more appropriate question is whether the possibilities Najmabadi can now find in Islam are not due to her eagerness to find them there.

The treatment of Western feminism by "Islamic feminists" is important not just because of its meaning for how people in this trend view "Western woman," but also because *what* they see is indicative of their understanding of women's rights, of what they consider appropriate for an "Iranian feminism." The recognition of "Western women," the legitimation of Western women and their movements for sexual equality, is undoubtedly a step forward in comparison with more conservative Islamic literature that basically dismisses Western women and the women's movement in the West as misguided, worthless, and even corrupt. But I do not share the enthusiasm of Najmabadi. Such tactics have been conventional in "modernist" Islamic writings. Remember the homage that Shariati paid to Western women scientists, artists, and professionals, as discussed earlier in the book?

How "Islamic feminists" assess Western feminism and Western women is more significant than their mere recognition of the contribution of Western feminism. Here one should constantly beware of censored and distorted translations. In the Persian translation of Marilyn French's *The War Against Women*, for instance, the section entitled "Religious Wars against Women" appears in Persian as "The War of the *Church* against Women" and more than three-quarters of that section is excised. French writes: "Today, when governments or religious leaders articulate policies extremely injurious to women, they rarely mention women directly" (French 1992: 18). In the Persian translation, "governments" is changed to "*some* governments" and "*religious* leaders" to "some leaders" (French 1994: 31). Later in *her* book, French continues her discussion of the religious war against women, this time examining the case of Islam. In the Persian translation, this entire section, as well as all other references to Iran, Algeria, Egypt, Afghanistan, and Jordan, are left out. One could argue, of course, that it's too optimistic to think that such "accommodations" should not be made in order to publish in a theocratic state. Perhaps. But we cannot overlook the fact that, for instance, throughout the book, discussion of legal abortion as an accomplishment of Western feminism is omitted. Early on, *French* writes: "Women possessed almost no human rights—to a political voice, to inherit, to own property, or to do business on their own. They even lacked rights over their own bodies" (French 1992: 11). The last sentence is nonexistent in the Persian volume (French 1994: 16).[10]

From this vantage point, we can observe that in fact, sharp edges of Western feminism are dulled in the Islamist reformist rendition. A feminist critique of Western society is presented, but feminist proposals for abolishing patriarchal gender roles are regarded with suspicion. In her "Feminism in Iran: In Search of an Indigenous Approach," Moti' criticizes Western feminists for considering "complete similarity between women and men." This emphasis, she argues, has caused women and men to become similar, but, since masculine culture is dominant in a patriarchal system, it was mainly women who have become like men (1997a: 24). "The growing likeness of women to men implies a grand revolution in values that has led to such developments as homosexuality, bisexuality, and the destruction of family" (24). Instead of this dangerous path, Moti' recommends that an indigenous Iranian women's movement promote "a change in the way we value traditional roles. In other words, we should equally value the emotional and instrumental roles that women and men play. In this respect, it is helpful to refer to Islamic values that consider equality between women's and men's emotional and instrumental roles" (24).

Feminist analyses of domesticity criticize this aspect of patriarchy for diminishing women's socioeconomic power, for limiting women's options in life to domestic roles of wives and mothers. That Moti' fails to make this pivotal distinction between the institution of domesticity and the housewife is no accident. To her, women's confinement to domesticity is not the problem. What she objects to is that their work is not appreciated (see my dialogue with her in *Zanân* Shahidian 1998; Moti' 1998).

Ebtekar also proposes that Iranian women undertake a "balanced approach, exactly the opposite of the speedy way in the West" where "the movement to ameliorate women's social status has led to tension and conflict between women and men" (*Zanân* 1997f: 5). Keyhânniâ provides a similar case. In his treatment, it is quite acceptable for Iranian women to learn from their Western sisters new ways of performing old gender roles—to learn, for example, when encountering a husband who is coming home late, to ask "Anything wrong?" instead of "Where have you been?" Yet it is inconceivable that they would also be inspired to transgress accepted gender norms. There, Iranian women are instructed not to "blindly" imitate Western women (Keyhânniâ 1996: 216).

Under the Islamic Republic, recognition of Western women's struggle for sexual equality lends legitimacy to the Islamist reformist women's call for sexual equality. This is an antidote to the conservative claim that exposure to the West has a detrimental impact on Iranian women. In the orthodoxy of the Islamic state, women who criticize the status quo are easily associated with the occidental enemy, and the sharper their criticism, the harsher the accusation. The problem is further complicated by the fact that the IRI claims legitimacy on the ground that it is an authentic, Islamic national state. Thus, contenders do not have much chance to compete. In pre-revolutionary Iran, one could claim "authenticity" by adhering to Islam. In the government of Islam, however, "authenticity" means adherence to the Islamic state. The trap of authenticity makes it difficult, if not impossible, for women to challenge the state without being accused of being "Westernized." Islamist reformist women discuss Western feminism to buttress their own grievances against patriarchy. In so doing, they also portray Western women as substantially less malignant than Muslim fundamentalists would argue. At the same time, however, they dissociate themselves from the "misguided radicalism" of Western feminism in order to protect themselves against potential charges of "guilt by association."

The same is true about Iranian women abroad. If the condition of women in the Islamic Republic is not entirely satisfactory even for believers, how can one expect people to feel if they do not believe in Islam, or are at least not religious enough to stay in the Islamicized homeland? Thus Iranian immigrant women are presented as a group who are not inimical, as women who are forced to leave because their homeland was not attentive to their needs and wants (Kar 1996a: 3).

Iranian women abroad become a bargaining chip in the negotiation between women in Iran and the Islamic patriarchy.[11] Besides, this approach is essential for reformist women to receive any recognition and support from the opposition to the IRI. Such support is crucial, as reformists' criticism of the Islamic Republic alienates them from many pro-government Islamists. Their success in attracting Iranian exiles and immigrants, however, has been relatively limited. Though some Iranian women abroad have been conciliatory toward Islamist reformists, many have remained critical of any Islamic treatment of women. Opponents of Islamist women's reformism can be found both in academic settings and among women activists (for some examples see Chafiq 1995; Daragahi 1995; Moghissi 1997, 1999; Mojab 1999, 1995; Royanian 1995. Also see various issues of *Zan dar Mobarezeh* and *Avaye Zan*).

AMENITIES AND DANGERS OF ISLAMIST WOMEN'S REFORMISM

I would like to reiterate a point that I made earlier regarding the difficulty of determining what this trend exactly is and who should be considered an Islamic reformist woman. To contribute to the comprehensiveness of this discussion, I have included any attempt, in government, the academy, or the media, to champion women's quest for sexual equality within Islamic ideological or institutional frameworks. It is then important to bear in mind that the Iranian cultural scene since 1979 has seen a growing body of literature (both original writing and translated) on diverse issues. These include: accounts of women's history (see for instance, Hejâzi 1991; Lâhiji and Kar 1992; Behnood 1995); children's rights (for example, Ebadi 1990); women's rights in divorce, women in the labor force and women and development (Moti' 1996, 1993; Kar 1994); a number of translated publications by the UNICEF (sometimes prepared jointly by various Iranian institutions) on such topics as women's education or the impact of developmental policies on women; women and politics (Kar 1997a); a growing body of literary production; analysis of women in Iranian culture (Lâhiji 1993; Sattâri 1994); of women in different societies, such as translations of Werner Thönnessen's *The Emancipation of Women*, Andrée Michel's *Le Féminisme*, Marilyn French's *The War Against Women*, and Barbro Dahlbom-Hal's *Leading Women: What Men Need to Know for Women to Grow*; women's psychology and pop psychology, such as a translation of Jean Shinoda Bolen's *Goddesses in Every Woman*. This incomplete roster serves merely to show the diversity of discussions on women—some authors and translators do argue in an Islamic framework, others employ an explicitly secular approach. Many authors who publish in magazines identified with Islamist gender reformism, like *Zanân*, are indeed secular intellectuals who may not have access to other channels. The recognition of these efforts is crucial since one might otherwise overestimate the role and contribution of the Islamist reformist women. Discussions of Islamist women's reformism in Iran have overlooked two crucial groups of Iranian women outside and inside this trend: the contributions of non-Islamic, secular women have been underrepresented to highlight the significance of "Islamic feminists," while among "Islamic feminists," the role of Islamists is downplayed to present Islamist women's reformism as a sociopolitical force independent from the IRI state apparatus.

That said, we should consider the scope and objectives of the Islamist reformist women's trend. My analysis in the last two chapters demonstrates that "Islamic feminists" aim primarily to:

• eliminate legislation that limit women's rights in the family;

• create legal and social provisions to guarantee women access to the social sphere;

• alter belief systems and cultural norms regarding women's capabilities and their contribution to society;

• ease and regulate social concerns for "morality," i.e., female sexuality.

If successful—and that is a big if—these adjustments effect a new patriarchal bargain that will ideally shift the locus of control over women from private to public domain. This agenda, markedly the reverse of the initial (and to some extent continuing) trend in the IRI, would give women a higher share of paid labor force, education, and politics. At the same time, it would regulate individual men's control over women. Women's confinement to domesticity would decrease by limiting men's supervision of their movements in family and society. Legal mechanisms of sexual control would also regulate the present lawlessness and haphazard interpretations of vigilante hizbullahis. Male violence against women would be checked. At least in some cases, women would have legal recourse to protect themselves against men's violence. These alterations, however, are not antithetical to IRI's segregationist-protectivist policy of creating a "safe," regulated social space for women.

The intention of Islamist women's reformism is to modernize and modify Iranian patriarchy that since the rise of the IRI has not only been strengthened, but has also become old-fashioned (*ommol*) in form and content. Men are taught to act civilly, to respect their wives' hard work, to give them gifts, to cuddle after sex, to express their feelings to them—in a word, to act "modern." Women are taught to be understanding, subtle, intelligent, conversational, and attentive in bed—in a word, "modern." Both, however, play conventional gender roles and create familiar gender identities.[12] To celebrate after a quarrel, she is instructed to put her traditional role to work, use "her cooking talent to bake him a cake." He, on the other hand, is advised to take advantage of his economic power by "taking her out for an afternoon cake and coffee or to dinner" (Keyhânniâ 1996: 233).

The new patriarchal bargain leads to a shift from private to public patriarchy. This is a return of patriarchal relations to the pre-revolutionary period, but in a more confined and outdated fashion than was practiced in the Pahlavi era. The "new" public patriarchy insists on restrictive standards over sexuality and morality, exposing a larger portion of the population to the conservative Islamic gender ideology than under the Pahlavis. Islamist women's reformism is, then, at best a "crisis-oriented movement,"[13] one that responds to problems arising from dysfunctions and imbalances of patriarchal relations in post-revolutionary Iran. It may lighten women's burden, but falls short of offering an alternative to patriarchal structure. No wonder that some IRI statesmen have been quite supportive of Islamist women reformists. As Melucci points out: "The dominant groups always tend to define movements as simple reactions to crises, that is, to a dysfunctional mechanism of the system. Admitting that they are something else would entail recognition of collective demands that challenge the legitimacy of power and the current deployment of social resources" (Melucci 1996a: 23). To accomplish the latter, a "conflict-oriented movement" should abolish sexual determination in appropriating social and economic resources currently at men's disposal. The acute gender crisis in the Islamic regime does bring to the surface the underlying gender conflict of Iranian patriarchy, but those manifestations of crisis must not be mistaken for the deeper conflict.

The constituency of Islamist women's reformism consists predominantly of middle and upper class, professional, gainfully employed, heterosexual (Muslim) women. Employment and educational reforms (especially at the post-secondary level) predominantly affect these women. By setting professional women as an example of women's capability, Islamist women's reformism attempts to refute sexism by showing that women's abilities in private and public lives do not fit the stereotypical images of them in traditionalist Islamic ideology. It is assumed that when elite or middle class professional women are guaranteed safe and lasting public presence, the rest of the sex will also benefit.

The legal reforms and provisions require so much knowledge of the law, intellectual and material ability to negotiate for a mutually respectful family relationship—one in which even *unemployed women* can demand equal treatment—that the negotiation ability of housewives, let alone uneducated women of the lower classes, is inadequately provided for. This is why, contrary to some observers like Mir-Hosseini (1996: 292), I am not optimistic about the legalization of the wife's demand for remuneration for her work during marriage if the husband demands a divorce. It is difficult for the woman to actually collect the material reward not only because of the man's bargaining power, but also because demanding her dues requires a degree of legal awareness not readily available to uneducated women. The problem is augmented by inadequate provision in the legal procedure for assessing her contribution, and by what she is entitled to considering the husband's economic power (see Kar 1996b: 38).

Women's control over their sexuality and morality, most notably in the case of hejâb, is downplayed as a compensation for higher social presence— as long as women can work, hejâb is more tolerable (Kousha 1992). This, however, not only ignores the harassment of female employees on the issues of hejâb and propriety, but also overlooks the problems of many unemployed women, especially younger women, high school and university students who constantly have to deal with the suffocation of compulsory veiling and the moral police.

Equally problematic is reformist women's assumption of heteromarital sexuality as the norm. This assumption defines sexuality, and more specifically female sexuality, only in the context of family life. Considering the continued presence of "motherhood" as a quintessentially feminine characteristic, women who do not wish to marry or to bear children will be deemed "less woman." Whereas men have always had licit and illicit channels for satisfying sexual needs, heteromarital sexuality restricts women's sexuality to the familial domain.

Finally, the normalcy of heteromarital sexuality continues to marginalize and victimize Iranian homosexuals. I do not suggest that Islamist reformists should champion homosexual rights in Iran. Nonetheless, I think it is important to note that overlooking such a problem limits feminist politics and theory. Reformist theorists in Iran do not need to defend gays and lesbians. Many do, however—though not necessarily in print. But reformists also do not need to write against homosexuals, presenting them, for instance, as "negative consequences of Western feminism." Theorists in Iran do not need to defend homosexuals, but there is no need for them to theorize based on biases.

Any women's movement that claims to represent Iranian women, that is, *all* Iranian women, must address not only the problems of upper and middle class women, but also those of working class, peasants, and national/ethnic minority women. The quest for these women involves not just class or national/ethnic issues, but feminist issues also. Different systems of oppression do not operate independently of each other. Nor do we, as subjects living in these systems, experience each in isolation from the rest. Individuals make and remake themselves, but only with resources that are socially available to them. Thus, just as we cannot sacrifice *women's* rights to enhance, say, class interests, we cannot subjugate the interests of *working class or national/ethnic minority women* to safeguard the rights of women of certain socioeconomic backgrounds, albeit under some general notion of "women's rights." This approach will also enable the Iranian women's movement to debunk a fatal premise of the progressives: that at every moment in history, activists have to fight either class exploitation, *or* sexual oppression, *or* national/ethnic oppression.[14]

Furthermore, as much as Islam is a constitutive part of gender relations in Iran, the problems of Iranian women are not merely the problems of Muslim women; they are the problems of *Iranian* women. Undoubtedly, the re-articulation of the shari'ah in a manner more attuned to women's rights *is* important because of both the precedent it would set in the theory and practice of Islamic gender relations and its practical implications for millions of women who live under Islamic laws. But, continued legitimacy of the shari'ah discourse on women and family, this time in the form of a women-centered Islam, denies the separation of religion from state, and subjugates not only non-Muslims, but also nonbelievers to a religion that has historically been anything but tolerant toward its "Others." In our assessment of Islamist reformist women, it is essential not to lose sight of the fact that though non-Islamists, even nonbelievers, have contributed to the development of this trend, *Islamists* have occupied key roles and sensitive positions. We should remember, for instance, that reformist women's journals are managed by people who are firm believers. Ziâ Mortazavi, the editor of *Payâm-e Zan*, is himself a clergyman. *Farzaneh* is published by the pro-government Center for Women's Studies and Research. *Zan-e Rouz* is blatantly pro-government. *Zanân* is run by a group of devout believers. Mohsen Sa'idzâdeh, a regular contributor to *Zanân* before his defrocking, used to be a clergy director of the legal division of the Discipline and Punishment Organization (*Ta'zirat*).[15] We should remember that many women associated with Islamist women's reformism hold authority positions in the Islamic government apparatus, and in many cases are related to statesmen in higher echelons of the government. Such cozy relationships does take its toll on the theory and practice of Islamic gender reformism. Indeed, as Abbas-Gholizadeh puts it, securing the integrity of the Islamic state—or the Islamic system (*nezâm*)—is a quintessential aspect of women believers. The IRI represents the very nature and value system of Allah; defending it is "the religious (*shar'i*) obligation" of any believer (Abbas-Gholizadeh 1995–1996a: 114). One example of the loyalty to the Islamic regime concerns the First National Report of the Women of the IRI, presented to the UN in preparation for the Fourth World Conference on Women in Beijing. The original draft, submitted internally to governmental organizations for review, apparently aroused anger among the statesmen. The committee had to draft a second version that ended up being a "propaganda" (*sho'ari*) piece, according to the members of the committee (Abbas-Gholizadeh 1995–1996b).

This is not an isolated example. Our discussion above shows to what extent Islamist reformist women are conciliatory toward Islam. Sholeh Irani's analysis of a discussion between editors of *Zan-e Rouz* and Mehdi Nasiri, editor of the hizbullahi newspaper *Sobh*, also shows that when the contenders come face to face, reformists are the party that gives in (Irani 1996).

Proponents of "Islamic feminism," especially those in Western academia, overlook this crucial relationship between Islamist reformist women and Islamists in power. This problem is particularly acute in Haleh Afshar's account of Islamist women's reformism because of her exclusive focus on women working within the apparatus of the Islamic state, particularly women deputies of the parliament (1996). "Celebrating" the success of these elite women, Afshar posits them not in the context of the development of the IRI's oppressive sexual policies, but in opposition to it. She overlooks that these policies were curbed in response to women's reaction and that the elite women of the IRI mediated that pressure for adjustment. Consequently, she blurs the distinction between what Iranian women have retained in the last two decades *despite the Islamic Republic* and what they have gained *because of* the Islamic Republic and "Islamic feminism."

Tohidi also obfuscates the political dimension of Islamic gender reformism. After a lengthy account of feminists' reinterpretations of Christianity or Judaism, she argues that if secular Western feminists could accept feminist theology as a discourse, why should secular Iranian feminists reject the possibility of a feminist Islamic theology (Tohidi 1997b)? She overlooks a pivotal factor in her comparative analysis, however. Whatever we may think about the possibility of a feminist interpretation of patriarchal religions, the point remains that in the case of "Islamic feminism," we are dealing with more than a reinterpretation by some women. *Here, the problem is a theocratic state.* Western feminists work within a long tradition of separation of church and state. In the United States, for instance, at least in written law, the state is responsible for protecting individuals from religious impingement of their civil rights. In the case of Iran, the entanglement of Islam with civil and political rights means continued marginalization of those who, though they may believe in Islam as a personal conviction, would not want their social and political life shaped by it; it means continued marginalization of non-Muslims; it means continued victimization of secularists; it means continued persecution of Bahaiis.

Moghissi points out a further problem: apologists for "Islamic feminists" fail to differentiate Muslim women on the basis of their political commitments, ideological fervor, social class, and ethnic and regional backgrounds (Moghissi 1997: 66–68, 78–79). Which group of Muslim women is Islamist women's reformism supposed to represent? Besides, we develop our identities in the context of a number of social relations. Making Islam the center of this identity, especially in the present Iran where such an identity surpasses individual lifestyles and affirms itself as a collective identity, reduces other dimensions of women's lives. Why must Islamist women's reformism be *the indigenous* solution to sexual domination for Iranian women? We have observed throughout this book the debilitating role of Islamic ideologies in addressing key issues of sexual oppression, both in their specific teachings and in their framing of the hegemonic culture. Here we see once again an attempt to reinforce Islam's hegemonic role. This time, however, hegemony stems not so much from consent as from resignation. The attempts of "Islamic feminists" and their advocates abroad will convey to Iranian women (and men) that there is no alternative but Islam, that they ought to seek their liberation only in the context of Islam.

Would donning the veil or adhering to "indigenous culture" protect women against the accusation of betrayal? Hardly. Like the sword of Damocles, the shadow of suspicion will continue hanging over women as long as the woman's body is the battleground of competing definitions of "authenticity" and "nationality." The alternative seems to rest with debunking altogether the dichotomies of indigenous and exogenous, us and them, authentic and inauthentic.

Defenders who are yet critical of Islamist women's reformism welcome them as a sign of burgeoning polyphony within Iranian women's movement. I join them in this. But, unlike those who believe that secular feminists should leave it up to reformist Islamist women to deal with Islam (see, for example, Tohidi 1997b: 144), I consider this approach tantamount to accepting Islam and Islamist women's reformism uncritically. Islamist women's reformism should be regarded for what it is—a modest effort to modify and modernize patriarchy, to create some open space for women to voice their concerns. Defenders of reformist women propose a dialogue between secular feminists and "Islamic feminists," but their treatment of the subject is marred with an enchanted enthusiasm. How else could we read Tohidi's blatant denial of valuable research by Iranian scholars abroad, including herself, and reference to the secular opposition of the Islamic regime abroad as "Stalinist and Maoist feminists" (1996)? How else could we construe Haeri's dangerous reduction of Western women to lonely, helpless employees, deprived of the support of an extended family or a husband (1996)?

If by feminism is meant easing patriarchal pressures on women, making patriarchy less appalling, Islamist women's reformism is certainly a feminist trend. But if I understand feminism as a movement to abolish patriarchy, to protect human beings from being prisoners of fixed identities, to contribute toward a society in which individuals can fashion their lives free from economic, political, social, and cultural constraints, then Islamist women's reformism proves considerably inadequate. I define feminism in these latter terms, and for that reason, I consider Islamist women's reformism a weak alternative to what exists in the IRI.

RECAPITULATION

This chapter offers an assessment of Islamist women's reformism. I emphasize that the Islamic imperative limits the horizon of reformist theory and practice. Regarding family, the Islamist reformist women's concern is to modify men's power and to guarantee a free zone for women. Reformists emphasize recognition of a woman's role in the family. The sexual division of labor is not questioned. Consequently, recognition of the housewife's role leads to a romanticizing of domesticity and sexual domination. The Islamist reformist interpretation of gender as socially constructed goes a long way toward promoting a modified version of the traditional division of labor. Regarding hejâb, the emphasis is again on moderation, on avoiding force to enforce hejâb. Modifications in family relationship, education, employment, and social control of morality will shift the locus of sexual domination from the privacy of the patriarchal family to the public sphere. This change may lead to women's higher share of the labor force, education, and politics. It will also ease and regulate individual men's control over women, making the state ever more responsible for women's conduct.

I have also discussed that Islamist women's reformism reflects the interests of middle and upper class, professional women; unemployed, minority, young, and working class women are marginalized or forgotten in "Islamic feminism." Islamist reformists' emphasis on being indigenous similarly marginalizes all who do not share their Islamic views.

I find little cause for celebrating the use of "catch terminologies" like gender and feminism. The articulation of these concepts in the context of the hegemonic gender ideology dulls their critical power. If successful, the changes proposed by "Islamic feminists" may alter the form and content of patriarchal domination: education and employment will remain segregated, control over women's sexuality and restrictive moral standards will persist. Male-defined God-sanctioned rules and beliefs, even in their modified version, leave women vulnerable to the discretion of men. The confinement of Islamist women's reformism in the hegemonic gender ideology leads to reinforcing ideas and priorities that will eventually contain, rather than enhance, women's struggle against patriarchy, patriarchal ideology, and the Islamic state. Islamist women's reformism defines the goals of the movement not far beyond the present situation. It may give women an outlet to whisper their anger, but it does not lead them far beyond that.

NOTES

1. For the significance of remaining loyal to the Islamic government, see Mahboobeh Abbas-Gholizadeh's interview with Shahlâ Habibi, advisor to former President Rafsanjani on Women's Issues and head of the Iranian delegation to the Fourth World Conference on Women in Beijing (Abbas-Gholizadeh 1995–1996b).

2. We recall that, contrary to Kadivar's claim, women's franchise was first introduced by the Shah, to which the Ayatollah reacted vehemently.

3. We can consider the example of Shirin Ebadi and Mehrangiz Kar's treatment in the monthly *Sobh*. Ebadi is discredited as a person frequently interviewed by BBC and the Voice of America (*Sobh* 1997a); Kar is characterized as a "corrupt woman with many faces," engaged in high class pandering for foreign diplomats and interviewing with the BBC. She is censured as a former member of the Shah's Rastâkhiz Party, and a secret agent of the SAVAK (*Sobh* 1997b).

4. Kadivar refers to Juliet Mitchell's discussion of gender construction in Peter Worsley's *Introducing Sociology*.

5. For feminist discussions that question the fixity of sexuality and the assumption of the biological bases of sexual distinction see, for example Archer (1985), Fausto-Sterling (1995), and Jacobs (1989). For arguments that question the fixity of sex distinction based on physiological differences, see Butler (1990; 1993).

6. *Tarh-e towse'eh-ye 'efâf* was proposed in the winter of 1998 by the Council for Cultural Revolution, at the request of the Women's Cultural and Social Council.

7. For further discussion, see Shahidian (1993a).

8. It is noteworthy that the IRI continuously emphasizes the cultural relativism of human rights. Afshari (1994; 1996) provides an excellent perspective on this, particularly in his discussion of the human rights of women and secularists.

9. In other words, that women are not allowed to attend a men's soccer match is *men's problem, not women's*.

10. I borrow these examples from Maral Rokni's review of French's book in *Faslnamejeh Zan*, a Persian socialist-feminist published in Sweden (Rokni 1996). In my commentary on Moti' (Shahidian 1998a), I have referred to another instance of mistranslation (in relation to the translation of Elizabeth Badinter) and its implication for the development of feminist theory in Iran.

11. This interrelated presentation of Western women and Iranian women in the West is a reflection of the general role Iranian immigrants and exiles have played in post-revolutionary Iranian politics and culture (see Shahidian 1996b).

12. On "doing gender," see West (1987); on gender as performative, see Butler (1990). I discuss both concepts in chapter 1.

13. The distinction between crisis-oriented and conflict-oriented movements is based on Melucci's (1996a) distinction. See chapter 1 for further elaboration.

14. I have explored this issue in more detail elsewhere. See Shahidian (1997c).

15. See note 2 of the previous chapter.

4

Dual Society: Gender Agonies in an Islamic State

Yesterday I was arrested by someone who was not even a Committee member. It was miserable. Simply because I was not wearing stockings, they arrested me. He was so insulting that I was too intimidated to ask for his ID card. Really, tell us what we are supposed to do in this country? Just because I wasn't wearing stockings, he hit my feet so hard that I got a bruise this big. My toe nails . . . it feels like somebody has put a burning cigarette on them. He squeezed my nails so hard that I had to spend the whole day in bed yesterday. Why should it be like this? Why isn't anybody concerned about our youth? How long are we going to live? I plead, for God's sake . . .

These are the words of a middle class woman in her early twenties, in an interview with a reporter from the Channel 2 network of the IRI TV. "I plead, for God's sake . . ." she addresses the reporter. Then she pauses momentarily, turns her face away from the reporter, looks directly at the camera as if looking at the world, and repeats her plea—this time, however, to a general audience: "I plead, for God's sake, *do something*. The people responsible for this . . . what sins have young people committed to deserve this? Give them some freedom. Help them a bit. Be a little concerned about them."

This interview is part of an untitled television series about Iranian youth and "deviant behavior" in Iran (I will refer to it as the "youth and deviance film"). The program was co-produced by Gorouh-e Ravâyat-e Fath (Group

for Narrating Victory) and the Nirouy-e Moqâvemat-e Basij (Basij Resistance Force). The production date is not specified, but based on allusions
to the upcoming election of Khatami to the presidency, it was probably
made around the summer of 1997. Though produced by IRI Sound and
Vision, the series was never aired. I have obtained a videotaped copy that
was smuggled out of the country. The tape contains some two-and-a-half
hours of the program. (For a similar report about "corruption" in Tehran's
streets, see *Jâm-e-jam* 27 July 2000. About runaway girls, see Tâheri
[1999]).

The "deviant" behaviors depicted in the film include failure to observe
the dress code; running away from home; membership in student cliques
(referred to among Iranians as *types*, in French parlance) such as *Rap* and
Heavy; wearing the "wrong" dress; attending parties; attending male-and-
female gatherings; addiction; and pre- and extra-marital sex. The striking
commonality of these instances is the narrow margins of normalcy and
legality that cause relatively easy slippage into what IRI officials brand
"cultural crimes": unspecified acts of transgression from not-so-clear behavioral standards.

Free self-expression is not congruent with a political system that from
the outset assumed the role of people's moral guardian. This is a clearly
stipulated role of the Islamic Republic. Early in post-revolutionary days,
the Bureau for the Prohibition of Immoral Conducts (*dâyereh-ye monkarât*)
states in two ultimatums to the women of the Qal'eh brothels that the goal
of the Islamic revolution is to "purify society from moral corruption."
Thus, Qal'eh and other products of the "dirty treason of colonialism and
the hated Pahlavi regime" are intolerable. The ultimatums urge "those deceived women" to repent and return to the bosom of their families. In
return, the Bureau would assist these women through their rehabilitation.
But, should brothel women fail to comply, the communiqués warn, should
these women "continue their dirty and immoral deeds that corrupt our
youngsters, betray the blood of our 70 thousand martyrs, and defy Koranic
edicts, they will be tried in the Revolutionary Courts and, in accordance
with divine laws, will be sentenced to the harshest punishment" (*Kayhan*
20 February 1979: 11). Since those early days of the revolution, the IRI
has maintained the role of moral arbiter for the masses. Believing that (as
a graffito reads) "a woman without a veil is like a garden without a fence,"
the state coerces women and men to put up fences around themselves or
their womenfolk and monitors movements to and from that garden.

If only things were that simple.

The IRI's "moralization" project has not been successful. Far from a
united community of moral, believing actors, the IRI has been wrought by
"cultural crimes." More than two decades after their triumph, Islamists
have not been able to suppress women's and men's hopes, expectations,
and lifestyles that emerged prior to the revolution. Pressure to comply with
Islamic moral codes continues in varying degrees, without yielding desired

results. Resistance has also forced the regime to modify policies in education, employment, and family law. More than two decades after ascending to power, the Islamic alternative has failed to secure women's cooperation. A *dual society* has thus emerged—one that the ruling clergy like to see and are obliged by women and men, and another, wherein women (and men) live out their own preferences (through cautious negotiations, of course), away from the watchful eyes of government officials. Indeed, IRI officials complain about "the corruption of belief and morality going underground" (Ministry of Islamic Culture and Guidance 1992: 7–8). Vulnerability, as discussed in *Gender Politics*, is the quintessential component of this arrangement, particularly for women. Any crisis in the Islamic Republic somehow affects gender relations by either tightening the ropes of gender control or easing the pressure.

Discussing the teleological Islamic gender, I argued in *Gender Politics* that in the Islamic Republic, men and women lose their individuality, essential for citizenry, and that coercion becomes ubiquitous. In *Gender Politics*, I argued that Islamists' gender policies have aimed to revive private patriarchy by returning women to the privacy of the home, but pre-revolutionary socioeconomic changes and women's resistance have made the complete realization of that agenda impossible. As a result, patriarchy has vacillated between private and public. Chapter 2 of the present book mapped out the ideological and political agenda of the reformist Muslim women activists—the "Islamic feminists." I assessed these attempts in Chapter 3 as a new patriarchal bargain, concluding that Islamist reformist women's recommend reforms to modify patriarchal relationships under the IRI, reforms that at best stabilize patriarchy in its public form.

In this chapter, I will discuss the dual society that has emerged through the Islamists' rule in Iran. I consider dual society the product of an unresolved sociocultural conflict that dates back to the Pahlavi era, but has intensified in the Iran of the Islamic Republic. Dual society emerges from women and men's defiance of dominant social relations, particularly predefined gender roles. Dual society constitutes the space for "being different," a nurturing ground for resistance and oppositional gender politics. I pay special attention here to the development of secular and leftist feminism.

Two important notes are in order. Discussing Islamist women's reformism earlier in this book, I cautioned about using an umbrella term to identify a heterogeneous group. A similar caution is in order here, too, regarding the IRI's gender politics. My treatment of Islamic gender ideologies throughout the book clearly rejects any essentialist Islamist gender doctrine. We recall, for instance, how IRI policies have emerged from the interplay of diverse objectives and exigencies. To clarify my discussion about dual society, however, I have to rely on ideal typical constructs of the IRI in this chapter. I feel justified in doing so, for I have already demonstrated the ebb and flow of the Islamist gender analyses; thus, the reader can easily contextualize this ideal typical image. Besides, we have also observed that diverse Islamist gender discourses have strong commonalities to warrant fleeting references to such overarching assumptions as women's domesticity, the centrality of the family, heteromarital sexuality, fixed sex, predefined sex roles, and social or spatial separations of genders. Insofar as the IRI's policies are concerned, despite the changes, women have been granted limited rights in the family, little access to social and political resources, and meager freedom of choice and movement.

Writing about "secular" or "leftist" feminists is even riskier because there is no easy way to identify these individuals. There are no organizations, no self-identified leftist journals or collectivities, unlike Islamist reformists, for instance, whose publications are easily identifiable. There is no systematic rendition of secular or leftist feminist politics. Written ideas belong to *individuals*, not collectivities, though they do undoubtedly express the beliefs and convictions of like-minded colleagues and comrades. These writings then should be regarded as *contributions* to secular or leftist feminist discourses rather than their summations. This dispersion is reflected in the style of this chapter, too, wherein ideas appear as pieces of a yet unsolved puzzle. I have chosen this style in order to remain loyal to the reality of people struggling against a serious historical defeat, a brutally repressive regime, and the heavy weight of past beliefs and values, to remain loyal indeed to the reality of individuals struggling through thick layers of their culture and politics to emerge as collectivities.

CONTESTED LEGITIMACY

Bertolt Brecht once wrote that on a bayonet one may rely, but cannot sit. IRI officials knew from the outset that they had to depend on a bayonet; but all along have also hoped that they would not have to sit on it. They knew, for instance, that the Islamic moral codes could not be implemented without the use of force, that women would resist mandatory hejâb. After all, as Haddâd 'Âdil puts it, "in every society, there are people who cannot be dissuaded from their paths by any logic or reasoning. With them, we cannot deal but in the language of coercion" (1995: 57). Yet, like many others in the Islamic state, he was hopeful that Islamists would win over the public: "If we fail to appeal to people's minds and hearts, the coercion of Revolutionary Committees and Pâsdârs [revolutionary guards] can accomplish nothing."

The Islamic revolution was supposed to build a republic of Muslims, enriched by the supposedly innate propensity of Iranians toward Islam. The IRI was meant to be embraced by its subjects, people who consented to Islam and the Islamists' moral and philosophical leadership. The IRI was to symbolize a love affair between Muslims and the Islamic leadership—at least after the infidels were eliminated and the anti-Islam, the misled, and the perverts were crushed.

Yet not only has that love not flourished, the intellectual and emotional gap between the Islamist rulers and their subjects has indeed continuously widened. Thus, in discussing gender politics under the IRI, we need to distinguish between dominant and hegemonic cultures. While dominant culture here implies coercive imposition of values upon the public, hegemonic culture involves consent and subscription to a "common conception of the world" (Gramsci 1971: 349). The politico-cultural contestation between the IRI and the people has effected what I call an *oppositional atmosphere*—a persistent, often instinctive, rejection by the public of the hegemonic politico-cultural structure, albeit disorganized, varied, and non-institutionalized. We need not dwell upon the severity and brutality with which IRI has responded to any "deviant" cultural and artistic expressions in order to gauge resistance to Islamists' agenda or how distant—and threatened—IRI finds itself vis-à-vis a considerable portion of the population. Nor do we need to focus upon Iranian exiles and immigrants, and many people, especially among the younger generations, who seek legal or illegal routes out of that "*jahannam*," that hell. There are plenty of other evidences. We can consider derogatory reference to the clergy as the *âkhoond*, the rank-and-file members of the clerical community without the authority and prestige of hojjatulislams, the ulema, *rowhânioun* (the spiritual leaders), or ayatollahs. Or, we can witness the bloody confrontations between students and government forces in July 1999, when the students called for Islamist rulers to step down and chanted that "20 years of silence has come to an end." Or, we can recollect the continued stream of criticisms, demonstrations, and strikes since the students' July movement, met by the banning of newspapers, arrests, and questionable trials. Or, we can hear the resentment in the unending stream of jokes about IRI officials and Islamic figures, usually alluding to their lack of intelligence, couth, and often laced with sexual innuendoes. Or, we can see the rupture in the Islamic order caused by the jubilating fans of the national team during a soccer match—women joining the spectators in the stadium, women taking off their veils in the auto-caravan of celebrating fans, young men and women dancing in the streets, even purportedly blocking the way to a clergy and not letting him pass until he joins them in dancing . . . all before the helpless eyes of the moral police (see *Zanân* no. 39, December 1998: 2–3). Or, we can observe the strong reaction to such practices as polygyny endorsed by the IRI. One woman in her early forties told me that upon learning that Mohammad Rezâ Shajariân, a prominent vocalist living in Iran, had married a second wife, she destroyed her rare collection of videotapes of Shajariân's private and public performances "because what he did was an insult to all Iranian women." Or, we can hear the constant reference to fear that the hizbullah and other Islamist organizations create in people, that people always had to be on the lookout. An immigrant woman in her mid-twenties related to me an incident that took place during the last days of her stay in Iran.

The day before I left Iran, I went to a government office to take care of something. As I rushed down the stairs to leave the building, I ran into a hizbullah man. Startled, he told me: "Oh sister, you frightened me!" With my passport, visa, and ticket ready, I felt quite sure. So, I said in response: "All my life, you frightened me. Once now, you fear me for a second."

The authorities are well aware of their failure, especially in light of the unsatisfied hizbullah zealots, the main supporters of the Islamic state. Ayatollah Yazdi, former Head of the Judiciary Branch, in a Friday Prayer sermon on 7 April 1995, expresses the agonies that permeate IRI:

We ask a government employee, a bazaar merchant, a citizen: How things used to be compared to now? We ask a devout person who knows nothing about politics, someone dogmatically focusing on religious matters. We ask how things used to be in your land? How did the call to prayer sound? How did *do'â* sound? How were naked, unveiled, half-naked women? How miserable were the conditions in most cities when colleges were closed? And how are things now? Now, when a young woman has full Islamic cover, wearing a manteau and a scarf—when every thing is perfect—I am confronted with complaints. "Why do you let these things happen? Why don't you prevent them? Why don't you make them wear the chador?" Certainly, chador is the superior veil. But this girl's mother and aunts, right before the revolution, would appear naked in public, would go naked from the beaches directly to the heart of town. The same women do not dare appear like that even on beaches. Why don't you [critics] consider that? Have you forgotten all that? Now you are worried why women only wear manteau? I am baffled. Is this fair? Let at least a generation be raised [in our system]. Has it been one generation? Mister Devout, leave politics aside, what status does Islam and religion have in this country? (Quoted in *Zanân*, no. 23, March-April 1995: 2)

Himself a conservative theologian, Yazdi is concerned about the zealots' dissatisfaction with the "leniency" of the ruling apparatus toward women. To these extremists, only the all-enveloping chador adequately hides women and secures simultaneously the honor of women, her family, and society. At the same time, Yazdi and his colleagues in the Islamic state have obviously proven ineffective in taming Iranian women and attaining their ideal gender relations.

I do not mean to imply that the IRI and Islamist sociocultural values are alien to Iranians. Quite to the contrary, many Islamist concerns about such issues as marriage, sexual morality, protecting women's chastity, do indeed reflect the sentiments of a considerable segment of the population. Yet despite these shared concerns, many among the urban educated middle and upper classes find Islamists "too extreme," "dogmatic," *ommol* (outdated), and *sonnati* (traditionalist).

This phenomenon can be understood better in light of what Barbara Myerhoff (1980) calls "domestic religion," that is, beliefs and practices embedded in a culture through their long existence and experienced at home and in the community. Domestic religion, writes Myerhoff, is "acquired in early-childhood, completely associated with family and household, blending nurturance and ethnic specificities." It is this "blend" that gives "heart-based religion such endurance and depth" (256). Leila Ahmed (1999) makes a similar distinction between folk and official religions, but in her vision, women are identified with the folk religion. This religion, Ahmed writes, is an essential part of how women make sense of their realities (121). Robert Redfield has similarly distinguished between "Little" and "Great" Traditions. While Great Tradition involves abstract, scriptural, and strict interpretation of a culture by official institutions, Little Tradition is the local, folk expressions of cultural beliefs that are by definition inconsistent and non-idealized. Little Tradition makes the thread of the quotidian, practiced constantly without external compulsion (discussed in Myerhoff 1980: 256).

In the Iranian culture, particularly among the urban, educated, middle and upper classes, this phenomenon has been referred to in the last few decades as *mazhab-e Âryâmehri* (Âryâmehri means attributed to the Shah who assumed the title Âryâmehr, the Aryan Sun). *Mazhab-e Âryâmehri* was initially used by the Islamists in post-revolutionary Iran to denigrate *Islam-e 'avâm*. Such an Islam, so believed the Islamists, practiced by the *'avâm*, the ordinary—that is, "uneducated" about Islam—people, replaced the outer shell of Islam for its true meaning. According to that Islam, one can, for instance, fast during the Ramadan, but consume alcoholic beverages the remaining 11 months of the year and still consider oneself a Muslim. Such a hodgepodge was unacceptable to Islamists; hence they delegitimized it as *mazhab-e Âryâmehri*. "Ordinary" people subsequently reappropriated and redefined the term to distinguish themselves from the rigid Islamists. The "Âryâmehri religion" is a "domestic," "folk" religion, a "Little Tradition," that is Islamic only in broad tenets. Its "Islam" is unsystematized and inconsistent; religious edicts are selectively practiced in juxtaposition with profane, often contrary to religious law. Some values and traditions of *mazhab-e Âryâmehri* are rooted in Islam, but they do not have the consistency and rigidity of the Islamist rendition of Islam (hence the Islamists' characterization of *mazhab-e Âryâmehri* as *islam-e âmrikâ'i*, an Islam contaminated by the United States). *Mazhab-e Âryâmehri* contains not only religious elements, but also other aspects of social life such as class, ethnicity, nationalism, and political orientation. Thus, imperatives of a changing society are reconciled by religious and traditional values. So, for instance, a person who consumes alcoholic beverages may also say prayers;

or one may fast and pray during Ramadan without observing other religious rituals during the year; families that consider themselves pious could accept their children dating; national holidays are observed along with— or are treated as more important than—religious ones.

The story of the book *Bâmdâd-e Khomâr* (*The Morning Hangover*) is quite revealing in this regard (Hâj Seyyed Javâdi 1996). This bestseller is a simple story about Mahboobeh, an upper class woman living around the 1920s, who fell in love with the neighborhood carpenter and married him against her parents' wishes. Her marriage failed and, with her father's help, she divorced her working class husband. She later married her reputable cousin whose admiration for her predated Mahboobeh's first marriage. He was already married; but his wife had lost her beauty to smallpox, and insisted that he marry his first love, as long as she maintained her lofty position as the "first wife." *Bâmdâd-e Khomâr* unfolds as Mahboobeh relays her life story to her niece who is about to repeat her aunt's mistake by marrying below her class. By the end of the story, the niece is persuaded not to marry her lover. (For more discussions, see *Zanân*, no. 33, March– April 1997: 26–31; and Karimi-Hakkak [1997].) People offer this popular novel—in both meanings of the term—as birthday gifts to young women and future brides. Though such incidents as the polygynous marriage depicted in *Bâmdâd-e Khomâr* are attributed to the "traditionalism of those days," the book functions as a surrogate mode of expression for values that are not exclusively Islamic, but nourished for their gender and class assumptions. The novel promotes chastity and warns about the hazards of gender and class rebellion, without being uttered by an immediate familial authority.

Many Iranians obviously find their ideas and sentiments reflected in *Bâmdâd-e Khomâr*. The book's gender message resonates with Islamic teachings discouraging contacts with members of the opposite sex. Yet many people who subscribe to this value also maintain their distance from many Islamist proposals on gender and gender relations, regarding them as inharmonious with the realities of today's society. The cultural sphere then becomes the site of conflict and competition among dominant, residual, and emergent cultures (see the discussion of Williams' classifications in chapter 1). Authors who write about Fatima and Zeynab do not monopolize the cultural field; Bob Dylan's lyrics are also available, as are the writings and biographies of Virginia Woolf and Rosa Luxemburg. If Islamists celebrate Fatima's birthday as Women's Day, many honor instead March 8, International Women's Day, at home, in small and informal get-togethers, or in public gatherings. At the same time that the public space is replete with Hejâb Avenue, Chastity Stadium, seminars on women's status in Islam, and conferences about women and anti-Islamic cultural invasion; acts of resistance emerge in private and public spheres to create an open space (Evans and Boyte 1986) for the development of alternative gender ideologies.

DUAL SOCIETY

Disparity between "ideal" and "real" cultures exists in virtually all societies. Islam, too, has entertained profound chasms between Islamic precepts and believers' practices by crafting interpretations that make actions compatible with the faith. Indeed, as Bassam Tibi argues, "behavioral lag"—a discrepancy between "held norms" and "everyday actions"—constitutes "an essential anthropological feature of Muslim culture" (Tibi 1991: 165). Maxim Rodinson (1981) convincingly demonstrates, for instance, how prohibited economic practices become acceptable Islamic practices through the use of alternative interpretations and terminologies. Gaining interest on one's savings is prohibited in Islam; but there is no reason banks could not "reward" somebody for their business. Similarly, abortion is illegal in IRI, but "miscarriage" is not and if incidents of "miscarriage" coincide with the state's concern for population growth, no one would feel the need to investigate the veracity of a physician's report. Interpretive innovations of Islamic law are so frequent that the Farsi expression *kolâh-e shar'i*—finding a "religious excuse" (literally, a "religious hat") for an action that otherwise is prohibited in shari'ah—is part of Iranians' daily vocabulary. These examples have been abundant in Iran before and after the Islamic Republic, and among Muslims in general.

But whereas the above innovations are designed to harmonize Islamic norms with social practices, or, in Tibi's words, to provide "cultural accommodations" for social practices, my reference to dual society in the IRI indicates *unresolved, and often irresolvable, differences* between the politics and culture of the Islamic state *and* the masses' practices and beliefs.

The roots of dual society must be sought in pre-revolutionary Iran. As I discussed in *Gender Politics*, gender relations in pre-revolutionary Iran underwent changes that offered women and men new, though limited, possibilities to refashion their gender identities. Educational and employment opportunities brought women a more active and visible role in society. Legal reforms altered women's status in family and society, offering them some mobility and limiting men's power in divorce and second marriage. Daily contact among men and women increased and new definitions of love and sexuality began to form. Many of the cultural consequences of these changes were still embryonic at the time of the revolution. Pahlavi reforms were not far reaching. New gender relations faced the opposition of old beliefs and values. Women and men who embodied emerging gender roles were unclear and unsure about the dimensions and the directions of these changes. Emerging notions of love and sexuality were often expressed through surrogate modes of the popular culture, rather than as personal testimonies of emotions. Thus, even before the revolution, emerging gender relations were now overt, now covert. The two coexisted, with varying degrees of acceptability; but both were legal.

After the revolution, however, many pre-revolutionary emerging relations were deemed counter-revolutionary. Besides, IRI's attempts to revert patriarchy to its private form have reinforced many weakening aspects of pre-revolutionary gender relations. We then encounter two contradictory cultural and gender patterns. One has flowed from the pre-revolutionary era, been reshaped in post-revolution, and become—simultaneously—more vulnerable and more resilient. The other, also existing prior to the revolution, has gained considerable power after the Islamic revolution. Deemed illegal, the former is forced to lead a predominantly clandestine life that becomes visible now and then, but only at the risk of liability.

Dual society emerges from a conflict between a project to reshape society along predefined roles, and women and men's access to different lifestyles and aspirations for "making" their own lives and reflexively forming their identities. Behaviors and beliefs emerge that range from modification of Islamists' ideals to outright refutation. Hejâb could be kept to a minimum, or it may be jettisoned altogether in "safe" zones. Cosmetics, fashionable dresses, ties, sunglasses, and Iranian- and Western-style pop music continue their existence. People may believe in the God and Prophet, but individuals also make pejorative references to Islam and Islamic leaders, ridicule, or even reject them. Alcoholic drinks are available. Mixed gatherings are quite accepted. Premarital amorous, in some cases even sexual liaisons are accepted. In sum, whatever Islamists deem antithetical to the Islamic revolution can be found in dual society. Yet this is not a "peaceful" coexistence, but the government's tolerance of "deviance." The dual society, then, is vulnerable to the forceful retaliation of the Islamic state.

Gender relationships in IRI have taken shape amidst constant tensions between genders preferred or accepted by Islamists (see chapters 6 and 7 of *Gender Politics*) and the subversive practices of women and men. The ruling clerics' gender preferences are dictated by the faith. These concerns are candidly echoed in Yazdi's sermon. *This is an Islamic society and Islamic it must look.* Such a society is incomplete without hearing the call to prayer (*azân*) from every corner, or without believers' heartfelt observance of religious rituals.[1] The reformists see the need for a relaxation of these rigid standards of gender, but they do not abandon these standards altogether. They may consider a less rigid dress code, but the obligation of wearing the hejâb—either in the form of an outerwear or the internally worn feminine "modesty"—is not rejected. An Islamic society with women roaming around as they please—"naked"—is incomplete; genders must maintain their appropriate "look" (see *Gender Politics* for a discussion). To fully appreciate why minute details of individual lives gain such prominence in the IRI, one must take these objectives of the Islamic state into consideration.

Capitalist modernity means the emergence of lifestyle choices (Giddens 1991; Melucci 1996b). For Iranian women, the reforms of the sixties and the development of public patriarchy have particularly played a pivotal role. Yet some post-revolutionary developments have also sharpened the conflict between rigidly defined Islamic norms and values and constantly changing lifestyles. Sex-segregated public spaces, for instance, afford women, especially from traditional families, the opportunity to utilize cultural resources (e.g., art or computer classes, sport centers, education, TV and videos) previously inaccessible to them. These resources expose young people to different lifestyles and encourage them to pursue goals that are not accommodated under the Islamists' rule. Living amidst multiple lifestyle choices thus breeds doubt about tradition and long held values and ceaselessly intertwines customary and innovative practices. Local and global interweave so that cultural "authenticity" and "purity" become impossible. "Where do you find your role models?" asks the reporter of the "youth and deviance" film. "Deviant" youngsters respond: at school, in the family, among relatives, through foreign media . . .

To be sure, there are Islamic alternatives to some contemporary hurdles; people may even use these alternatives as pretexts of their actions. But there are also numerous occasions in which these alternatives are rejected. Consider sexuality, for example. Recall that Islamists condone early marriage, but realize that starting a family at an early age is seldom feasible in contemporary society. Recall also that men and women experience pre-marital sex. Islamists have tried to solve this dilemma by proposing *siqeh* or temporary marriage, but the public has overwhelmingly rejected their solution despite Islamists' concerted effort to attract people's approval. The daily *Zan* (published for a short time by Fâezeh Hashemi Rafsanjani), for instance, in its issues of the second week of Shahrivar 1377 (late August and early September 1998) asked readers' opinions about whether temporary marriage could reduce young people's barriers for marriage by allowing them to interact freely. Readers were overwhelmingly opposed to *siqeh*: 80% responded negatively, expressing particular concern about the future of young, single women who would drastically diminish their marriageability if they accepted a temporary marriage contract. People's reaction to *siqeh* prompted authorities to salvage this Islamic institution. The following week, Ayatollah Bojnourdi offered a solution: virgins could specify in the contract that sexual relationship would not be part of their temporary arrangement (*Zan* 7 September 1998). At the end, *Zan*'s editorial basically dismissed public opinion and responded to the higher call of shari'ah: "At any rate, we must accept temporary marriage like a thousand other religious edicts, but that does not mean that we cannot add conditions to it" (6 October 1998). The persistent popular rejection of temporary marriage is particularly noteworthy in light of the Islamists' considerable efforts to "clarify" misconceptions about *siqeh*. In one such attempt, the author goes as far as rejecting the significance of virginity. In this day and age when "virginity" can be easily restored through reconstructive surgery, we have to emphasize a woman's *moral* intactness. There is a difference, he argues, between a woman who does everything but keeps her *pardeh-ye bekârat* ("curtain of virginity" or hymen), and someone who loses her virginity in a shari'ah-sanctioned "temporary join up" (see Zeinali 1998: 84–90). There are obviously people whose concerns about virginity do not dissipate simply by Zeinali's logical explanation. But even among those who reject virginity as a criterion of a woman's dignity, *temporary marriage*, not premarital relationship, perhaps not even losing virginity, remains objectionable. They, for instance, regard *siqeh* as "legal prostitution," or they see no need for a religious validation of their sexual choices.

The existence of dual society is particularly evident among the urban middle and upper classes. Familial background enables the younger generation financially *and* culturally to adopt alternative lifestyles. Pierre Bourdieu and Jean-Claude Passeron (1977) have argued that education reproduces social stratification because it turns parents' economic capital into children's cultural capital, a resource that influences their future placement on the socioeconomic hierarchy. A modified version of this argument is helpful for understanding the development of dual society among middle and upper class urban Iranians. Though formal education is controlled by the state, parents' economic abilities do influence children's access to myriad other cultural resources. Here, parents' economic and cultural privileges distance children from the Islamist alternative, a lifestyle they deem "outdated" and "old-fashioned." Financial power enables these families to gain access to—or buy—a cultural space unavailable to those without means. Economic privilege becomes a resource in preserving social relations that Islamists are determined to eradicate.

The economic factor plays a role in the expression of difference. "Being different" is costly in more ways than one. Attending language or art classes, learning music, participating in such sports as skiing and horseback riding, attending parties, adhering to fashion—these require financial resources not available to all. Furthermore, authorities deem many forms of "being different" as more than mere expression of difference; they are illegal or illegitimate conducts, acts of defiance. Those engaged in these acts are thus susceptible to the prosecution of the moral police and have to either pay fines or bribe the officials.

A more significant factor, however, is the accumulated cultural capital within the family—a tradition of secularism, relaxed familial supervision, challenging Islamic moral codes, and acceptance of non-mainstream gender relations. In Ayatollah Yazdi's sermon quoted above, the *badhejâb* middle-

or upper class girl whose "mother and aunts, right before the revolution, would appear naked in public" utilizes her family's cultural capital. The lifestyles of these classes have differed fundamentally from that proposed by the Islamists, making IRI both culturally and politically unappealing.

These people were initially a primary target for Islamists, often subject to humiliation, demotion, dismissal, and even persecution and imprisonment. Yet, as I discussed in chapter 6 of *Gender Politics*, Islamist technocrats who enjoyed the security of being a part of the establishment have emulated the lifestyle of this "Westernized" group. In recent years, the persecution of a "decadent lifestyle" has considerably subsided. To be sure, the class scare—condemnation of the upper class lifestyle—continues to carry weight because it ensures the state's legitimacy among its supporters and can be used as a weapon in political fights.

Living under the Islamists' rule has nurtured resilience in many who have found themselves suddenly "strangers in their own country" (Esfandiari 1997: 119). That is especially true about women who had to undertake major economic responsibilities, particularly when their men lost their jobs, became depressed, suffered from deteriorating health, migrated, passed away, or were executed. For many of these women, meeting family responsibilities—an arrangement contrary to the Islamic doctrine that makes men the sole family breadwinners—has entailed, as Esfandiari puts it, "reconstructing" their damaged lives. In the process, they have realized that they have "to fight back and to negotiate" (115).

The pronounced presence of dual society among middle and upper classes is, therefore, understandable: they have both cultural and economic means of creating a space that distances them from Islamists. To be sure, however, economic capital is only one factor. Though economic considerations are significant, they are not debilitating. Not all habits of living "differently" are expensive—planning the family budget or other creative means can accommodate different expenses. Clothes, for instance, are expensive and there are stores where only the wealthy can shop. But those on a limited budget can also survive. They can shop, for instance, at retail stores. Friends may share clothes. Families may also eagerly forego certain comforts to provide for their children's educational and artistic development. Besides, available cultural and recreational resources in poor neighborhoods—some even the results of IRI's cultural and urbanization policies—have diminished differences in the aspirations of upper and lower class youth, making them express "similar grievances and complaints" (Amir Ebrahimi 1998: 40). This is not, of course, to minimize sociocultural differences across classes. Crossing class boundaries often requires a spatial and cultural journey to uncharted territories, going to an unfamiliar environment where alienation is accentuated by complex social psychological dynamics of class. Yet, as new social spaces become available to the lower class young, they gain more opportunities to question established norms and vie for alternative living arrangements. Public parks, for instance, enhance interactions between the sexes. College life offers young people, especially young women, anonymity and less parental control in daily life.

Workplace politics reveal a similar conflict between prescribed relations and individuals' actual potentials. One woman worker, for instance, recalls that when women in her factory started a co-op, elder women were reluctant to join, believing that such activities do not suit women. Gradually, this notion was challenged and their co-op grew in number and resources (Hosseini 1998). Workers' intervention in the politico-economic management of daily life is a direct challenge to dominant class and gender politics by individuals who are not part of, or at least approved by, the Islamic establishment. These practices have an obvious implication for gender politics by proving to both women and others that women are capable of attending to the economic needs of themselves and their families.

The simultaneity of two sets of political and cultural principles requires the individuals to constantly move between appearance and their "real lifestyle," assuring safety in public by displaying compliance to values of the state while appropriating one's own values in private.[2] Lying preserves the truth. Lying about one's beliefs and practices, or at least concealing one's realities from untrustworthy preying eyes, has become a constant in a system that assumes moral guardianship. Parents are left with no choice but to give children contradictory messages: on the one hand, parents teach children the value of being truthful; on the other, the virtues of lying. Young children have become quite skillful in safely representing family realities. A middle class, nonbeliever teacher in her early thirties who is married to a believer writes in a letter of 23 May 1997:

I don't want my son to grow up religious, but I want him to adhere to honorable moral standards. Neither his father nor I pull him in our respective direction. He himself says: "Mom, I don't believe in religion. What business is that of our Religious Education teacher whether I pray? *You don't*, but that doesn't make you a bad person." At this point in the conversation, I tell him: "Son, do not ever tell anybody I don't pray." He wonders why. I explain that if they find out, they will fire me. He says: "That is none of their business!" His father says: "Son, *this is the Islamic Republic*, they want everybody to pray." And I wonder that if not praying is a sin, we have to compound that with the sin of lying! Our final word to him is that whether you pray or not is a decision that you have to make after you study the options. But really, see where we stand: until a few years ago, I couldn't conceal anything with a straight face, but my son's classmates tell only those they trust that, for example, they have a satellite dish.

Her frustration is loud and clear, frustration about living in the "republic of morality" where lying is a means of subsistence. Her narrative also reveals the political character of the private. In fact, as we shall observe throughout this chapter, the private sphere plays a pivotal role in the preservation or emergence of secular lifestyles, even oppositional politics.

The Islamist and non-Islamist aspects of the dual society are not separated by an inviolable line; they coexist and interfuse both materially (as in a married couple with divergent beliefs) and intellectually. Obviously, the existence of a dual society signifies that the Islamic state had to make concessions to people resisting its agenda. This means that the state's policies contain both Islamic ideals (however defined by competing groups) *and* what they can realistically expect to achieve—compromises that many Islamists deem bring the profane side-by-side with the sacred. As in the policies of the helpless state, conflicting tendencies similarly coexist in the lives of the unsympathetic public. Not subscribing to Islamist ideals, for instance, does not mean anti-Islamic or even anti-religious beliefs. Prime examples include the spread of mysticism or individuals turning their backs on Islam as a systematic doctrine but believing in an "idiosyncratic god."[3] Here, god could appear in such forms as "beauty," "nature," or "pure energy"—an entity that simply "exists" and provides moral support for the believer, but has no other practical implication for the individual; a god that does not share Allah's characteristic power. Individuals are then left free to define morality, values, and their social relationships. They may even selectively observe Islamic practices, but see their "Islam" as different from the Islam of the Republic. One female high school student interviewed in the "youth and deviance" film clearly expresses this separation of personal and religious spaces in her life:

If I tell you that I am a hizbullahi, I'd be lying . . . No, I'm not neutral either. That is, you see how I'm dressed now, but if you see me outside of the school, you may not recognize me . . . I am a Heavy. But, see. I tell you, I believe in Islam, do all my prayers on time. You may not believe that. But I tell you something, god has his own business, I have mine. They are not going to put me in the same grave as a hizbullahi. If I've sinned, I'm accountable; if I haven't, again I am accountable.

If anything, more than two decades of constant exposure to Islamic propaganda has affected people's attitudes. In some cases, old beliefs have been strengthened; in others, people have gradually adopted Islamist interpretations. While dual society indicates a compromise on the part of the state, it also tells of concessions by opponents. A secular intellectual referred to a process of *sâyesh-o-farsâyesh*, friction and smoothing (private correspondence, summer 1999). She uses this metaphor, inspired by the collisions of sharp rocks that gradually soften sharp edges. Iran's relatively young secular movement, she suggests, has suffered considerably under the IRI. Resistance is inspiring and positive, yet weakness of articulating secular ideas and lifestyles—not just in private gathering, but in public—makes secularists (and one could add, leftists) quite weak and vulnerable. What is worrisome, she emphasizes, is not just the compromise; rather that in this exchange, it has been the *secularists* who have paid more than they earned. She offers as an example intellectuals' treatment of Forugh Farrokhzad, the famous poet of the 1960s. Secularists and leftists now read and revere Farrokhzad, but resist defending her free spirit in public; they restrict their praise to the sensations of her poems, attributing her amorous and sexual relationships to "historians' distortions."

When I asked a sweet 15-year-old girl what she liked about Forugh, she replied, with much embarrassment, her free spirit. This response angered her mother: "These are lies people say about Forugh." You see, people who called Forugh a whore before the revolution because of her free sexuality, now present her as more chaste than Mary. What does this mean? To me, it means the seepage of traditional Islamic culture into our thoughts.

These incidents once again reveal the inadequacy of manipulating existing symbols to express disapproval of the regime's gender policies. Though such tactics are worthy as *one form of the struggle*, they cannot substitute for the more daunting task of crafting an autonomous secular women's movement. The IRI's history attests that the government's tolerance of such maneuvers is contingent on its sociopolitical needs rather than acceptance of gender equality and personal freedom. Dual society might provide a temporary refuge for some, but also works to the detriment of others in society at large.

IRANIAN YOUTH: "THE CANCEROUS TISSUE"

Despite IRI's hope to raise a new generation of devout Muslims, youngsters have become, in the words of a university student, "a cancerous tissue that had to be removed or replaced." According to one observer, "cultural crimes"—failure to comply with the dress code or use and possess illegal cultural objects such as nail polish, sunglasses, and unapproved movies— are particularly aimed to control young people (*Goft-o-gu* 1998: 18). Middle class Tehran high school students in the film state that power in their educational institutions tilts in favor of nonbelievers. One female student says: "In our school, out of 1000 students, perhaps only two wore the chador; we controlled the environment." Though this may not be an accurate estimate of the exact composition of believer and nonbeliever students, it reveals the existence of division, as another student comments upon:

There are 3 groups in schools. One group is the ordinary kids; they've got nothing to do with any groups, just mind their own business. Another, are very religious and participate in every school activity. A third group is completely opposed. . . . Whatever school officials say, they do the opposite.

IRI officials acknowledge their failure in gaining legitimacy among the young, who now constitute a considerable portion of the Iranian population. According to Ayatollah Mohsen Qarâ'ati, students' enthusiasm for prayer decreases drastically as they advance in their education. "Students who go through our system," he said, "break from religion as soon as their knowledge increases" (quoted in *Iran-e Fardâ* 49 1998, no. 49: 45). According to IRI's reports, some 1,200 people were arrested following the July 1999 unrest. Among the detainees were about 200 university and 600 high school students (*Neshat* 28 August 1999). Reflecting on this fact, Golpâyegâni, Head of Ayatollah Khamenehii's Office, refers to a "serious threat to the revolution" and ponders what the regime has done to attract the support of young Iranians (*Khordâd* 28 May 1999).

Narrowly defined normalcy, double standards for boys and girls (often practiced to "protect" daughters from public and police harassment), and rigid control both within the family and throughout the society, all contribute to the making of a social milieu wherein young individuals can easily slip into the realm of "deviance." "My family was too rigid," a teenager interviewed in "youth and deviance" says. "Her father hits her fiercely," a mother says. Another mother explains to the reporter: "I told her she should go only to places that I take her." And the father emphasizes: "When you tell a child don't go out, she ought to say '*Yes Sir!*' " "Our principal was a tyrant, everything had to be done her way. Nobody dared to talk to her." "There are supervisions that leave negative marks on the students' spirit . . . For instance, when they pay so much attention that your nails must be short. Well, it may happen that a girl has long nails for no particular reason." And slippage is deemed not only as breaking the rules, but also as moral failure that threatens the entire "Islamic system" (*nezâm-e islami*). A young woman says, for example, that she has been detained frequently, sometimes for not adhering to the dress code, *badhejâbi*, but mostly for "insulting the system."

Various groups or types, such as Rap, Heavy, Metallica, and Techno, often compete for recognition and legitimacy among peers. Though no type is clearly defined, each is associated with distinct behaviors, appearance, and linguistic expressions. When individuals join a group, they are expected to act out the (alleged) characteristics of that group. "I was with the Rap folks. Kids brought whisky to school and we drank it in the restroom. We smoked, exchanged sex films and photos." "In a Rap group, everybody is a leader, but a Heavy group has only one leader." The Heavy wear long boots that always have locks hanging on the side, and bat-like manteaus with wide, bell-shaped sleeves that in windy weather resemble bats. Boys pluck their eyebrows; girls put on heavy makeup. Rap people "are obsessed with their looks. 'Do these shoes go with this dress?' I even saw boys with pierced ears." "Rap folks are homosexuals." A young woman who belonged to a Rap group explains: "Well, we did things to attract students' attention at school. Our clothes were different . . . the way we spoke was different. . . . We had our own lingo." The reporter asks her about the expressions that distinguished them from others. Embarrassed, she utters their English lingoes that place them on the border of committing a cultural offense: "shit, fuck, motherfucker." Though tattoo is illegal, "we tattooed words like *Rap*, *Heavy*, or *Techno* on our hands using a glass to make incisions. Then before the wound is healed, another cut, and then another, until the wound marks become permanent."

But the wounds of the flesh are more tolerable than those inflicted by the brutality of interpretation. The wheels of control are set in motion the moment the youngsters are defined as "deviant," as ill individuals contaminated by the "West." The "youth and deviance" film is dotted with images of youngsters infected by "Western culture"—boys pretending to play the guitar; a man with several rings on his fingers; a girl and a boy exchanging glances; several boys standing by a boutique; boys doing fancy footwork for the reporter; clips from MTV; a boy's room with a poster of "The Wall" and Persian and English writings on the wall . . . Interviewees acknowledge that their looks and deeds may not be right, but "we are so deprived that we compensate for it this way." Yet the official interpretation chooses to ignore this explanation. An expert (not identified in the film) expresses that, if gone unchecked, the danger these youngsters cause could be serious. It could spread so much that gradually "the corruption of society and generations expands and has very negative effects on the formation of our identity as Muslim Iranians." If an epidemic or an illness spreads, numerous people may become contaminated. "Other societies, both Islamic and non-Islamic, have felt that young people's inclination toward non-native cultural manifestations" has caused detrimental consequences for economic growth and social well-being. "These are parasites," the expert says, "that can spread consumerism, deepen dependency, chaos, and insecurity. I ask you, can we expect these people to defend our society if it is invaded?" The expert fails to ask what alienates these young people from their environment, what makes them indifferent toward "our identity as Muslim Iranians."

What is to be done? More Islam. The comments of the expert are followed by frames that show a young boy in the mosque, preparing for prayer. In the background, music echoes that sounds like *azân*, the call to prayer. But this "remedy" is nothing but the cause of the problem itself. In an environment where a "crisis of happiness" persists and "living happily is synonymous with living sinfully" (Foruzandeh 1992: 21), offering more religion as a solution to young people's low morale, lack of motivation, depression, and aimlessness would only augment the problem. Thus it should be of no surprise that, according to a study by President Khatami's Office of Women's Affairs, "young women in the conservative holy city of Qom are more depressed than those in the more liberal capital of Tehran." Zahrâ Shojâ'i, advisor to Khatami on women's affairs, attributes this discrepancy to the "suppression of girls' interests and existing restrictions" (quoted in *Defenders' Newsletter*, vol. 3, no. 8, August 1999). What interviewees in "youth and deviance" express is not atypical at all: "It's all over. Life has no significance for me any more. . . . I'm happier in prison . . . There is no future; I have no hope . . . wanted to kill myself in prison . . . swallowed broken pieces of glass, but wasn't enough." "I'm less than cigarette ashes." "I'm like a tableau, everybody points at me."

GENDER AND THE DUAL SOCIETY

It is true that the policing of gender brings public compliance, but many people's observance is neither out of conviction nor uncontested. Women constantly transgress the dress code; men and women negotiate "appropriate gender appearance," and engage in "illicit" liaisons. The contradictory tendencies of the IRI and women have created distrust and antagonism between the two. Islamists frequently complain about compromises of the dress code or continued tolerance of interaction among the sexes (see, for instance, letters to the editor, quoted in *Zanân*, 1996, no. 31: 50–51). Encounters between the young and school authorities or the religious police—always coercive, frequently violent—testify to that. Islamists' persisting concern about the clash between Islamic "values" and non-Islamic "counter-values" is indicative of IRI's failure to gain cultural support among the masses of the population, especially women. Disparity between Islamists' and people's norms and values has caused conflicting behaviors among the public that at times border on absurdity. For instance, female students occasionally unveil in class before a male professor, but make sure that their hejâb is always fixed when the female instructor of morality approaches. Departure from Islamic sexual morality is also vivid. The reporter in the film asks informants about their get-togethers. One person says these events usually include alcohol and drugs—hash, marijuana, cocaine, and LSD. Boys and girls mix freely. "How did your parties begin?" the reporter asks. "We started with a game called Spin the Bottle." The person the bottle points at must remove an item of clothing. Baffled, the reporter asks: "Did you go all the way, or stopped at underwear?" "Sometimes even all the way, when boyfriends and girlfriends were together."

Dual society has thus profound implications for gender politics. At an immediate level, dual society creates a "safe" zone for feminists. Besides, new activists emerge primarily through experiencing the conflict between real and pretend lives. Though the youth countercultural behavior does not always result in visible oppositional action, it nevertheless nurtures a new generation whose life experience encourages resistance to Islamist values and venturing beyond the mainstream (Islamic) boundaries. Dual society allows the expressions of gender alternatives; makes visible the diversity of women's roles, experiences, and identities; and legitimizes grievances and causes. Consequently, dual society enhances the scope of the women's and other social movements beyond immediate political grievances to include undercurrents of social life. The political scope of such deep-rooted conflicts goes far beyond any reinterpretation of gender ideology or modification of patriarchy within the Islamic framework.

Though dual society signifies a compromise by the Islamic state, one cannot overlook that such an arrangement is in an *oppressive* state, that *Islamic mandates* shape the structure of gender politics in the Islamic Republic. Islamism, I argue in this book, is a movement to secure men's prerogatives at home and in public by reviving private patriarchy. It is also a movement that vies to achieve its goals within the context of Islam. That precondition limits how far Islamists can drift away from Islam's prescriptions—or what they believe those to be. However defined, *Islam* constitutes the outlook of these people and shapes how they perceive problems and imagine the solutions. In the words of Weber, material and ideal interests shape individuals' action by acting like a switch operator, determining "the tracks along which action [is] pushed by the dynamic of interest" (1981: 280).

And it is along the Islamic tracks that these actions are interpreted. Revisioning life as a process that forms as one lives and makes decisions, rather than following a predetermined path to a "true" womanhood or manhood, challenges many forms of social control. IRI's re-strengthening of private patriarchy and its rampant policing of gender enhance the control of gender. This project is thus antithetical to a reflexive construction of autonomous individuals. If the dispersed, indirect, and more flexible control of public patriarchy cannot entertain free choice for women and men, the widespread, idiosyncratic, direct, strict, and brutal control of private patriarchy is even less accommodating.

Policing gender has obviously failed; so socialization ought to produce consent among the Iranian youth, convincing them that compliance with gender roles are to their benefit. A report on parental control and daughters (*Zan-e Rouz* 15 January 1993) consoles young girls (*dokhtarân*) unhappy about their parents' double standards that superiority in the eyes of God stems from piety and nothing else. "Girls must be more responsible because of the mothering task they have to shoulder in the future" (43).

Undoubtedly, the report concedes, sometimes "conditions" dictate certain restrictions on young girls, but that is only for their own benefit— after all, girls are "more vulnerable."[4] Temporary social conditions notwithstanding, modesty and shame are beautiful ornaments on any person, but "particularly on girls it is more becoming and more protective, securing them against invasions." Granted, there are undue restrictions in institutions and bureaucratic organizations, but why waste one's time: "Why spend our time making comparisons [of how men and women are treated], comparisons that bear nothing but the erosion of our morale? Why do so, instead of dealing with our essence and bringing to the surface our talents and abilities from the depth of our human nature?" (43).

The reporter asks psychologist Sousan Seif if the definitions of "control" and "freedom" should change. She replies: "What our children, especially our daughters, call freedom is distancing from our authenticity. They consider 'special provisions' for women a 'denial of freedom.' These special provisions mark the limits of girls and boys in society" (*Zan-e Rouz* 22 January 1993: 44).

The differential treatment of male and female children is, of course, hardly an invention of the IRI. The significant point, however, is the blessing of these practices by an official gender ideology that tolerates little dissension. Divinity prescribes roles; roles justify differences; justifiable differences make unwarranted discriminations appear insignificant. Islam blesses patriarchy; patriarchy validates Islam. Both come to the rescue of the state that, in turn, is a steadfast supporter of both.

The teenagers interviewed are quite unhappy about their treatment in the family. A 14-year-old girl, for instance, complains that parents are more indulgent about sons than daughters (44). Parents, on the other hand, are convinced that double standards are necessary to secure parents and children in that society; but they, too, have to frequently acknowledge the absurdity of their actions. A 42-year-old mother of three says that she does not allow her daughter go out with friends whom she does not know: "For, after all, she is a girl. I know she is impressionable, might be influenced by the various factors present in environment, and what should not happen, happens. Despite all these, I also trust her completely, but . . ."(44).

She does not complete her sentence. Though she does trust her daughter, she knows she has to supervise her. The unarticulated doubt in her remark is indicative of a space for contemplating counterhegemonic gender politics. Dual society thus becomes the space for not only experiencing oppression, but also realizing wants and cultivating hope and negation. The plea of the young woman that begins this chapter is echoed frequently in the narratives of others interviewed in the film, expressing asphyxiation under heavy social pressure. A young incarcerated woman, for instance, conveys the frustration of an independent individual living in a Republic whose objectives include preserving the sanctity of the family and the rule of morality:

I don't want to live here. Even when I'm out of prison, I feel like a prisoner. I don't remember anymore how many times I've been imprisoned—13, 14, or 15 . . . I'm charged with *monkarât*—immoral conducts. "Why do you talk to boys? Why is your hair showing? Why don't you stay with your family?" I don't *want* to be with my family. They are religious and restrict. They want me to wear a chador, not to wear colorful dress, do only what *they* like. But I like to act differently. . . . Every time I'm incarcerated for 6 months, 7 months, 2 months . . . Then out, then back in again. . . . Since I was a child, I liked to be independent—go where I liked, talk to any boy I liked. But the law says that is illegal. What can I do? What am I guilty of?

"What do you wish now?" the reporter asks. The young woman responds: "My wish is that this country would change. Just that!" In the solitude of her prison cell, this young woman has made a commitment to herself: "I promised myself not to go back on my words. I mean that even if they take me to the gallows, I want to say that I remained a Heavy; that I didn't change here."

It is in moments of doubt lingering in a parent's voice, or in the resilience of a young incarcerated woman that the legitimacy of the Islamist gender order becomes vulnerable. As doubts grow, they nourish discontent and refusal. Dual society creates a space where men and women can forge a different and autonomous identity.

FROM FRIENDSHIP CIRCLES TO COLLECTIVITIES OF RESISTANCE

Gender resistance is present in all aspects of life. The tension between IRI and women stems from rights and prerogatives women have experienced in contemporary Iran and the patriarchal order IRI officials wish to impose on society. Resistance is informal and unorganized *as well as* formal and organized. It includes manipulation of the dress code; expression of anger and frustration in private and public; active presence in art classes, sports, and women's circles; IWD celebration; women's tour groups; and crafting revisionist interpretations of Iranian history and culture. It includes both crisis- and conflictoriented movements. *Women simultaneously shape and resist dominant and residual cultural and social systems.* A secular woman activist, poet, and scholar who was purged from the university during the "Cultural Revolution" of the early 1980s, writes to me about her resolution, not unlike the buoyancy and resourcefulness with which countless other women have dealt with the Islamic Republic:

I am very stubborn. I don't give up easily. When I find this door shut, I search for another. If they don't let me in through the door, I'll climb in through the window. Wherever I am, even in prison, I try to open a window . . . or a crack to breathe. Perhaps that is why I am still active. . . . I am seriously considering opening a publishing house. Even have done some preliminary work. We also had meetings with several NGOs, hoping to create some unity. But in practice, we realize the temptation for many of these groups to become official, which is another way of saying become affiliated with the government. We believe there is a miniscule chance that ours would get any official approval, that is, they would allow us to register our group. But if that happens, our every move will be controlled. (Private correspondence, August 1997)

Feeling isolated for resisting Islamists' hegemony is not, of course, confined to women. I asked a middle-class, 23-year-old university student to tell me his experience of living in the Islamic Republic. He wrote about what he calls "old youngsters," young people who feel old, "suffering a gloomy past, an uncertain future and an unstable present life":

Young people my age spent most of their childhood in the shadow of a hideous war. Many lost their closest friends and beloved relatives, some were killed or suffered mental trauma. At the same time, they were the very aim of Islamic radical rulers who saw their future survival in capturing their minds. This, they admitted openly. Extreme religious control, close observation, and oppressive pressure on youth became part of everyday life. The situation was and is in many ways similar to what Orwell described in his *1984*, but of course in a more realistic atmosphere. Young people also experienced the postwar period during which the war's devastating economic and cultural consequences became more conspicuous. (Email correspondence, 6 April 1999)

Frustrated young and old, male and female, have built discrete communities, autonomous from the regime and its supporters. This division is evident both in the realm of ideology and worldview and in practice. Gender appearance becomes a site of resistance through the expressions of masculinities and femininities that do not fit rigid Islamist molds. These autonomous communities are both real and imaginary. People constantly categorize those around them into hizbullah and non-hizbullah, dogmatic or flexible, or believer and nonbeliever (as do the Islamists classify people as *khodi* and *qeyr-e-khodi*, in-group and strangers). In these imagined communities—to borrow from Anderson (1991) and Rushdie (1991)—individuals appropriate legitimate and subversive symbols and practices to express their unmediated selves. People recognize each other as distinct from the hegemonic Islamists, without necessarily assuming an undifferentiated, unified bloc.

Members of these communities create networks, draw inspiration, and gain support from each other. Friendship circles, research groups, formal and informal associations, cyber communities, contacts abroad—these communities flourish in innumerable forms in all corners of the society. The exchange of ideas and experiences creates awareness about common problems and inspires a search for collective solutions. Giti Shâmbayâti, for instance, writes about the content of 532 messages exchanged among members of a Web-based discussion group called the Anjoman-e Tasâvy-e Hoquq-e Zan va Mard (Association for Equality between Women and

Men). She observes that often members were unaware of such problems as sexual abuse of children or mothers' malnutrition.

Raising this issue on the Web would create quite an excitement. As soon as a message would circulate about these topics, the Web would become flooded with messages of objection, accusing the author of being unaware or extremist. At the same time, however, a considerable number of participants would offer evidence supporting the author's claim and guiding the objector or objectors. (Shâmbayâti 1997: 474)

Political conditions or financial resources permitting, some communities evolve into collectivities of resistance, though with different degrees of articulation. For years, these individuals have held discussion groups, planned activities, or celebrated International Women's Day. Some secular and leftist feminists have related to me that, lacking financial resources and acting semicovertly, they meet in each other's houses—"with much fear and trembling" (private correspondence, August 1997). Yet here and there, overt expressions are detectable. At times, informal groups crystallize into such entities as research centers, publishing collectives, and magazine circles.

The idea of publishing an independent, secular feminist journal goes back to the mid-1980s. Years before *Farzaneh: Journal of Women's Studies and Research*, published in 1993 by Muslim women reformists, a number of secular intellectuals searched for ways to publish a forum for research on women's issues. A number of original and translated articles were distributed in informal circles. Later, some essays on women and literature and art appeared in print in *Zanân* and other similar magazines. *Zan va Sinemâ* (Women and Cinema) is among the earliest efforts to publish secular feminist literature, prepared in 1996 and published shortly after (Najm-e-'Erâqi et al. 1998). This anthology mainly aimed to fill a theoretical void. These authors, as articulated in the introduction to the anthology, believed that analyses of women in Iranian society would be incomplete unless women's-studies scholars benefited from feminist theoretical achievements in other societies. *Zan va Sinemâ* contained predominantly translations, including works by Wendy Kozol (1994), Frigga Haug and Brigitte Hipfl (1995), Annette Kuhn (1994), and Michelle Royer (1990). A section of the anthology was devoted to defining feminist terminology. As one contributor wrote to me:

This was something we proudly aimed to produce. It gave us an excuse to write short paragraphs about feminist jargons. We were discussing these issues for the first time in Farsi. We also meant to suggest Persian equivalents for expressions that did not exist in our language. (Personal correspondence, July 2000)

Zan va Sinemâ clearly targeted intellectuals, particularly university students. It was to be followed by similar collections in other areas—an anthology on women and literature is in preparation.

Around the same time, several activists recommended *Farhang-e Towse'eh* to publish a special issue on women, which was published in March 1998 to honor International Women's Day. But after *Farhang-e Towse'eh* magazine showed reluctance to publish a second special issue, the idea of publishing an independent secular feminist forum grew stronger. *Negâh-e Zanân* (Women's Outlook) collective was immediately formed with the mandate to publish articles on and by women. The anthology was collectively prepared, financed, and distributed. To bypass the difficulty of obtaining a magazine license, the collective decided to publish it in the format of a book. The collective anticipated that with its objective (as stated in the introduction) to reflect the needs and problems of low-paid workingwomen, *Negâh-e Zanân* might not survive beyond a single issue. Yet, in search of sustainability and the privileges of a journal, they decided to pursue the option of obtaining a license. Meanwhile, however, one member of the group collected materials on her own initiative and published *Jens-e Dovom* (The Second Sex) individually. The collective subsequently dissolved, especially since *Jens-e Dovom* was almost in the same format as *Negâh-e Zanân*.

Secular feminists are, of course, politically fragile and financially frail. Unlike Islamist and Islamist reformist women groups that enjoy political and economic support from the government (or factions thereof) and its near and distant supporters, secular groups have little leverage in official politics and skimpy financial resources. Though resilient, these individuals are fragile; their effectiveness must not be overemphasized. They are isolated and cliquish, and in the absence of freedom to establish organizations with wider constituencies, these collectives thus remain limited in number and effectiveness (Ahmady Khorasany 1998a).

Lack of freedom and security is, of course, only one problem facing secular women. So far, these women have not formulated their overall agenda. They seem not to have clear collective identities; they have not delineated their objectives, commonalities and differences with other trends (e.g., Islamist reformist women), and their aims and methods of intervention in Iranian politics. One example related to reactions against a domestic violence case is illuminating. In the summer of 1997, news about the tortuous death of a 12-year-old girl named Ârian by her family shocked the nation (see *Zanân* no. 37, September 1997). The incident evoked several public reactions. Magazines publicized the news. A group of female journalists issued a communiqué, criticizing the judicial system for its failure to take action against the violence inflicted upon women and children within the family (*Akhbâr* 7 October 1997). The National Association for Defending Children's Rights called for a demonstration on 17 September

1997. "A large crowd" of women writers, reporters, and artists gathered, shouting: "The law must be amended" (*Jâme'eh-ye Sâlem* no. 34, September-October 1997: 88). Some participants related to me in our correspondence that though the protest had an impact on the public opinion about custody laws, that event did not lead to broader strategies of a sustained, feminist political intervention.

Secular women see in this limitedness the danger of lacking clear political identity and objective. A secular writer offers another example: "When A'zam Tâleqâni called for celebrating the second anniversary of Mr. Khatami's presidency, so many women attended it without any attempt to show their separate identity" (personal correspondence, May 2000). This form of activism has serious practical consequences. Shortly before the spring 2000 election, Shahlâ Lâhiji and Shahlâ Sherkat called for a gathering of women MPs, new candidates, secular women, and the press. The meeting was advertised as a "free discussion" session. The secular women who were at the meeting were surprised to find out that it was instead a propaganda meeting to promote the participation of women in the election without a definite secular identity (the report of this meeting appears in *Zanân* no. 60, February-March 2000: 14–16).

Paucity of information makes a definitive judgment difficult, but several women have expressed to me that they consider intellectual disarray (*parishân andishi* or *âshoftegy-e fekri*) and the ambiguity of their collective identity to be a major setback for secular women. This problem is particularly acute among women who have questioned the fundamentals of the leftist politics of the revolutionary days of the late 1970s and early 1980s; most of their energy is devoted to self-education.

Most secular women's collectivities are still in the formative stages; they are active and emerging nonetheless. The evolutionary process of these collectivities has often been reflexive, involving assessments about the theories and practices of women's movements worldwide and in Iran (see, e.g., Jalali Naeini 1997). Mahin Khadivi, Zhâleh Shâditalab, and Mansoureh Ettehadyeh, for instance, discuss aspects of such concerns during a summer 1997 interview with the Farsi program of BBC Radio. They emphasize the need for legal changes and sustained social involvement to be essential for changing gender relations. Ahmady Khorasany (1998a) suggests that for a genuine women's movement to develop in Iran, women's collectives must remain autonomous from the state and avoid cliquish (*mahfelgarâ*) tendencies.

As I discussed in *Gender Politics*, autonomous feminist organizations have not had a chance to emerge under the Islamists' rule, making direct approach to some feminist demands quite difficult, if not impossible. This condition has prompted roundabout politics among secular and leftist activists. These activists support and participate in causes that are not directly confrontational, but that directly or indirectly promote social justice, freedom, democracy, and nonviolence. This maneuver is, of course, not merely due to political repression, but also because prevalent beliefs may not allow overt identification of demands and objectives, particularly those that are countercultural. Consequently, feminist activism is not limited to *working on* identifiable grievances; it also includes *working toward* concerns that are not yet verbalized, vivid, or within reach. Lesbians and gays, for instance, are extremely discrete because of their vulnerable position under the law. Unable to form organizations that advocate their causes, they involve themselves instead in activities to advance women's rights and tolerance toward difference. A weakened patriarchy or more tolerant public opinion would create an opportunity for these activists to voice their own cause in the future. Similarly, many feminists engage in activities that lead to *pishraft-e farhangi*, "cultural progress," toward a future when they can directly further their own cause. Activities such as participating in national and international agencies to promote antiviolence or environmental concerns for these activists mean far more than working for the specified goals of those organizations. Activists aim to eventually effect a new culture and social system that advocates freedom, equality and values difference.

Roundabout politics is inevitable under repression, a valuable symbol of the activists' resourcefulness. But roundabout politics has its drawbacks as well. Often ultimate concerns remain unnamed and unrecognized, a condition that further masks the undercurrent conflicts of gender relations. Besides, lack of public identification and debate isolates activists and causes uneven theoretical (and practical) development. Many sensitive topics, especially those related to morality and sexuality, are merely hinted at, or, as one activist put it, "signaled": "We use 'signals' to indicate our differences," she says, "but can't say much beyond that—at least not yet." Mokhtâri calls communication through signals *pushidehgoï*, concealed-speaking, and points out that *pushidehgoï* is antithetical to critical, realist understanding of phenomena. In *pushidehgoï*, he writes, "both a portion of reality remains concealed and a segment of the citizenry . . . does not find the chance to speak its reality; both a part of discourse (*bayân*) finds a tendency toward silence, concession, and distortion, and the subject of discourse becomes limited" (Mokhtâri 1998: 117).

Despite limitations on self-expression, the desire to counter the dominant system has not been crushed. Noteworthy is the presence of younger activists (early 20s to early- to-mid-30s) side-by-side with veterans. And though predominantly female, men also participate—one notable example being the late Mohammad Pouyandeh who translated several books on feminism, a victim of political murders that shook the nation in late 1998 (see Moossavi 1999). The young age of these activists deserves further in-depth studies, because this is the *nasl-e enqelâb*, the "revolution generation," raised in the Islamic Republic. For the officials, this is indeed a sore sight, as a young male university student and a frequent contributor to women's magazines explains it eloquently:

Some young people got totally involved in the ups and downs of everyday life in the early days of their youth and took life as it came to them. A minority enjoyed a high social status and wealth, thus rarely played an active role. But there were others who cared more. They couldn't leave it all to fate or to others to decide for their lives. These were certainly the least welcome. More pressure was concentrated on them since the ruling system looked at them as a potential threat—a cancerous tissue that had to be removed or replaced. They were not easily moved by religious stimuli anymore. The war was over and in a society now desperately seeking stability, these doubted the faultlessness of their preachers—something that could not be tolerated. The condition got even more serious when those who pulled the strings virtually realized that their plan in having the next generation of the revolution under their control didn't prove as successful as they had expected. The irony of its adverse effect was not something easy for them to digest. (E-mail correspondence, 12 May 1999)

What of the Left? The organized Left of the revolutionary days was crushed through imprisonment, execution, and exile. Though some exiled Marxist organizations allude to their revival inside Iran, there is no evidence as yet to their organized presence. Nor is there any sign of new groups. But, as is often true about defeated social movements (Sztompka 1988: 188), activists seek alternative modes of expression for activism. Individual leftists have actively participated in the reshaping of oppositional movements. In a sense, the "old" Left has continued in two ways. First, many veteran activists participate in new oppositional efforts; and, second, the goals of the emerging movements include demands such as democracy, freedom, separation of religion and politics, and social justice that continue from the past. This, however, does not mean the repetition of the old politics. As I have discussed elsewhere (Shahidian 1996a; 1997a), the dissolution of the organized Left lifted the pressure of "total movement ideologies," official ideologies that claimed to have answers for any and all personal and social questions. Social, economic, political, and cultural priorities have been reshuffled. The new generation of activists experiences emerging conditions that underline the significance of sexual politics. Many newcomers and veteran activists have reassessed the theory and praxis of the leftist movement regarding women's rights—from the Left's understanding of patriarchy to its understanding of women's position in Islam, to leftist organizations' reaction to mandatory hejâb, and to the Left's stand vis-à-vis the autonomy of the women's movement. Consequently, many leftist women and men have modified or abandoned old beliefs and values. The effects of these revisions on the politics of future leftist organizations remain to be seen.

IN SEARCH OF ALTERNATIVES

Oppositional politics under constant persecution requires skillfulness in covering one's track; crafting an oppositional movement under a police condition that not only persecutes, but also targets the very sociocultural foundations of that movement, requires facility both in concealing *and* revealing oneself. Activists need to at once be and not be. They ought to appear nonthreatening while envisioning an alternative society. To claim legitimacy, they need to rediscover themselves and their position in history and politics; to remain unseen, they need to utilize existing symbols. As discussed earlier, for instance, whether one wears a *maqna'eh* (a black scarf completely covering hair and chin) or a scarf; the choice of scarf color; wearing a dark or colorful manteau; the use of makeup; and the choice of words and terminologies—all exemplify symbol-borrowing and negotiating symbolic meanings.

The *creative* use of existing symbols offers some actors a comfortable distance from their orthodox meanings. Yet this is satisfactory only for those who "somewhat accept" dominant Islamic symbols, not for all activists. Consider, for example, Islamist reformists who believe in "modified hejâb" and question the effectiveness of compulsory implementation of the dress code. For them, forcing the government to ensure that the hizbullah would not bother women for *badhejâbi*, or expanding the spectrum of accepted colors and designs might appear a considerable accomplishment. In this case, symbols are accepted, but manipulated to better relay actors' intentions. But, in a conflictual relationship—albeit a contained and cautious discord—manipulation of symbols is not to express creative adherence, but rather to indicate reluctant ritualism in the Mertonian sense— "leave us alone, we're complying with the bare minimum." "They want us to lie," a recent university graduate summarized as her "central" life experience under the IRI.

And sometimes, not even reluctant ritualism suffices for oppositional expression. Particularly in politicocultural fields, we find serious limitations to symbol borrowings; the "multiaccentuality" (Vološinov 1973) of hegemonic ideological signs proves quite limited for oppositional politics under the IRI. A reporter from a European TV station expressed his desire to interview an Iranian scholar in her home office. But, she was asked to wear a scarf:

I accepted to be interviewed about my work. I even accepted that he would come and film me in my house and my simple, little life. But I am not willing to wear the scarf in my home. When I go out, to a governmental office for instance, I have to wear the scarf. I'd be crazy not to. But I cannot do it at home, even in order to appear on a television program. I am not willing to wear a manteau and a scarf in my house, sitting in my study room, behind my desk. That is what I told him. He said the Ministry of Islamic Guidance would not allow that. I said in that case, he had to interview me in the street, or at my workplace. (Personal correspondence, summer 1998)

Negations of existing symbols are not limited to hejâb, or even to IRI policies or Islamic beliefs; they include all aspects of life. Linguistic analyses, for instance, question the benignity of daily language. Faribâ Rofugarân (1999) uses *Loqatnâmeh-ye Dehkhodâ*, the authoritative Dehkhodâ Persian dictionary, to investigate the meanings and connotations of *zan* (woman) and *mard* (man). She concludes that *mard* is defined as masculine *ensân*, masculine human being, while *zan* appears as his opposite. *Mardân* (men) appear as productive and socially active beings, but *zanân* (women), "in the confinement of a limited space, have no social or historical identity outside their gender role (*naqsh-e jensi*)" (11). She proposes that "if we intend to make a new way of thinking, a new culture, and a new history, we need new vocabularies, a new language" (15). Notice the magnitude of the historical mission she envisions—not simply avoiding sexism in language, but refashioning the language as a step toward creating a new culture, a new history.

Repudiating—quietly, of course—the Islamist claim that the "Muslim woman is *the* Iranian woman," scholars have exhumed the past, revived censored or forgotten figures, and explored various experiences of Iranian and non-Iranian women. These attempts contribute to establishing a collective identity, finding continuity between themselves and other women. Various articles in numerous magazines and several books are dedicated to uncovering the diversity of Iranian women's lifestyles and their dedication to combat sexual injustice throughout history. Since the Iranian year 1377 (1998), Ahmady Khorasany has prepared women's calendars that chronicle Iranian and non-Iranian women's history. Her effort has evoked objections among the Islamists. *Negâh-e Zanân* and *Jens-e Dovom* dedicate sections to oral history, interviewing pioneer women in education, the women's rights movement, and business. Particular attention is paid to working-women narratives. Indeed, workingwomen are regular contributors to anthologies. In addition, workingwomen's accounts of their time and work are recorded as a part of women's oral history. Women's domestic role is criticized for restricting financial independence and imprisoning women in household roles (Keshâvarz 1998). Employment, on the other hand, broadens women's social vision, empowers them, and allows them to develop an independent identity that is nurtured by a multiplicity of experiences and interactions. Women's employment also benefits the whole family, by making women better role models, "especially for daughters," creating a "democratic family structure," and strengthening the friendship with the spouse (Keshâvarz 1998).

Even the term "feminism" is reappropriated. Nayereh Tavakoli (1998) writes that as soon as a woman crosses the borderline of accepted thoughts and deeds, she faces the belittling surprise of people around her—"What? Don't tell me you've become a feminist, too?" And the word *feminist* is uttered as if referring to "plague or some other contagious and dangerous diseases" (129). But, she asserts, feminism is merely explaining the world from the women's standpoint; feminism is a monster only for those who deny women their most basic human rights, by considering them a "minority," even if statistics tell otherwise (130).

"Women's nature" is dismissed as a "stereotypical conception of womanhood," relying on an age-old division of human characteristics into masculine and feminine. Iranians hold on firmly to these outdated beliefs because, "as customary in traditionalist societies, we are accustomed to regarding more valuable and authentic whatever that is older" (Najm-e-'Erâqi 1998: 82). Yet, both scientific investigations and social practices testify that there is too much diversity in men's and women's behaviors and capabilities to classify them in rigid molds.

Liberated from the "natural" task of mothering, women then can envision living outside existing family structures. Mahvash Qahremâni, for instance, discusses problems of the nuclear, two-parent family and argues that the persistence of this type of family as the only legitimate option denies the fundamental rights of the very people it is supposed to serve: children who live in single-parent families or with relatives; women heads of household "who have no interest in remarrying, but are discontent because they live outside societal norms;" couples who do not wish to have children but are stigmatized; and "women who wish to be single" and enjoy education or work, but because of social pressures have to "give in to unwanted marriages" (Qahremâni 1998: 34).

Deconstructing gender molds that Islamism and tradition have revered requires an unyielding intervention in cultural politics. Mohammed Pouyandeh, for instance, has translated three books that address gender clichés: Elena Gianini Belotti's *Du côté des petites filles*, which investigates the socialization of girls and offers tips on avoiding the reproduction of sexism in raising children; Andrée Michel's *Non aux stéréotypes*, which discusses children's books and the reproduction of sexism in the educational system; and a volume by Benoite Groult analyzes men's ideas about women. Manizheh Najm-e-'Erâqi (1998) points out that the persistence of sexist stereotypes reflects a system of inequality that pushes women to the margin. Herein lies, she argues, the key to understanding women's personal and social behavior. Living on the margin, women learn to constantly see themselves through two cultural prisms—their own and that of the dominant culture. Thus, women are both connected to their society and feel alienated, *motefâvet*. They know that their every action is under scrutiny. Any act of an individual woman, especially if in violation of norms and laws, is taken to disqualify *all* women. Consequently, "she feels proud for every accomplishment made by others of her sex, just as she feels ashamed by the vile (*forumâyegi*) of every woman" (85). Being at the center of attention makes her vulnerable to others' opinions. Her attention is focused more on how others judge her ideas than on her thoughts. She becomes sensitive and compromising toward criticism—what is commonly believed "women's ir- ritability" results "at least to some extent from this sensitivity" (86).

Marginalization also has sociopolitical implications. Marginalized groups may identify with the oppressor and develop exaggerated sensitivity, even hatred, toward their group, as happens among racially oppressed groups or the condescending attitude of some women toward other women, especially of educated women toward uneducated ones.

The fact that many women resolutely distance themselves from women's associa- tions cannot be explained simply by resorting to women's instinctive inclination to associate with the opposite sex; it is more because [some] women cannot tolerate a gathering of what they consider "pitiful creatures" like themselves, as if they see their own picture reflected in a mirror. (87)

Women are located at the margins of the public world. In the labor force, for instance, they are concentrated only at certain peripheral fields. Their labor is remunerated at less than its actual value. Their male fellow-workers may even see them as a threat, unless women remain content with their second-rate position in the labor market.

But marginalization also breeds discontent. People who suffer from eth- nic, racial, national, or sexual discriminations "thirst for equality and hu- manism around the world" (87). "Thus," Najm-e-ʿErâqi proposes, "if we accept that humanity moves toward humanism, democracy, and interna- tionalism (*jahânvatani*)," marginalized groups play a vanguard role. This general characteristic, she warns, should not prevent us from realizing that *not all women* undertake the grand responsibility of fighting against op- pression. Some women become content with what they can achieve within the patriarchal system. They deny the structured nature of inequality and see differentiation result from women's own failure (87–88).[5]

Najm-e-ʿErâqi aims to liberate the woman from symbolizing collective honor—family, ummat, national, etc.—and instead posit her as an individ- ual being who, though connected to her community, does not need to uphold her community. This approach goes contrary to the dominant Is- lamist perspective where a single individual could elevate or devastate a nation (see chapter 6 of *Gender Politics*). Similarly, this orientation con- tributes to a critique of the Left's politics of representative revolutionism, predominant in the 1979 revolution. Revolutionaries then could not only base their activism on a universal quest for justice—or, in the Left's par- lance, the liberation of the Proletariat—but also see their own liberation as worthwhile and essential for human emancipation.[6]

Discussing clashes between traditionalism and modernity set the background for these discussions. A translated chapter of Kumari Jayawardena's *Feminism and Nationalism in the Third World* (in *Jens-e Dovom* no. 1) discusses the history of the women's movement in Iran since the late nineteenth century. Some authors discuss the development of modernity and its implication for discourses and social practices that affect women, comparing traditionalist and modernist approaches to women in law and culture (see, e.g., Sami'i 1999; Najmabadi 1998a; Ebadi 1999). Some analyses posit traditionalist outlooks in opposition to modernist ones: "The most important characteristic of traditionalism is looking toward the past; the most significant trait of modernity, gazing into the future" (Ebadi 1999: 31). Ahmady Khorasany (1999b) criticizes regressive criticisms of women in the West (echoed in Islamist, Islamist reformist, and postmodernist renditions) or the ill fate of women under capitalism (as in some leftist analyses). Women's rights are articulated as human rights, unfettered geographically or by cultural idiosyncrasies, rejecting the cultural relativist argument that oppression must be defined only in localized cultural contexts (Shahidian 1999c).

In contrast to the dominant Islamists' discourses that emphasize "cultural invasion" and cautiously distance themselves from non-Islamic cultural trends,[7] secularists consult the ideas of a diverse group of non-Iranian scholars to reflect upon oppression, development, freedom, democracy, and gender politics in Iran and elsewhere around the world. This orientation equally stands apart from the "cultural imperialist" approach of the Iranian Left at the time of the revolution (see chapter 5 of *Gender Politics*). Feminist analyses propose a connection between the oppression of Iranian women and social injustice worldwide, arguing that "it is impossible to engage in theoretical issues and avoid searching in other cultures" ("Introduction," *Negâh-e Zanân*: 6). Ahmady Khorasany identifies *bigânehtarsi*, xenophobia, as an obstacle to the formation of a national women's movement because it limits dialogue and criticism (1998a). M. Hâjar (1999) dedicates her poem "A Woman in Me" to Shania Twain and composes about the ties connecting her to Joan Baez, Shania Twain, Federico García Lorca, and a long stream of Iranian folk songs and poetry. She sees herself wandering in Rwanda, losing her child in Zaire, becoming a victim of Saddam Hussein's chemical bombs, losing her husband in Southern Lebanon, and being raped in Srebrenica. These efforts go beyond translating other cultures or identifying with other "oppressed people around the world"— an admirable yet not-so-novel effort since Iranian intellectuals in the past century have maintained an active relationship with intellectualism and sympathy for the oppressed around the world. Efforts to look outward are significant because they are also part of a search inward to assess "our" problems and envision "our" future.

Reconsidering cultural borders has also changed the relationship between activists inside and outside Iran. Whereas in pre-revolutionary oppositional politics, a hierarchy posited an unquestionable leading role for activists inside Iran and a supporting role for those "outside," the hierarchical gap has diminished considerably in recent years (Shahidian 2000). Exilic publications find their way into Iran and contribute to ongoing debates. Activists in Iran have in fact recognized such cooperation (e.g., Ahmady Khorasany 1999c).

Though lines of demarcation between the Left and other secular activists are not often clearly drawn, one can already detect some changes in leftist cultural politics. Noteworthy here is a rupture from the 1970s emphasis on cultural imperialism that sought the roots of Iranian cultural dilemmas in foreign influence, rather than internal cultural politics (see chapter 5 of *Gender Politics*). Two decades of Islamists' emphasis on the "authentic," "pure" Eastern, and Islamic alternative work like a mirror, showing to the Left the limits of identity politics and the hazards of not challenging "national culture." A number of translated and original articles in *Farhang-e Towse'eh* and *Adineh*, inspired by the ideas of such Marxist thinkers as Eric Hobsbawm and Ellen Meiksins Wood, reflect this position. But the sentiment is also reflected in non-Marxist writings. Qazzâleh Alizadeh (1996), for example, expresses her problematized relationship with her homeland in a short prose work entitled "The Dream of Home and the Nightmare of Destruction." Mediocre individuals hold the frontline while people, at large or in exile, hold tightly to their house keys. "When was our bright home winded away from us?" she ponders. "Homes of deception and hypocrisy are dark. We are dedicated to bright houses. At home, I dream and in sleep, I dream of home; without home I have nightmare and in nightmare, there is destruction—destruction that has already started."

Simultaneously, leftist intellectuals have ventured beyond the orthodox base-superstructure model of culture, as evident in the translation and (re)reading of unorthodox authors like Gramsci, Lukács, Althusser, Goldman, Adorno, Horkheimer, Bakhtin, Derrida, Eagleton, and Jameson. These readings have generated deeper understanding about the role of culture in social change (see, for instance, the works of such prominent authors as Mohammad Mokhtâri and Mohammad Pouyandeh). The broadening scope of cultural politics also increased interest in studying gender politics in literature and art (e.g., Najm-e-'Erâqi et al. 1998). New readings of Marxist and non-Marxist cultural criticism have also introduced a new conception of social injustice that goes beyond capitalist exploitation of workers and recognizes diverse forms of social inequality, particularly sexism.[8]

In the absence of organized activism in Iran, it is impossible to assess the actual implications of these rereadings for leftist politics. Nonetheless, these revisions signify a pivotal turn in the cultural politics of the opposition. In the past, "conditions" dictated that "more pressing and serious issues" would have "priority" over "petty" concerns (e.g., discussing the exclusion of women in our definition of the human being). Nowadays, however, the arbitrary prioritizing of issues into major and minor, principle and peripheral is seriously questioned. Based on the historical lesson of the Islamic revolution, authors argue for reassessing the process of "prioritizing" in social movements and in the process of social change. Ahmady Khorasany argues that nowhere can we find an instance in which women's needs were actually met when they were postponed to sometime "after solving fundamental problems" (Ahmady Khorasany 1998a: 77). I have argued that class, national, and sexual oppressions constitute an intricate system that cannot be overcome consecutively; various forms of oppression interlock and thus must be opposed simultaneously (Shahidian 1999e).

Debunking "priorities," secular intellectuals have turned their attention to individual rights, conflicts between tradition and modernity, and sexuality—issues hitherto deemed "irrelevant" or "taboo." Mehri Behfar (1999) challenges the notion of love and the lover in Persian literature. She argues that in classical Persian poetry, love is a suprasocial, metaphysical feeling that one experiences in *his* isolation. Such love, Behfar demonstrates through poetic analyses, creates a passive lover who tolerates any and all abuses. In contrast to this understanding, she asserts, new meanings of love have emerged in contemporary poets like Ahmad Shamlu and, most notably, Mohammad Mokhtâri. Emerging definitions assume a social character for love and reject master-slave roles in amorous relationships. She goes even further and criticizes some modern poets for their "masculinist language." Reflecting on some lines from Shamlu, Behfar writes:

Shamlu ... explicitly condones the feminine-masculine distinctions of the patriarchal mind and demonstrates that his thoughts and mind have not escaped our androcentric social structure when he considers women as refusing to be fellow-travelers (*hamsafargoriz*), instead of choosing a common fight (*hamsangargozir*), and when he considers being *mardomi* [fair and popular] to connote and related to being a man. ... (37)

Though analyses of this sort do point to the birth of a real individual as the object of an amorous relationship, they do not explicitly address the sexual dynamics of relationships. Indeed, though the taboo character of sexuality as a political topic is gradually being questioned, the subject is rarely acknowledged publicly. One such rare reference, for instance, merely points out that sexuality is an aspect of male domination and that "the formation and continuation of sexual relations between a woman and a man and factors for their dissatisfaction or satisfaction" has attracted scholars' attention (Moossavi 1998: 69). Considering the character assassination technique that has dominated IRI's encounter with its opposition, and the lingering conservative sexual attitude among Iranian intellectuals, activists find discussing sexuality too dangerous, if not outright impossible. Remember: "We use 'signals' to indicate our differences, but can't say much beyond that—at least not yet."

DEBATING THE FUTURE OF THE ISLAMIC STATE

The futility of IRI's stifling pressure has led some Islamists to the realization of Brecht's advice that no government can sit on the bayonet. Islamists have taken divergent paths in confronting a society boiling from the heat of suppression. Conservative ideologues—characterized in the Iranian press as the "traditionalist right," "monopolists," and "power-seekers"— enjoying the implicit and explicit support of the Supreme Leader Ayatollah Khamenehii see the solution in tighter control, closing even the tiniest open spaces. Another orientation, led by the President Khatami and broadly known as the moderates or the *jebheh-ye Dovom-e khordâd* (the May 23rd Front),[9] proposes to protect the rule of Islam by allowing a wider range of tolerance. (See, for example, Saeed Hajjarian's (2000) essays on the "abnormalities of political behavior" in Iran (56–67) and the rule of law (68–74). Also see Mohammadi [1997: 73–158].) Hoping to acquire the initially desired cultural and moral leadership of a considerable majority, Khatami seeks to gain legitimacy for the Islamic system through "giving freedom" in his proposed "Islamic civil society." In December 1997, in his opening address to the Conference of Leaders of Islamic Nations in Tehran, Khatami states:

In the civil society we envision, though the axis and circle of thought and culture is Islamic, there would be no sign of individual or group tyranny, or even the dictatorship of majority in an effort to dissolve the minority. In that society, human beings are revered and honored as human beings and their rights are respected. The citizens of the Islamic civil society will have the power to determine their destiny (*haqq-e ta'iin-e sarnevesht*) and control over the management of their affairs and hold authorities accountable. The government in such a society is the people's servant, not their master and must answer to the people whom God has given sovereignty over their lives. (*Kayhan Hava'i* 17 December 1997 [*vizhehnâmeh*]: 3)

In his address, Khatami frequently specifies that the "civil society" he desires is an *Islamic* civil society, that it is "*our* civil society," modeled after "the Prophet's Medina" (*Madinat-un-nabi*), and in which "Koran is the unifying factor." The Islamic character of the reformists' or neo-Islamists' ideal system is quite emphasized in the expanding literature of this trend (see Ganji 1999: 90–106).

Though struggling for freedom has temporarily brought together different political forces to elect Khatami over his "hardliner" opponent, Khatami's emergence also divided those seeking an alternative to the IRI from searchers for a remedy within the state. This crossroads has even led to differentiation among secular activists. Those concerned with immediate changes and optimistic about achieving their goals in Khatami's Islamic Republic have actively supported him. This tendency opts to achieve a greater degree of freedom and sexual equality through "legal complaint" (*e'teráz-e qánuni*) effecting "little differences and incremental progress" (Ahmady Khorasany, in *Zanán* no. 51: 4).

Others criticize the step-by-step orientation. They hold that limited demands cause conservatism, and that supporting a faction of the Islamic government jeopardizes women's autonomy. One activist expressed her criticism during a telephone conversation with me in the spring of 1999:

No doubt there is less pressure now than before Khatami's election, but the relaxation is more due to popular pressure than the possibility of freedom under this regime. We must use the easing of pressure to our benefit, but we need not be content with minute changes that "legal complaints" can create, nor need we become a "Khatami supporter," lauding him and participating in events organized by his people as if we are one of them. Distributing cookies to celebrate the anniversary of his election—how could this exemplify an autonomous women's movement?

These activists argue for a distinction between struggling for freedom and supporting Khatami, or any other Islamic alternative. These critics welcome working with Muslim women on specific issues, but see a fundamental difference between their objectives and those of the various reformists. While Muslim women activists attempt to ameliorate a genuine solution gone awry, these activists see Khatami's promised "rule of law" as inadequate. They also distance themselves from the secular allies of Khatami, believing that enthusiasm for variations within the Islamic system muddies the fundamental differences they perceive between their ideals and Islamists'.

Reformists' alternative to increased tolerance under the rule of law indeed does not fundamentally alter the existing order. Hajjarian, for instance, refers to the Constitution of the Islamic Republic as the protocol of the national unity (2000: 21–28). Yet, as a woman worker comments on this dilemma in a round table discussion about women and civil society: "The rule of law, that is, putting an end to some people doing what they wish, is definitely to our benefit. But we don't merely face problems that stem from poor implementation of the law, *we have problems with the law itself*" (*Farhang-e Towse'eh* Special Issue on Women, March 1998: 22, emphasis added). Her colleague explains workingwomen's relationship with the law and civil society eloquently:

I believe the problem is that even if the rule of law is established, how secure will people be under the existing law? In effect, there are two problems here. One is the implementation of these laws. The other is that suppose these laws are implemented, what will be accomplished and how will people succeed in voicing their opinion and achieving the demands they, their groups, or classes have? Now, focusing on women, the question is if these laws will protect women. (21)

It is unclear how secular feminist supporters of Khatami would reconcile the objective of, as Ahmady Khorasany (1998b) put it, "revolution in life-style" with the minute relaxation of the Khatami-type "Islamic civil society." Even in the most liberal rendition of the "Islamic civil society," though Islam is to be a personal conviction, the system remains Islamic and upholds the Islamic shari'ah. The contradiction is not resolved: if Islam is merely a personal conviction, then why should the political apparatus ruling over the nation be the *Islamic* Republic of Iran? On the other hand, if the system is supposed to uphold Islam, what is so "civil" about its proposed social structure? The *Islamic* civil society seems to be, at best, nothing but a peaceful coexistence of various *Islamist* factions, with some tolerance toward some of Islam's "others."

RECAPITULATION

In this chapter I discussed the development of secular opposition to the IRI and its implications for gender politics and the ever-present oppositional atmosphere that has led to the formation of a dual society in Iran. Though the two societies share some commonalities, there are also profound contradictions between the Islamists' Republic and others' everyday lives. The chasm between official and actual society is created by a fundamental conflict between the self-reflexivity of individuated persons and the disappearance of individuality in the concept of ummat—opting for an undifferentiated collectivity wherein individual identity derives from disappearance in the group. Conditions encouraging the development of reflexive individuals who aspire to choose from diverse lifestyles are products of capitalist modernity in the twentieth-century Iran, especially following the reforms of the sixties and the emergence of public patriarchy. Despite IRI's efforts to combat this trend and impose a predefined gender identity, some of these conditions, especially as far as the young are concerned, have become more pronounced. The coexistence of the two societies is possible through compromise—IRI demanding that people do not publicly contradict the shari'ah and the public being discreet about their defiance of Islamic rule.

I argued that among the young, conflict with Islamic values is quite pronounced and covers a wide range of behavior, from quiet disbelief to countercultural use of cultural objects, alcohol and drug consumption, and sexual encounters. The conflict is most detectable among the young middle and upper classes who benefit from their parents' accumulated economic and cultural capital. Yet even the lower classes experience unresolved conflicts with IRI's class and gender projects. Gender and sexuality is another site where dual society is most visible. Here, the conflict is expressed through subversive manipulation of symbols like the hejâb and unsanctioned interaction between the sexes.

Dual society has also provided a space for the development of oppositional politics. I delineated the process that secular feminist politics has undergone from isolated, individual reactions to Islamist gender politics to the emergence of feminist collectivities—all this, despite economic, social, and political barriers. These "groups" have ceaselessly engaged in diverse practical and theoretical efforts—from organizing women's cooperatives to active participation in politics, from forming informal study groups to establishing publishing houses. (I use "groups" because these are often unrelated individual efforts with similar goals, not formalized collectivities.) Secular feminist politics has tried to reappropriate women's history by uncovering a tradition of activism that did not define itself as *Islamic*, but instead found its strength in adhering to modernism. Free from the economism of the orthodox Left, activists investigate the intricacies of cultural politics: Iranian culture and history is reassessed; definitions of humankind reconsidered; the relationship of individuals to their society and to each other (as in love, for instance) reexamined; cultural politics redefined, especially as it related to designations of "us" and "them," "insiders" and "outsiders"; "priorities" debunked.

But these activists are also hampered by dispersion. Political pressures prevent forming nationwide organizations and having sustained, systematic political intervention. There is as yet no secular women's group; individuals write and translate on their own. Contacts are among authors qua individuals, not as part of an organized effort. Even then, they have to be extremely careful to keep their meetings to a minimum. Under such conditions, they cannot hold regular or lengthy discussions. The separation of like-minded activists leads to repetition and ineffective management of intellectual and material resources. Some authors have also communicated to me that limited feminist or womanist consciousness (*khodâgâhy-e feministi yâ zanâneh*) poses a barrier to their works. At the same time, political differences cause further splinters. Though such differentiation is inevitable in a movement and could potentially lead contestants to a richer understanding of respective objectives and politics, it may also become a burden if not resulting from enlightening dialogue.

NOTES

1. Consider, for instance, the significance of fasting as expressed by the then-Attorney General Khu'inihâ: "If our society does not fast, we have to fear Satan

every day. But if we fast, we fear not any treachery of the enemies of Islam, never be concerned about the rise and fall of the oil price" (*Kayhan* 20 May 1986).

2. On the sociology of deception, see Barnes (1994) and Galasinski (2000).

3. "Idiosyncratic," that is, in the eyes of individuals, people who consider their god unique because he or she is not the same as Islam's Allah. As a sociocultural phenomenon, however, this type of god reveals a trend, not idiosyncrasy.

4. This view is expressed most recently by some Majlis representatives while debating single women's study abroad. Mohammad Reza Dowlatâbâdi believes that since women are more emotional, they are more susceptible to corruption (*Zanân* no. 67, September-October 2000: 13).

5. Najm-e-'Erâqi here singles out women for becoming co-opted into the dominant system. It is not clear if she means to separate women from other oppressed groups or if she simply intends to focus on the topic of her essay—women.

6. See also Shâhmorâdi (1998b; 1998a)

7. Reformist Islamists have been considerably more open in this regard. In addition to the discussion of Islamist reformist women's approach to Western feminism, consider, for example, the "dialogue of civilizations" proposed by President Khatami and other reformists.

8. I write "particularly sexism" because, in the tradition of leftist movements worldwide, national chauvinism has been long recognized by the Iranian Left.

9. The May 23rd Front refers to June 1997, the day President Khatami was elected.

5

Pushing the Boundaries of Political Culture: The Cultural Politics of the Iranian Women's Movement

The Iranian Woman at the Threshold of the Year 2000

This was the theme of the Tenth International Conference of the Iranian Women's Studies Foundation.[1] Thinking about Iran and Iranians at the threshold of a millennium that symbolizes progress, I experience contradictory feelings. Our sociohistorical problems make me wonder: "Is it really us at the doorstep of the year 2000, or are we merely looking at others a few centuries ahead of us?" I recall, for instance, that we—or at least a part of our population—are concerned whether riding a bicycle compromises a woman's virtue. Yet what is our world on the eve of the year 2000 but a geography of diverse times looking, side by side, at the future? Then we, too, can join others in our own historical time and envision a future. We can ponder our limits, not as the bars of a historical cage, but as conditions we must overcome to escape that cage. Social conditions can work both as justifications for a low and short flight *or* as reminders of how high and far we must fly to transcend our present difficulties. And I prefer the former option. Social realities not only demonstrate what exists here and now, but also reveal deficiencies and wants that can be met only by transcending—fleeing—social realities and changing existing conditions. Limitations are not eternal damnation; they are unrealized possibilities, ready to be utilized.

The necessity of reassessing Iranian culture became urgent for many of us immediately after the 1979 revolution, for we witnessed both the blossoming of the flower of revolution and mourned its quick wilting. Though the victory of the Islamic Revolution did not result in the complete defeat of modernism, many Iranians believed it was a defeat for modernists. It then was very natural for us to ruminate: "What has happened? Why have we ended up here? Why, after about a century of conflict between old and new, traditionalism and modernism, has Islam come to power?"

For Iranian women, cultural reevaluation was doubly urgent, because the rise of the Islamic Republic of Iran (IRI) not only did not bear the promise of an improved lot, but, quite to the contrary, denied them much of what they had gained through years of struggle. Consequently, the women's movement has faced dual tasks in post-revolutionary years. One relates to maintaining women's rights or struggling for specific advantages. This task stems from confronting a political system that aims to increase men's power and their dominance. The other task goes beyond challenging IRI's gender policies; it involves the totality of our culture and social relations. Here, the women's movement transcends specific demands and opts for relations that can accommodate new lifestyles. Such exigencies result from the incompatibility between imposing predefined gender and sexual identities and a modern arrangement in which individuals—albeit gradually and unevenly—attain fresh resources to invent new identities and redefine their roles. This conflict cannot be reduced to policies regarding, say, employment or family law; they emerge from a fundamental conflict. Two ways of life, two understandings of humankind and society stand face to face. Improvements in policies might ameliorate crises in the existing structure, but they cannot resolve the contradiction between that structure and ceaselessly emerging identities. The cultural tasks of the women's movement must be defined in the context of this conflict. Such re-visioning requires rethinking the assumptions of politicking. In other words, intertwined with recasting culture is a refashioning of political culture, that is, acceptable methods of politicking, influenced by the complex interaction of such factors as class, gender, race, ethnicity, religion, and culture.

Let me reiterate here that though we all affiliate ourselves with the "women's movement," we are not dealing with a singular movement. Rather, we have women's *movements* (Shahidian 1997c). Thus, our cultural outlooks differ based upon the women's movement with which we are affiliated. For me, that perspective takes shape in the context of a secular movement aiming to eradicate sexual injustice and remove prefabricated frames for human development.

I believe in an autonomous women's movement, mobilizing side by side with other struggles to end sexual, racial, ethnic, and class inequalities. The cultural project I propose has thus two characteristics. First, I call for a complete rupture from the old social relations. Such an endeavor undoubtedly requires calm and calculated social and political actions. In other words, we must avoid extremism and, without losing sight of our ultimate goals, patiently and flexibly determine our immediate objectives. This is important, because my proposal for a complete break may appear unrealistic to some. But, I repeat, every social reality provides untapped resources for a reordering of social life. The break I refer to is far less "abrupt" and "alien to present conditions" than it first seems. Much of the currently evolving social relations call for such a breach; changes have already effected now deep, now superficial apertures in our society. We can cautiously tread along these openings and remain enslaved to social bonds. Or, we can widen these orifices to create fields for new ways of living. I emphasize the delicacy of our task also because of the vastness and complexity of it. The development of a new culture is a protracted, maze-like, conflict-ridden, difficult process. We must distinguish between this project and hurried actions, lest we mistake any angry pronouncement for levelheaded analysis, lest we replace acrimonious statements for the rigorous study of, and struggle against, oppression.

The second characteristic of the present analysis is that some of my proposals are also applicable to struggles other than the women's movement. This is only natural: the women's movement does not evolve in isolation and cannot succeed if it overlooks pervasive social relations. The women's struggle thus has common concerns with other social movements. Yet we must remember that even in relation to issues affecting all members of society, the women's movement must adopt a gender outlook.

Cultures evolve from the depth of social life. For this reason, discussing tomorrow's culture reveals optimism, if not idiocy. Yet we can, and we must, study the problems of our culture. My goal here is not to offer an inventory of cultural demands, but to paint, with broad strokes, an outlook of the cultural challenges I see before us in our strife for sexual equality and democracy.

THE WOMEN'S MOVEMENT AND CULTURAL INNOVATION

Among the first challenges for social movements are the cultural beliefs and symbols that render meaningful those relations that movements opt to alter. Symbols and beliefs are defined differently across times and thereby add a new overlay to previous layers of the culture. A social movement must be mindful of both the (re)invention of symbols and beliefs and the social structures within which these renovations take place. Examining existing language and popular beliefs constitutes a vital task of the women's movement, because these are instruments with which human beings give meaning to their daily lives and through which they form and express feelings, ideas, mundane activities, or abstract thoughts (Gramsci 1971:323). Language is not a simple communicative device; it also enables us to "see" our world (Shotter 1993). Axiomatic principles that survive in popular beliefs (often unconsciously) do not merely reflect the reality; they also shape it. So, words and premises that appear harmless and neutral play pivotal roles in the perpetuation and reproduction of sexual inequalities. Language, popular beliefs, and "common sense" reflect male dominance because they are all rooted in various layers of androcentric symbolic systems and patterns of meaning. The cultural politics of the women's movement thus goes beyond fighting for equality in such spheres as employment, education, politics, and law; it also involves language and other social relations of the everyday life (see, e.g., Rofugaran 1999; Najmabadi 1998a).

Linguistic politics are particularly important in today's Iran. The ruling Islamic discourse avails itself of word-games, double-talk, symbolism, and romanticizing male domination in order to conceal patriarchal power relations. Remember, for instance, that men—the same people whom the divine script gives "authority over women" (Koran 1988:370, surah Women)—are called women's "servants," and their economic power in family and society is presented as an "obligation" toward women, symbolizing Allah's mercy and compassion for females. In the words of ʿAmid Zanjani: "Islam has relieved women from economic endeavors. This does not mean that a woman must not work; it means that whatever she earns belongs to her. But if she decides not to work, nobody can force her. Islam has given women this great advantage that even if they do not work, they are provided for" (*Zan-e Rouz* 25 December 1993: 14). Unequal power relations are masked by such words as "obligation;" "it does not mean . . . it means;" "nobody can force her;" and "great advantage." Linguistic symbolism—a popular Islamic genre—makes social relations opaque. This ambiguity allows Muslim ideologues to interpret Islam in ways they deem suitable. Authors are not obligated to speak clearly and specify their demands, values, and conditions, especially when they hover over historical conditions, or ignore, ensconce, or distort historical specificities. The moment this rhetorical shroud is pulled aside, patriarchy feels threatened. No wonder when such issues as "malnutrition" or "painful sutures of child delivery" are discussed in *Zanân*, Islamists find the issues "negative and bitter." The mere use of words of pain—even in the context of nutrition or a surgical procedure—signifies a potential problem to these observers. They fear that this women's magazine constantly addresses discontent and violence, instead of "increasing kindness among couples, consoling them, and raising their hopes for a warm family life" (Bâdamchiân 1994: 11).

Linguistic politics are also important for a movement because its language displays the commonalities and differences of that movement with others. Both the activists of that movement and the onlookers comprehend it and discern it from rivals through its vocabulary. The more precise the language of a movement, the clearer is its beliefs and objectives—for advocates and spectators alike. Contrary to those who propose utilizing familiar terminologies and concepts to enable women's rights activists to establish closer ties with all Iranian women, I find more perils in such a blurring of ideas and goals. Using customary codes and clichés could cost a movement its autonomy and freedom. A clear example is the approach of "Islamic feminists" to the Islamic discourse. These reformists try to re-define words like *zaraba* (beat) and *qavamun* (have authority), or employ concepts like gender, sexuality, man, woman, masculine, and feminine in a modified Islamic framework. Yet if our goal is to freely experience new ways of being and becoming, adjustments in the existing settings—no mat-ter how pervasive those alterations—cannot offer security for new identi-ties. We must create spaces that not only support new definitions for, and relations among, "men" and "women," but also allow questioning the "naturalness" of classifying humans into rigid genders and sexes, or defin-ing sexuality according to heterosexual "norms."

BETWEEN MEANING AND STRUCTURE

We give meanings to symbols in our social relations, redefine them, or use them in new contexts or in different structures. In this regard, a tension exists between the symbols' meanings and the structure within which sym-bols are used; the intensity of the tension depends, of course, on a society's cultural-social characteristics. For a woman in a colonized society, wearing a native dress can be an anti-colonial crusade. But clothes can also offer a meaning more complicated than a national symbol. For a Muslim woman who sees her society as inimical toward her faith, hejab may indicate cul-tural independence and distinction from a heretical environment. Hejab may even provide her a protected space for social involvement. Here, the meaning of the hejab crosses religious regulations, possessing a new socio-political function. In other words, a symbol, in a new structure of symbols, in the context of a different framework of patterns of meanings, offers a newly fashioned meaning. Some conclude from this that the hejab is not necessarily a symbol of the Islamic patriarchal oppression, but that it can indeed have an emancipatory function, symbolizing equality and freedom. Yet we must not forget that the original meaning of the hejab is not elim-inated altogether; it has simply gained a different function. The old struc-ture that gives a symbol its original meaning is still there. People can modify symbols as they use them, or give them functions beyond their original purpose. Yet redefining symbols whose original meaning is rooted in a rigid structure and pattern of meaning does not always create a fundamentally different meaning and function. A Muslim woman can use the hejâb to create for herself a new space for social activities, but her presence in those areas is still defined within the Islamic framework. She appears as a Muslim woman in her environment—a human being whose moral, intellectual, and behavioral patterns, as well as the symbolic structure that constructs her gender and sexual identity, all remain Islamic. Her redefinition of the hejab as a protection in public spaces may open to her new avenues, but we must not mistake this expansion for women's liberation. And it would be an even graver mistake should we conclude that the hejab is not an institution of control, but a symbol whose personal and social consequences depend only on women's interpretation (Shahidian 1997b).

This mistake occurs when we consider social structures rigid and inflexible; that is, if we have a preexistent definition for the "Muslim Woman," and adopt a narrow definition for Islamic patriarchal oppression. Consequently, any change in meaning and function of the "Muslim woman" is interpreted as the destruction of her mold, just as any change in the Islamic patriarchal relations is construed as the relations' demise. But for Muslim women and men—similar to any other women and men—there is not a singular identity, but a spectrum of various behaviors and definitions from which one can pick and choose, mix and match, or even redefine a feminine and masculine identity. Nor does the Islamic patriarchy have a solitary structure and form. But both the behavioral spectrum of Muslim women and men and structural alterations in the Islamic patriarchy still reproduce unequal gender relations. There is no reason why a Muslim woman-wife or woman-mother should be confined within the house; but even as an active member of society, her role as a wife or mother is the basis for defining her gender and sexuality.

OPPRESSION AND THE STRUCTURE OF OPPRESSION

It is therefore possible to give different compositions and meanings to cultural symbols and social structures without breaking existing cultural and social frameworks. The evolving social conditions inspire individuals toward new material and intellectual purposes, and people pursue their aims through the paths determined by their (to use Weber's term) cultural switch operator. The women who were expected to stay home and live under their men's direct control may enter public spaces, earn a share of education and employment, and attain some rights in family and society. But such changes may not necessarily pulverize the foundations of sexual oppression. One cultural task of the women's movement is, thus, offering a definition of sexual oppression and stipulating conditions that ensure sexual equality.

I define oppression as a social condition that systematically bars the growth of distinct social groups, shuts the doors of free experience on them, dismisses their feelings and thoughts, and denies their control over their lives. Such a condition indicates the domination of one group or groups over others; it indicates, in other words, the institutionalized denial of control over one's life.

The dominance of one group over another does not occur through only one social mechanism; a set of different relations makes oppression possible. Sexual oppression simultaneously applies several methods: exploitation, marginalization, disempowerment, cultural control, and violence (Young 1990). Whether as members of working or middle classes, or in interpersonal and familial relations, women are subject to economical exploitation. Patriarchy also strengthens sexual inequality by marginalizing women and men who wish lifestyles different from the customary living arrangements and societal norms. Disempowerment is another mechanism of oppression. Patriarchy denies women's mental and physical capabilities, limits their educational and intellectual opportunities, and opts to socialize them into passive roles—patriarchy thusly portrays itself as invincible. The production and perpetuation of sexual inequality would not be possible without the use of overt and covert violence against women. It is the collection of these relations that comprises the structure of sexual oppression; reducing sexual oppression to any one mechanism means inability to perceive the complicated totality of oppression.

The dominant perception in the Iranian political culture rejects oppression, but fails to provide a sufficient analysis of oppression and its mechanisms. Exploitation, particularly economical exploitation of the proletariat, is often presumed the root of oppression. In this perception, oppression and domination become the generic manifestations of inequality, outgrowths of class exploitation. That is why for the Iranian Left, sexual oppression was mainly the inequality imposed on workingwomen. Economic exploitation of working-class women constituted the core of women's oppression; around this nucleus formed an appendage, created by cultural backwardness and oppressed non-working-class women. Due to the Left's preoccupation with the economic factor, it paid attention to those social relations—particularly education and employment—that retarded women's productive role. But that approach ignored sexual politics—the reproduction of patriarchy in family relations, and violence against women—unless it was in a general and ambiguous treatment of "the residue of feudal culture" or "cultural imperialism" (see *Gender Politics*, chapter 5). Though this narrow perception has been criticized in the past two decades, unfortunately many leftist activists still consider—"in the final analysis"—the abolition of sexual inequality to be contingent upon the eradication of class exploitation, this time, however, with a greater emphasis on the "cultural campaign." According to this point of view, what will finally make the dissolution of sexual oppression possible is the equal distribution of resources.

But we must not think only about even distribution of resources, but must also consider reconstructing the structures that make the context of our present and future actions. These relations go beyond the common understanding of the "relations of production" in the Marxist theory and entail the structure of social action in its entirety (that is, including, but not confined to, economical action). These relations involve such elements as language and assumptions, elements with whose assistance and in whose contexts we think about our present condition, organize our observations, and plan our future. In other words, we may speak about just distribution of resources, without re-assessing the very structure that plays a part in the production of inequality and the unequal distribution of resources. The structures and institutions that must be equally distributed are not predetermined. Nor are those structures and mechanisms that make "fair distribution" possible formed outside social relations—they thus reflect existing beliefs and cultural values. These beliefs and values, their resulting social actions, and the institutions established on their foundations, all are tainted by unequal gender relations. That means both the decisions and principles on which decisions are based must be questioned. *What must be shared? How must they be distributed? Who must distribute them? And what are the consequences of such a distribution?* None of these issues is an obvious and simple matter, and only in light of a sexual critique would our replies cease to reproduce patriarchal relations. Each and every process of fair distribution of wealth must be examined so that no mechanism could appear "natural" and "self-evident." It is in this process that cultural meanings and concepts—those layers set one atop another that function as our behavioral switch operators—step forward.

Sexual oppression is not reducible to economic exploitation. Marginalization, disempowerment, cultural dominance, and violence are tightly linked to economic inequality, but none of these dimensions of inequality can be reduced to economic exploitation. We cannot efface such inhumane relations by the eradication of economic exploitation. Women's feeling of self-worth and empowerment, and control over their own lives cannot be explained by alienated labor, or treated as problems that will be "automatically" resolved through control over production or a heightening of cultural awareness. Here, once again, cultural values and meanings act as the "switch operators" to determine the content and direction of social action. Culture must be reviewed, criticized, and reconstructed with respect to which aspects of social life require reevaluation and reorganization, and how this reevaluation and re-organization must be accomplished. This way, the social and cultural outlook of the women's movement goes far beyond reducing sexual equality to a betterment of women's roles in the labor market and educational institutions, or to mending this or that legal injustice.

But ambiguity in the meaning of oppression does not affect exclusively the leftist movement. Since our history has always been mixed with dictatorship, there is an implicit tendency among us to make oppression synonymous with violent and unrestrained acts of political rulers. Though this approach clearly points out the prevalent political trend in our society, it also causes several hazards. First, it equates oppression with violent and unrestrained control, while this sort of control is merely a form of oppression. As a result, a decrease in the degrees of violence is easily mistaken for the abolition of oppression. That is why colorful scarves and uniforms, or the authorities' forbearance about women's "violations" of the compulsory dress code appear to some as freedom of dress.

The popular interpretation also mainly conceives oppression as arising predominantly from the political rule, paying little attention to how oppression is interwoven throughout life's varied sociocultural dimensions. In other words, this approach can detect oppression when concentrated and bare, but fails to distinguish it when dispersed all through society and less visible. This confusion raises two reactions that seem contradictory but are in fact quite similar. In one, the observer denies any change in the structure and methods of oppression. Things may appear different, yet everything remains the same. All relations are summarily defined as "oppressive," without any need to examine distinct mechanisms of oppression or the changes in the oppressive system. From the "opposite" orientation, analysts see the donated "tolerance" of the oppressor as signaling the dawn of freedom and democracy. To these individuals, the oppressors' contrivance or ruse—due to changes in their belief about ruling or in response to popular pressure from below—means the realization of the *behesht-e mou'ud*, the promised heaven. Despite apparent differences, these two methods indeed follow a common principle and logic. Both assume a distinct form of oppression as the only form; the difference is that the latter denies new forms of oppression lest its spiked reproach dulls, while the former loses the spininess of its analysis as soon as it acknowledges change.

The common understanding regards oppression as something that "they" inflict upon "us," primarily through state institutions. Such a conception overlooks oppressive relations in the quotidian, or these relations become simple "consequences" of the (state) oppression. That explains the tendency to oppose the violent and inhumane punishment of *zena* (voluntary sex outside marriage or adultery), or to renounce the violent policing of male-female interactions, yet leave our beliefs about relations between the sexes intact. Here, too, decentralized power renders it undetectable. This orientation identifies manifestations of oppression, but falls short of recognizing the structure of oppression through its instances. No wonder in most analyses of women's status in Iran, reference is made to something vague called *mardsâlâri* (patriarchy), without ever defining patriarchy. Patriarchy is a general problem produced and perpetuated by everybody, without any specific body being culpable for its persistence. This is particularly true about the "Islamic feminist" discourse, where any discussion of patriarchy is immediately followed by an avowal about the innocence of IRI's statesmen. Patriarchy does not exist only in faceless structures like the labor market or the law. Men—individually and collectively—reap the benefits of patriarchy and, thereby, work to perpetuate it. Doubtless, Iranian patriarchy does have negative consequences for men, too. Yet that does not preclude men's role in the production and reproduction of patriarchy.

Oppression, of course, need not result only from some groups' conscious and purposeful acts. Modern institutions such as the law, education, medicine, or psychiatry—often despite practitioners' humanitarian intentions—perpetuate patriarchal relations. Those staffing these institutions may not view their jobs as oppressive, nor may they even condone oppression. Nonetheless, since these professions are founded upon androcentric assumptions, they propagate patriarchal thoughts and practices. The inability to detect dispersed oppressive relations makes us either overlook the functions of these institutions or reduce them to men's machinations. Either way, the complexity of social relations remains hidden from us.

OPPRESSION AND POWER

Oppression is not possible without power; but the oppressed are not powerless either. A most urgent task of the Iranian women's movement is reconceptualizing power and the relationship between the oppressor and the oppressed. This step is crucial for us in order to demystify social life, to construe our culture and society as influenced by the social relations of power. This new vision must demonstrate women's creativity in their struggle against patriarchy, without downplaying the oppressive and structured nature of male domination.

Power is not an object that one party possesses at the expense of another. Power is a social relationship among various groups. Just as the oppressive power is dispersed through different institutions, resistance to oppression is also present in various individual and social relations (Foucault 1980). Regarding power as a social relationship is also important in order to portray the oppressed not as passive victims, but as powerful actors who resist oppression and fight for social justice. At the same time, however, there is a risk that recognizing women's skillful resistance and battle against oppression may distract us from the structured nature of oppression (Hartsock 1983). Women's inventiveness in wearing the hejab may cause us to belittle the hejab's role in the structure of the Islamic patriarchy; or housewives' ingenuity may be used to justify the patriarchal institution of domestic labor.

Patriarchy presents the Law as a set of rules and regulations that transcend social relations. The Law is an indifferent arbitrator, judging based on criteria severed from time and space. The "Legislator," that is, an unidentifiable entity, discerns between right and wrong: "The Legislator (*qân-ungozâr*) has determined that we must prevent the destruction of the family" (*Zan-e Rouz* 18 December 1993: 17). Thus, legal and political decisions that directly affect people's daily lives are insulated from social relations, left to the discretion of politicians and lawmakers. This is a serious problem under the Islamic Republic because the Legislator is not only ultra-social, but also divine and timeless. That is why when explanation fails to prove the merits of *siqeh* (temporary marriage), the editor of

Kayhan-e Andisheh (the monthly cultural publication of Kayhan Publishing) states unequivocally that people cannot dispute Allah's wisdom:

> Temporary marriage must be a subject studied by the clergy and the experts, away from sentimentalism and pseudo-intellectualism. The legislative branch must determine the parameters and dimensions of the *siqeh* and the executive branch must implement it. This is a technical matter and experts must discuss it from the proper religious (*fiqhi*) and social perspectives. (*Kayhan* 24 December 1990: 5)

The women's movement ought to critique this perspective to reveal that law and culture are not divorced from social relations and, as such, must be assessed in their societal contexts. Sexual equality is not possible without demystifying law and culture. Until the earthly foundations of social life are uncovered, we may succeed in replacing one sort of "meta-social" order with another, but we will never locate these arrangements in their proper social contexts and make them subject to public debate.

Law, culture, and politics emerge from a power struggle among various social groups. As with the law, patriarchy aims to portray culture as apolitical. Culture is described as omni-powerful and inviolable; cultural change is deemed impossible or undesirable if it violates sacred values (read: it is injurious to the patriarchy). No wonder Muslim authors repeatedly emphasize that Islamic laws on gender reflect the "law of nature," for what merely reflects "nature" and is immune to the interests of various social groups can hardly be challenged. These are not human-made laws, thus unaffected by earthly interests—these laws enjoy the authority of "nature."

But neither society nor culture is stagnant. The mystification of social life aims to defend unequal sexual power relations under the disguise of identity and cultural authenticity. Iranian patriarchy tries to discredit attempts to redefine gender and sexual norms by such accusations as "Westernized," "cultural imperialism," or "cultural invasion" (Ahmady Khorasany 1999b). As I have discussed elsewhere (Shahidian 1999a), at stake is safeguarding the traditional sexual division of labor, not protecting tradition or culture. Patriarchy thusly fights progressive aspects of culture that inspire new relations, definitions, and values. This suppression leads to the cultural exile of non-Islamic and anti-traditionalist approaches. To create a legitimate space for its demands, the women's movement ought to contest arguments founded on claims about "cultural authenticity," "cultural imperialism," or "cultural invasion." The domain of feminist struggle thus includes overt struggle, organized action, political and intervention through existing official and unofficial channels, as well as challenging dominant cultural symbols and structures of meaning. The latter dimension of the women's movement may not at first appear political or interventionist, for though it does stem from inequality and oppression, it is not reducible to the divergent interests of the sexes. But cultural contestation is an urgent political task under the Islamists' rule in Iran: the state's sexual ideology (both its "formal" and "informal" articulations) and the Islamic state's support for patriarchy have made challenging dominant culture political.

OTHER WAYS OF BEING AND BECOMING

Why can't we articulate new gender relations using old concepts and vocabularies? Why can't we reconcile between old symbols and new meanings so that our ideas would find security in existing symbols and patterns of meaning? Why can't we analyze power relations between the sexes and feminist challenges to them within the present cultural framework? Why can't we assess oppression and the struggle against sexual inequality within the dominant cultural horizon? Why can't we turn reinterpretations of the institutions and symbols into our refuge in the standing social structure?

I seek the answers to these questions in the objective conditions of our society. I remarked at the beginning that though the triumphant Islamic Revolution was a defeat for modernists, it was not the defeat of modernism. Many modern trends have survived the Islamists' rule and bred conflicts that cannot be resolved within the structure of the IRI. I situate the cultural tasks of the women's movement in the context of such frictions.[2]

The discord between modernism and traditionalism in Iran dates back to the late nineteenth century, especially to the rise of the Constitutional Revolution at the turn of the twentieth century. From the start, women's struggle for equality was an integral part of this movement. Iran's developments in the twentieth century, especially the reforms of the sixties, led to new gender relations. Women secured higher shares of the education and the labor force. Reforms in family law—despite its limitations—signaled initial steps to curb men's unlimited power. Franchise for women and the abolition of the husband's permission for a wife to obtain a passport or to leave the country promised easier geographic mobility for women. These changes marked a shifting of the patriarchal structure, which transferred the locus of control over women from the privacy of the family to the public sphere. Both the declining and the emerging structures were patriarchal and could be characterized, to borrow classifications by Sylvia Walby (1994), as private and public patriarchies.[3] (These are, of course, analytical classifications; in real life, it is quite difficult to draw clear lines of demarcations between these structures, especially in transitory times.) Private and public patriarchies demonstrate two different gender relations and distinct mechanisms of control. The sexual division of labor in private patriarchy makes the family the primary domain of women's activity. Women's access to formal education, employment, and politics is minimal, if any. Patriarchal control over women is implemented by specific male relatives. Under public patriarchy, women enter educational institutions, the labor market, and formal politics, and their roles expand beyond their domestic tasks as wives and mothers. Nonetheless, women do not participate in the public sphere on an equal footing with men. Instead of the seclusion of private patriarchy, women are subjected to segregationist policies. They are concentrated in certain fields and ranks. Individual men continue to control women, though some limitations are placed on them. Social control over women's lives, however, increases. Various social institutions—the law, the state, dominant ideologies and beliefs, and the media, each in its own way—control women's thoughts and deeds, especially in the realm of morality and sexuality.

The transformation of patriarchy from private to public does not necessarily better women's lives; making that assessment requires empirical research into each case. But the reforms that opted to refashion Iran's patriarchal relations created conditions for some women to enjoy more control over their lives. Traditionalism and Islamism were reactions to alterations in gender relations, intending to guarantee men's power in the family and to secure private patriarchy against the perils of real and perceived changes that Islamists assumed inevitable. The Islamic Republic has attempted to revive private patriarchy, though the pre-revolutionary social changes have made a complete restoration of private patriarchy impossible. That is why the patriarchal structure in Iran under the IRI has witnessed dissonance between two internal tendencies.[4] One is a *sonnaty* (traditional) patriarchy of the Islamic Republic seeking to revive private patriarchy; the other, is a contemporary vision that, though adamant to maintain male domination, considers the traditional relations outdated, extremist, and incongruent with the realities of today's world. I consider "Islamic feminists" in this context, since they opt for a strengthening of public patriarchy so as to control and regulate male individuals' unrestrained power over women.

Though public patriarchy continues to assign women lower status in society, it nonetheless offers them more varied gender roles. Education, employment, and exposure to the ideas of equality and freedom encourage women to look beyond prefabricated "feminine" roles and yearn for new forms of being and becoming. The realization of these aspirations—that are indivisible from modernity (Giddens 1991)—requires freedom of thought, expression, and deed so that women—humans—may make of themselves what they want, so that they can question themselves and others in order to transcend their creation toward a newer form of being. Even the relatively greater freedom of public patriarchy is incapable of accommodating such a project, let alone the restraining private patriarchy. Women searching for novel forms of being do not find conducive an arrangement that a priori defines them as "women" and considers their duty to learn and practice that predefined identity.

The Islamic society is a teleological system that does not grant humans the freedom to choose their ultimate objectives. "Girls" blossom to "womanhood," just as "boys" grow up to "manhood." These essentially different people have two distinct "natural" roles. This difference in identities and functions creates a hierarchy of power in which men not only have financial "authority" (*qavâm*) over women, but are also their moral guardians. Ahmad Beheshti comments about this in one of his articles about Islam and marriage:

The husband must know the religious edicts about marriage and teach them to his wife. . . . He must teach her the conviction of God-lovers (*ahl-e haq*) and purge her heart of any [doubt or] innovation (*bed'at*). If she shirks her religious duties, he must put the fear of God in her and educate her about her duties. . . . If a woman does not know an edict concerning women and her husband fails to teach her, the man is guilty. (Beheshti 1985b: 40)

A qualitative difference exists between this Islamic approach and the project I have referred to above. To some Muslim theorists, Beheshti may be exaggerating about the moral authority of a Muslim man over his wife. But even after modifying Beheshti's views, it remains irrefutable that the wife's "chastity" and "faith" mirror how manly and God-fearing her man is. Yet neither the man nor the woman can transgress the predefined Islamic borders. In other words, though responsible for her morality, he has no sovereignty over his own moral choices; he lacks independent, autonomous, and decision-making qualities.

What Islamist advocates of the "civil society" propose differs from the Islam of the followers of the *valy-e faqih* (the religious leader) only in the degree of flexibility of pre-made gender identities and roles. There is no fundamental difference in how they envision the future of our society. In both, Iran remains fundamentally Islamic; the proponents of the "Islamic civil society" merely underemphasize that quality by tiptoeing around the issue. In his *What Share Do Women Have in Civil Society?* Mohsen Sa'idzadeh offers an opaque picture of gender relations in his ideal system. Refuting the responsibility of the *fiqh* (Islamic law) in shaping social life, he writes: "Women's participation and presence [in society] is a social matter; it is left completely to people's discretion. If women are eager to participate in social activities (and men welcome them with open arms), fiqh cannot prevent" (Sa'idzadeh 1998: 10).

He thusly assigns a dependent role to *fiqh*; Islamic law becomes an innocent factor, a mere reflection of social reality with no bearing on its development (37). Nothing prevents women from an active social role if they so desire and, of course, if men welcome their participation with open arms. Women's desire and men's response are not socioculturally shaped by the *fiqh*. Islamic laws have no function in shaping men and women's social spaces. A more optimistic reading may be that Sa'idzadeh suggests that the *fiqh* should no longer intervene. For a fleeting second, one finds hope for the birth of independent humans who settle their differences solely based on their earthly relations. Yet he ruins that optimism by stating "our model is Islam" (92). He writes:

As evident from the meanings of "civil society" and "Islamic society," the two are not at all incompatible. There is no antagonism between "civil society" and "Islamic society." Because referring to an Islamic society, we mean a society wherein individuals organize their personal-religious (*fardi-'ebâdi*) lives. And speaking of a civil society, we propose a community of people who manage their affairs based on social responsibilities and rights. (63)

Beyond the linguistic trickery of this statement, no fundamental change is propounded. In this amalgam, though the political system remains the Islamic Republic of Iran, the state is not Islamic. People are free to manage their society, though the society stays Islamic, and individuals continue to think and worship according to Islam. Proponents of the *velayat-e faqih* declare: "We'll implement Islam from above. Those at the bottom would be forced to comply." Adherents of civil society suggest: "Everything shall remain Islamic, but we won't publicize it to avoid antagonizing the public. Those at the bottom would think their observance is volitional." The latter have no choice but to loosen the limits of freedom. But this inevitability is an achievement of popular resistance and struggle against Islamists; a valuable achievement we must defend. Yet the policies "civil society" reformers promote do not produce new relationships between individuals and their society, nor do they alter citizens' rights and role: all members of Iranian society, irrespective of creed, are subject to the laws of Islam. Arguing that "religion is a private matter, divorced from politics, but the state shall remain Islamic," or "the state is Islamic though people can do as they please" both lacks logical consistency and is fundamentally antithetical to democracy. This animosity is irresolvable by any stretching of the limits of "individual freedom" in an "Islamic civil society." An "Islamic civil society," even if it blossoms to the fullest ideal of its advocates, cannot be a free society, for one precondition of a democratic and free society is the freedom to doubt one's "personal religious" lives, choose a different religion, or not believe in religion at all. Freedom and democracy won't actualize until individuated humanity becomes possible; that is, when humans, unimpeded by oppression, exploitation, and ideological teleology can freely shape their individual and collective identities.

Without the recognition of people's unconditional right to create themselves, freedom will be meaningless. Human freedom is based on autonomy and choice. They are undoubtedly related to their society, but they are not its subjects. Their relation to their society stems from the social dialogue of free individuals who consider being and becoming different an undeni-

able right and a usual pattern of living. The realization of such a relationship is not possible within the old culture. What we need is a fresh perspective on novel social relations that guarantee people freedom to make
their own lives. I do not deny the delicate nature or the practical complications of such a task for the women's movement, or any movement. But
I do propose that instead of searching for solutions in the prevalent obsolete
settings, we must entertain clean ruptures from much of our cultural and
social past. It is time we subject our society and culture to a radical and
uncompromising critique. We must decisively break from what dooms us
by circling the beaten path.

RECAPITULATION

In this chapter I argued the significance of reexamining axioms of political culture. Relying on insights by such theorists as Gramsci and Shotter,
I emphasized that dominant political language and beliefs, just as language
and popular belief generally, play a major role in perceiving sociopolitical
issues and political praxes. Reexamination becomes still more urgent due
to word-games, double-talk, symbolism, and romanticizing male domination in Islamist politics (reformist and non-reformist alike).

I also discussed the tension between the symbols' meanings and the structure within which symbols are used. I particularly cautioned against over-
emphasizing the importance of symbolic interpretation at the cost of
overlooking sociocultural arrangements. In this regard especially, I studied
attempts to "redefine" hejab without proper attention paid to the patriarchal structure that lends hejab its original meaning.

I also proposed redefining "oppression" to denote conditions that hinder
the growth of certain social groups, that dismiss their experiences and sub-
jectivities, and that deny their autonomy. This approach enhances the current perception of "domination" and "oppression" in Iranian political
culture as an outgrowth of economic inequality and class exploitation.
Though strongly linked to economic inequality, such aspects of sexual inequality as marginalization, disempowerment, cultural dominance, and violence are not reducible to economic exploitation.

Further, I criticized two common Iranian political concepts—namely,
equating oppression with extreme forms of violent control; and conceiving
oppression as primarily limited to the political rule. To discern oppressive
operations through various sociocultural domains sensitizes us not only to
the diversity of such mechanisms, but also to reproducing oppression in
our own practices. Integral to this re-vision is redefining power as social
relationship. We must then construe law, culture, and politics not as apolitical and unhistorical, but as emerging from a power struggle among diverse social groups. Under the IRI, what stands out is Islamists' hostility

toward collective and individual attempts to secure spaces that recognize—not simply tolerate—one's right to freely *make* oneself.

But, as I discussed in chapter 4, the path before a secular, leftist feminism in Iran is quite uneven, the tasks daunting. How far can a fragile secular feminist movement proceed? What role can it play in daily politics? How effective can it be in a movement to end Islamists' rule in Iran?

NOTES

1. This chapter was presented to this conference, held July 2–5, 1999, in Montreal.

2. I discuss this tension as "dual society" in this book, but even Islamists acknowledge this sociocultural chasm. See, for instance, 'Abdy and Goudarzy (1999).

3. For elaboration on private and public patriarchies as applies to the case of Iran, see my *Women in Iran: Gender Politics in the Islamic Republic.*

4. Feminist challenges that aim to eliminate patriarchal structure are obviously not considered here.

6

Toward the Future: Gender and the Possibilities of Cultural Politics

History . . . is a nightmare from which I am trying to awake.

These words, uttered by Stephen in James Joyce's *Ulysses* (Joyce 1961: 34), echo a familiar sentiment felt among many Iranians. The raindrop that dropped into the swamp tries to defy gravity, move up to the surface and jump out. Rising from the depths of the swamp is not unlike waking up from the intensity of a nightmare. Both involve shocking moments, horrifying experiences, and stifling pressures. Our nightmarish swamp lies in the depth of our culture, at the bottom of symbols, values, and beliefs. Parts of this "stratified hierarchy of meaningful structures" (Geertz 1973: 7) nudge us to awakening, others become "webs of significance" (5) that, though we ourselves have spun them, now trap us and make our fleeing more difficult. Just as awaking from a nightmare entails disorientation and unrest, rising out of the swamp is a discomfiting process. Yet—many of us feel—just as the comfort of a nightmare is unimaginable, the tranquillity of a swamp is illusory. We know that though we have survived it, the swamp is not the dwelling we have dreamt of . . . nor deserve.

To understand our fall into a nightmarish world—the world we deemed familiar but realized was too unknown to us—we have become our own ethnographers. Determined, we have contemplated "thin" and "thick" descriptions of our culture, we have opted to hear how "small facts" are made to "speak to large issues" (23); we have ventured to unravel "the conceptual world" in which we live (24). Yet, unlike most ethnographers, we cannot leave our swamp behind. We cannot peep into other people's night-mares and then desert. The swamp is *our* nightmare; at the end of each round of ethnographic dissecting, we find ourselves back at the starting point—still at our starting point, in the swamp of our nightmare, in the depth of our culture and history. Our ethnographic task is incomplete, not only because of the "intrinsic" incompletability of such an endeavor (29), but also because interpreting our nightmarish swamp is only one part of our task; the other is to change it. We study our "world image" to under-stand how the switchman of our culture has chosen "the tracks" along which we choose a way out (Weber 1981: 280).

So, our challenge is not just finding the hidden meanings of our "con-ceptual universe" through excavating various cultural layers. We must also deal with concrete social relations: actual power politics related both to our ethnographic self-study (what we can study; how unorthodox our ap-proach and how daring—"heretical"—our conclusions can be) *and* what we decide to do with our world. We have challenged sacred cultural zones of not only Islam, but also of secular ideologies. Untangling how revered traditions, religious sentiments, political beliefs, and cultural values con-verge in gender relations, we have realized how deeply power relationships are embedded in seemingly benign and self-evident conceptions of gender, national honor, political responsibility, freedom, equality, and democracy. Embarkation upon a new journey out of the swamp requires re-visioning and redefining the concepts that craft our vessel, choose our route, and determine our destination.

To be sure, we do not have monopoly over this effort. Many advocates of Islam, too, have experienced discrepancies between their ideals and what has unfolded in the IRI. Yet, as I have discussed in this book, there are fundamental differences between secular, feminist, or leftist visions and the variety of Islamic projects. I proposed critiquing predefined Islamic genders, not because they are Islamic, but because they are *limited* and *limiting*.

Let me leave no room for misunderstanding: we are aware of our weak-nesses. But we are also aware of the responsibilities that fall on our shoul-ders. For us, concerns that ended the previous chapter do not dictate whether we should act; rather, they merely reveal the difficulty of what lies ahead. We ponder, thus, not just "how far a fragile secular feminist move-ment can proceed," but also how far we *must* go *despite* our frailty. We do not wonder if, considering our fragility, we can be effective in daily politics of challenging Islamists, but *how* we must counter Islamisms *even though* we are weak, dispersed, and under attack. There are undeniably more questions than answers, more concerns than hopeful prognoses. There are presently more scattered activisms than organized and unified move-ments. Much of what secular feminists propose relates more to potentials and possibilities than to actualities.

These are not worries unique to the women's movement; many existing and emerging social movements in Iran wrestle with these concerns. Yet the chores are accentuated for the women's movement because this movement challenges so many aspects of our social and personal lives. Can a movement emerge, form, and consolidate to effect, or welcome, a next social upheaval? If so, can it set its own sociopolitical agenda? Would it have ample time to build itself and to form its cadres? Would it be intellectually and organizationally capable of facing the challenges of a gender crisis in post-IRI society? These questions may sound ominous. Nonetheless, no realistic account of contemporary gender and cultural politics in Iran can avoid these issues. There are no ready answers to these and many similar questions. One thing has become clear, however. We must question many things in Iranian culture and society, a provocative and disturbing venture. Waking up from our nightmare requires grand undertakings.

THE SISYPHEAN PUNISHMENT

I stated at the beginning of this book that a lingering question among post-revolutionary progressive movements in Iran concerns their repetitive failure, a Sisyphean punishment of much sacrifice and little gain. "Why is it that," I asked, "after decades of hard work, the destiny of a revolution, intended to attain equality, freedom, and democracy, fell into the hands of those with no respect for these ideals?" Based on preceding chapters, I would like to suggest some problems in women's and leftist movements. This is, of course, not a comprehensive discussion by any means, as my primary focus is on gender and cultural politics. These are pertinent issues to both leftist and feminist politics because, despite their tensional history, the two have maintained close ties through common causes and activists.

The base-superstructure model in progressive politics deemed "peripheral" any cause not directly related to class politics. Individual rights, cultural freedom, women's rights, and the student movement became significant only if they related to class struggle. Problems like sexism, deemed rooted in the cultural realm, were expected to resolve once their economic foundations disappeared. These reductionist politics, then, saw limited justification for fighting sexual inequality. In fact, even when the Left opposed IRI policies injurious to women, its criticisms did not venture beyond specific politics to indict patriarchal domination.

The consequence of this orientation goes even deeper. As I discussed in chapter 4 of *Women in Iran: Gender Politics in the Islamic Republic*, the notion of "cultural imperialism" dominated cultural analyses in the 1979 revolution. Thus, contrary to earlier generations of activists who searched inward for sources of sociocultural problems, opponents of the monarchy located their cultural foe outside Iran's politico-cultural borders. Fighting against imperialism and its internal ally—the Shah—not only spared issues *within* the Iranian culture from critical appraisal, but also nurtured a hostility—or, at the best, an indifference—toward emergent social relations and cultural patterns (consider, for example, the Left's critique of women as "Western dolls"). When the Left did consider internal cultural issues, it attributed problems to "remnants of the feudalist culture," but failed to develop plans to combat those "remnants." This failure was in part due to the belief that once new, socialist, economic relations emerged, the vestiges of the old culture would disappear. But the inaction also resulted from the Left's fear that it might offend people with traditional beliefs and values. Indeed, as Mahnaz Matin observes, it was in part out of "the fear of losing the support of this group that the Left stood in opposition to the Islamic Republic—*but as a 'competitor,' not an 'opponent'*" (1999: 297, emphasis added). This also explains why the Left was ambivalent about discussing religious matters: such debates were considered divisive and inconsequential compared to the "main cause," that is, fighting against the Shah and imperialism.

Regarded as "superstructural," culture was divorced from the daily politics of the revolutionary movement. Culture became "oppressive" only insofar as it promoted certain practices of the ruling class. The "oppressive culture," then, stood in opposition to the culture of the "masses" who miraculously remained immune to the dominant "corrupt" culture. The oppressed were "instinctively" opposed to, even distant from, oppressive gender relations. Whereas middle and upper class women ("Western dolls") of the Pahlavi era were the prey of cultural imperialism, "toiling women" remained outside of that consumerist culture (see Matin 1999: 307). Militants hovered over the historical processes they challenged—desexed and de-gendered, ahistorical beings championing a better future. The transformative process was to take place outside existing cultural and social relations. Activists thereby paid little attention to how sexual injustice and oppressive cultural beliefs were reproduced by the very movement that aimed to construct a new society—those problems wreaked havoc "out there," at a safe distance from leftist activists.

Uncritical adherence to axioms like "women's emancipation is possible only under socialism" made it nearly impossible to experiment with new politics. The evils of economic injustice were emphasized at the expense of other injustices. Women constituted a cause only when they participated in production. Consequently, the "woman question" in reality was the "*working*woman's question"—even working-class women were considered for mobilization predominantly if they were directly involved in production (see chapter 6 of *Gender Politics*).

The theoretical orientation of the Iranian Left and progressive movement led political activism along clear "tracks" that paradoxically regarded everything as political while defining politics quite narrowly. The primacy of fighting against the Shah's dictatorship and, after the downfall of the monarchy, the anti-imperialist struggle constituted the prism through which all social phenomena were observed. Political activism was defined as "bringing political awareness" to sites of sociopolitical unrest. Activists were to make politically sensitive individuals aware of the "real problems." In other words, rather than detecting the political in daily sociocultural relations, the "political" was to be injected into the quotidian.

Rather than considering sociocultural problems as challenges to be taken up, they were considered irremovable barriers to action, limitations within which the progressive movement had to operate. Victims of an unjust politicoeconomic system, old beliefs, and uncertainties of a changing society, activists joined the movement as representatives of "other" social groups— "workers, peasants, toiling masses"—not their cause. Representative revolutionists subscribed to a political prioritizing that could not accommodate any autonomous political expression, including an autonomous women's movement.

Post-revolutionary cultural and gender criticisms have pointed out the limitations of the base-superstructure model and the prioritizing of the political causes that spring from such a model. Yet, these criticisms are not tantamount to the demise of old politics. Critics have at times merely transferred the base-superstructure paradigm to the sexual sphere. Accordingly, issues that affect women's employment overshadow concerns for other aspects of gender politics. So, though the recognition of the "cultural factor" and the necessity of fighting against "sexual discrimination" have grown commonplace, little has been done—sadly—to reinvent a leftist praxis that integrates cultural politics and feminist awareness. Many exiled leftists whom I interviewed acknowledge that sexism is much more pervasive than the pre-revolutionary Left understood; but they consider fighting against patriarchy primarily women's responsibility. They claim more tolerance toward homosexuals, but deem struggling for homosexual rights of minimal implications for socialist struggle. Problems of this sort still remain "out there," affecting "other people"; it is, then, "those people" who have to fight for "their rights" beyond but close to the Left's borders.

THE WOMEN'S MOVEMENT AND CULTURAL RUPTURE

The cultural politics of the Iranian Left in the 1979 revolution has been disarming in two ways. First, the base-superstructure model postponed the resolution of problems deemed cultural (e.g., sexism) to an undetermined future. Thus the Left overlooked fundamental social problems. Second, the Left did not acknowledge the reproduction of existing sociocultural relations in its own praxis. As a result, activists rarely questioned how they reinforced "cultural problems" within their revolutionary movement. Limitations of this cultural politics, to be sure, became apparent time and again. As I discussed elsewhere (Shahidian 1996a), individual activists did experience tensions between their ideological commitments and daily experiences. The Left's political morality that emphasized self-sacrifice, Puritanism, and a denial of personal concerns contradicted the middle-class, mostly college-educated activists' experiences. Yet, activists learned to either ignore such discrepancies or explain them away on ideological grounds. Though there have been some tendencies toward proactive cultural politics since 1979, the Left has not yet articulated its theory and agenda about such politics. Developing such praxis is essential for the Left to challenge the IRI and promote an agenda for—as it opts—a fundamentally different social order.

As the idea of the autonomy of the women's movement takes root, Iranian feminists face the task of cultural innovation with even greater urgency. In the immediate post-revolutionary years, opposition to the IRI functioned as a unifying factor in political, social, and cultural realms. Feminists regarded critiquing Islam and repudiating traditionalism—however defined—integral to women's struggle in Iran. But in later years, the emergence of reformist Islamist women and the political currents that led to the election of President Khatami have caused disunity inside and outside Iran. Some remain steadfast in their position that even a modified Islamic government is antithetical to sexual equality, while others argue that a revised Islam could accommodate women's freedom. Rupture from the dominant culture, these individuals argue, would alienate feminists from the majority of the people who have a propensity toward Islam.

I believe that such cultural politics contributes little toward the eradication of sexual injustice. My analyses demonstrate that a revised Islam merely modifies patriarchy without resolving the conflict between gender equality and Islam—or any predefined gender arrangement, for that matter. Thus, I argue in favor of a rupture from existing Islamic patterns. Many of women's basic rights cannot find politico-legal expression or sociocultural support without such a rupture from the dominant—that is, coerced—and hegemonic, that is, consensual—cultural norms. Women's secondary status in the family, for instance, cannot be successfully challenged unless the institution of the family is stripped of its sacred aura and reconstructed as a diversified historical entity. Women's social and political participation cannot be guaranteed unless freedom of lifestyle choices is accepted and the institution of domesticity is contested. Equal education and employment cannot materialize unless the "naturalness" of sex, sex roles, and the sexual division of labor is questioned. Resistance to women holding key judicial and political posts will persist unless the rational-emotional dichotomy is challenged and the "natural" foundation of sex and gender identity is questioned.

Furthermore, the women's movement can maintain the radicalism of many of its demands only if they are defined in the context of a cultural politics of rupture. Take hejab as an example. Fighting the Islamic dress code has been a goal of the women's movement for more than two decades now. But the most radical component of this struggle is not its mere refutation of the *imposed hejâb*, but *freedom to choose*, including freedom to choose one's appearance. To achieve this goal, we must not only defeat Islamists' coercive gender policies, but also develop a fresh outlook on gender, individual rights, and individual identities. We ought to challenge cultural clichés about "gender-appropriate" behavior, just as we deconstruct "honor" and its intertwining with femininity and masculinity. Or, consider the issue of *zena*, adultery. It is one thing to fight against the inhumane stoning of "adulterers" in accordance with the Islamic law, yet quite another to debunk distinctions of licit and illicit sex. So long as our bodies are the property of a supernatural entity, we lack the power to define the terms of our existence. To liberate our sexuality from the marital bed, we must challenge not only Islamic sanctions but also convictions about sexuality and sexual morality. As a major part of this project, we must re-evaluate the vocabulary (e.g., sanctity, value, virtue, moral, honor, shame, man, woman, family, and love) with which we have constructed and experienced our social existence.

Without a cultural rupture, the women's movement runs the risk of trivializing its demands. Repeating an argument made at the outset of the IRI's coming to power, some observers reject the urgency of fighting the imposition of hejâb, arguing that the injustices Iranian women experience involve more serious issues. It goes without saying that sexual oppression in Iran cannot be reduced to hejâb. But unless seen in the larger politico-cultural context of freedom and democracy, hejâb's significance would be missed. Viewed merely as an isolated phenomenon, the veil would be an item that the women's movement could forego in exchange for more urgent demands. Yet, such a compromise overlooks that the veil may be "merely a piece of cloth," but its *imposition* is a denial of women's rights. A movement can of course be flexible toward a "piece of cloth," but not toward denial of the very rights it aims to defend. We cannot fight for freedom and democracy in the abstract, leaving its concrete manifestations unattended. Only by positioning the hejâb in its proper cultural and political contexts can we understand its significance—and discussing the issue from that perspective requires fundamental revisions in cultural beliefs that shape our understanding of femininity, masculinity, politics, and individual rights.

As women's resistance grows stronger, as they succeed in pushing the limits of IRI's tolerance, it becomes more essential to make a rupture from the dominant politico-cultural order. Such politics aim at creating free space for individuals to define and shape their genders and sexualities, instead of modifying the dominant teleological order. We must create a sociocultural space that allows redefining cultural borders and gender identities to be inclusive, not only of marginalized groups of today, but also of emerging ones of tomorrow. We must join the worldwide effort to create a world free of dominance and hierarchy, "a world that is truly human," to quote Gerda Lerner (1986: 229), not simply to inch away from the oppressive conditions that compromise our human rights. To achieve that, we *must* be "unrealistic," we *must* make far-fetched demands, without being blind to the harsh realities that condition our every step. We live in nightmarish times and only a sober, collective, polyphonous call to awakening can liberate us from that nightmare. The more oppressive our situation, the more inclusive and "unrealistic" must our demands be. We must leap forward through realistic steps, but the realism of our steps should be situated in our ideals.

This emphasis on the limits of Islamic "alternatives" is vital, especially because IRI's coercive measures make the emergence of the smallest breathing spaces appear much more significant than they actually are. The lure of "every bit is better than nothing" is indeed quite strong, as there has been such extremism under the Islamists' rule that every bit of relaxation is a welcome change. But it is also exactly at this juncture that the strength of women's resistance could become a potential Achilles' heel. Individual and collective negotiation of existing rules, or ideological innovation in the Islamic context may lead to valuable gains within the patriarchal system, but can also easily make us content with a "peaceful coexistence" with sexual domination.

Iranian cultural politics is at a critical moment, when a "disturbance in the moral order" (Wuthnow 1989) calls for reassessing sociocultural relations. At times Islamism employs every possible means to remain in power, when the progressive movements of women, workers, and young people are under pressure; reverting to tactics that opt to effect incremental change is indeed tempting. But I believe it is exactly at such a moment that these progressive movements can make their marks on society. It is precisely at that point that progressive movements must transform their limitations into power by making their agenda reflect not their weakness, but their strategic objectives. Sociopolitical action confined by weaknesses reproduces weaknesses—a sure prescription for future defeats. Yet a movement inspired by its strategic goals, by what it deems a necessity, aims to transcend the existing order. While cognizant of its limitations and striving to overcome them, such a movement envisions its radically different ideal future.

Feminists must equally emphasize the need for a rupture from prevalent politico-cultural trends within the revolutionary movement. Without such a breach, women run the risk of repeating the failed experience of participating in a movement that ultimately shuns their freedom. As in the past, women could contribute to a change within the male power structure, unless the movement's objectives, symbols, and expressions reflect a firm commitment to eradicate sexual inequality. This danger became abundantly clear during the July 1999 student demonstrations. In those days, students repeated the slogans of the 1979 Islamic revolutions, even after they turned into a movement against the Islamic Republic in its entirety. "I'll kill, I'll kill whoever killed my brother" or "Stick, club, or knife / won't be effective any more / tell my mother / she no longer has a son"-like slogans not only pushed to the side some 20 years of women's resistance against the IRI, but presented the coming revolution as a transaction between different groups of men (see Shahidian 1999d and various articles in the *Journal of Research and Analysis,* 15.2).

CHALLENGING EVERYDAY VIOLENCE

I have argued that violence has been integral to the IRI. Physical punishments (e.g., amputating hands for theft, retribution, and capital punishment) have made violence a routine practice in the Islamic governance. Gender-related violence is made abundant through both the laws assigning women inferior familial and social status, and the paternal role assumed by the Islamic state and its official and "independent" representatives (the moral police and the vigilant hizbullah). The ambiguity and elasticity of "proper gender behavior" afford the Islamists a free hand in inflicting violence upon the public.

A first step to eradicate violence against women is obviously the abolition of laws that give men controlling power over women. Defeating private patriarchy could provide women some degree of security against family violence and blatant forms of vigilantism in public. Any law that relegates women to a subservient or inferior position in the family or society exposes them to violence. Barring violence against women then requires the abolition of all such opportunities in the law and the institution of equal treatment of the sexes under the law. The Islamic punitive law of the Iranian regime is violent in nature. Thus, equal treatment of women under the law will not by itself end violence against them. An entirely new legal system that excludes physical punishment must replace the Islamic law.

Violence is too intertwined with the IRI to be uprooted through legal statutes alone. Terror has played a key role as Islamists erected a system that, in the ever-changing modern times, declares allegiance to rigid moral and ideological standards. The construction of an Islamic state has involved the use of modernist political rhetoric and institutions such as the republic, Majlis, and civil society. In other words, to implement Allah's plan on earth, Islamists have been forced to utilize political institutions and concepts devised to enhance *people's* role in determining their destiny. Popular participation in politics has become a double-edged sword for the IRI officials. On the one hand, the regime needs to demonstrate adherence to mass political involvement to claim popularity and legitimacy. On the other, a teleological system in which future objectives as well as daily affairs are subject to prefabricated laws can hardly accommodate people's input. Such an inherently contradictory order cannot survive, save by the use of force. Even the seemingly more flexible statesmen like Khatami constantly remind the people about the *Islamic* nature of the system within which they are to "freely participate."

So, Islamists' coercion can be eliminated only by an arrangement that does not subject popular political will to theocratic edicts. Uprooting vigilantism requires an order capable of obliging both popular political expression and individual rights. Women and men can be protected against gender-related violence when the state is denied the role of the moral guardian and no social entity can self-righteously "bid others unto good and reject the reprehensible." The prerequisite to such a system is redefining morality to reflect the sensitivity of decision-making individuals in search of self-actualization in the context of social interaction. To break the circle of violence against women, womankind must be redefined as autonomous decision-makers—individuals who do not need guardians.

DUAL SOCIETY AND RUPTURE

Yet cultural rupture does not mean the substitution of existing cultural patterns with rootless values and beliefs. Quite to the contrary, cultural rupture is necessary in light of the existing gender relations. The development of public patriarchy, as we have observed in preceding chapters, has stimulated changes in gender relations that cannot be accommodated in a patriarchal structure. The revival of private patriarchy in the Islamic state has reinforced many patriarchal beliefs and practices; yet the IRI's agenda has also paradoxically revealed the limiting nature of *any* patriarchal structures—private or public. Many mute practices and beliefs of the pre-revolutionary days that disturbed Islamists (praxes that might have continued their silenced existence for some time) have been forced to articulation simply to protect themselves against the IRI's coercion. The accent on Islam's role in the production and perpetuation of sexual injustice, for instance, is a direct response to Islamists' overzealous attempt to protect Islam from the growing apathy of the pre-revolutionary era. Gender relations promoted by both the IRI and the oppositional movement—their differences notwithstanding—have brought to the fore conflicts between the free development of individuals and upholding existing social arrangements. The interweaving of gender identities with politico-ethical symbolism under Islamists' rule has paved the way for claiming individual identity to be a reflexive, personal choice.

These tensions have given rise to a dual society in the Islamic Republic. While the Islamists hold power and define politico-legal boundaries of "acceptable conduct," women and men have negotiated those limits. As a result, two groups with divergent orientations and unequal power appear to "coexist," though in reality a vast group of Iranians have remained exposed to the ruling Islamists. Securing the Islamists' "Others" requires the resolution of the dual society through a fundamental change in power relations—so long as Islamists hold sway, their challengers remain assailable. Thus, dual society warrants a politico-cultural rupture, both to subvert the dominance of the patriarchal triad and to provide favorable conditions for the development of emerging cultural patterns and gender relations. As is, the dual society demonstrates the resourcefulness of men and women in combating Islamists; yet, the political dominance of the former bars the development and victory of "subversive" genders and sexualities. The dual society has provided a free space for varied expressions of gender and sexualities. Though some of these expressions are *tolerated* in varying degrees under the Islamic state, many others would remain constantly vulnerable, at worst, to Islamists' coercion and, at best, to the pressures of sociocultural relations reinforced by Islamists. Islamists might, for example, ease the restrictions on male-female contacts, or choose to ignore same-sex relationships, but sexuality outside its presently enforced heteromarital context shall remain at odds with the "moral" foundations of this theocratic state. No innovative interpretation of Islamic shari'ah could render sexual relations outside marriage *mashru'* or legitimate—let alone the offspring of such a liaison. A weakened Islamism may tolerate "illicit" liaisons, but such sexuality would always remain vulnerable. We must oppose predefined Islamic genders, sexes, and sexualities not because they are *Islamic*, but because they are *inadequate* and *restrictive*.

The politico-cultural scope of these conflicts, then, falls beyond the Islamic border. The IRI officials have proven reluctant to abandon their project of reviving private patriarchy, as records of women's presence in education, employment, politics, and law indicate. But even if a maneuver toward public patriarchy succeeds in improving some women's social status, the deeper conflicts imbuing the undercurrents of social life in the Islamic state will remain unresolved. The objective is not to ameliorate symptoms of the gender crisis with reform in aspects of patriarchal relations. The resolution of patriarchal oppression necessitates fundamental changes that acknowledge diverse identities, grant them equal rights, and include them in citizenry. This is a politico-cultural project inherently subversive in the teleological Islamic gender relations.

The obvious example is homosexuality. Though some renditions of Islam have *tolerated* discreet homosexuals, they have not proven accommodating of homosexuality as a social identity. Presently, Iranian homosexuals gain their collective identity and become socially visible only after they leave Iran. Various homosexual groups have emerged in the past few years among Iranian immigrants and refugees in Western Europe and North America. These groups organize events, participate in political demonstrations, and publish books and journals. Homosexual rights have gained considerable support among Iranian leftists and feminists abroad. Thus, though due to politico-legal constraints, homosexuals cannot organize *inside* Iran, discussions of homosexual rights have already emerged within the Iranian women's movement abroad. This concern will undoubtedly find its place inside Iran sooner or later, not only through exchanges with activists abroad who have the security to do so, but also by gays and lesbians inside

Iran. That is why I deem it pivotal for the Iranian women's movement to address patriarchy and sexuality beyond its critiques of (Islamic) heterosexuality and the patriarchal structuring of law, education, labor, and politics in the IRI, to include heterosexual limiting of gender and sexuality. Again, as I discussed in earlier chapters, it is understandable if feminists in Iran would refrain from openly raising this issue for the time being. But even under the current situation, we must be alert about the hobbling effects of this exclusion on feminist theory and praxis. More than anything else, we must remain critical of any formulation of feminism as a heterosexual—worse yet, homophobic—project. There would no doubt be differences between feminists without and within Iran on this issue, but debates of this sort would only enhance and strengthen Iranian feminisms.

This is not merely a gay and lesbian's problem. It has implications for how feminists envision the future of gender and sexuality. A consistent critique of the "legitimate" (*mashru'*) Islamic sexuality (one that exists only within the shari'ah-approved marital relationship) needs to debunk the assumption of "natural" heterosexuality in order to liberate sexuality from its presumed reproductive role. Without recognizing the diversity of gender and sexuality, we cannot open any space for men and women who wish to live (temporarily or permanently) outside a marital union. Reformist trends like "Islamic feminism" that base their outlooks on the "naturalness" of gender and sexuality have failed to accommodate diversity in gender and sexuality.

I do not want to denigrate the significance of reform, but reforms proposed by "Islamic feminists" must be rewritten in the context of a radical transformative project. Those proposals must be evaluated both in terms of the real improvements they can effect and their contribution to the eradication of patriarchal oppression. Yet, working within Islam's ideological and IRI's legal frameworks, the Islamist women's reformism encounters structural limitations at every crucial corner. To be sure, those who believe in such perimeters or are forced to work within those confines have no choice but to make the best of their conditions. But this does not preclude those working outside of those limits—both ideologically and geographically—from critiquing the inadequacies and perils of this reformism.

THE PATRIARCHAL TRIAD AND THE ISLAMIC STATE

There is certainly more to politics than the state. But when a state places itself at the center of all dimensions of gender relations, dealing with that state constitutes a central task of the women's movement. Patriarchy in Iran cannot be reduced to Islam because various institutions and sociocultural factors contribute to the perpetuation of patriarchal relations. Under the Islamic Republic, as in earlier times, these cultural and structural relations are intertwined with religious beliefs. Unlike before, however, as the state ideology, Islam—or some interpretations of Islam—has found a more pronounced role in gender politics. Islamist interpretations of gender not only reinforce sexist assumptions, they provide the bases for laws and social policies. Until Islam consecrates patriarchal structure, and until the IRI safeguards the two, struggling for sexual justice in Iran means fighting against the patriarchal triad. The women's movement cannot combat patriarchy without at the same time opposing Islam; nor can it oppose Islam without simultaneously targeting the IRI.

The dual society indicates that an antagonism between gender inequality and the Islamic state commenced immediately after Islamists' ascent to power. Daily rejection and modification of Islamic policies with a deliberate care to sidestep or outmaneuver the Islamic authorities polarizes the state and the public. Thus, in post-revolutionary times, the "historical separation between the 'state' and 'anti-state' in Iran's political culture" not only did not disappear, as some observers (e.g., Najmabadi 1998b: 49) argue; it has indeed heightened. The antagonism between the state and people has been nourished, as Shahrzad Mojab (1999: 50) comments, by IRI's brutal suppression of any oppositional gesture.

Optimistic prognoses regarding an amicable relationship between the state and anti-state in Iran stem from regarding reformist Islamist women as capable of feministizing Islam, if not eradicating patriarchy altogether. Had reformist women been so proficient, it would appear reasonable to assume they could accomplish their objectives without confronting the government. Yet, their reformist project has not altered Iranian patriarchy enough to justify such an assessment. And if Islamist reformists have remained within the political framework of the Islamic state, it is not because they see no ultimate division between the state and anti-state. Rather, it is because the IRI—albeit a modified version of it—*is* their ideal state. Islamist reformist women have no reason to oppose the state because the realization of their reformist agenda is quite possible within an Islamic framework. What is better suited for an *Islamic* feminism than an *Islamic* system? Thus, at least for the believers among the reformists, the preservation—and not the dismantling—of the state is desired. In other words, Islamist women's reformism exemplifies the persistent antagonism between the IRI and its feminist opponents, not the erosion of dividing lines. That is why following the July 1999 anti-state demonstrations, a *Zanân* editorial expresses concerns for the safety of the Islamic system. Sherkat Shahla, the editor of *Zanân*, wishes to ensure that the opposition does not go "too far," that the "harness" is not completely abandoned, that the hairline fracture does not become a complete break-up of the system (see *Zanân* August 1999: 2).

The complete separation of religion and the state is a prerequisite for the success of the Iranian feminists. The emergence of an open space wherein various movements—women's as well as other progressive movements—

can form and articulate their demands requires the absence of not only the tyrannical IRI, but the tyranny of any theocracy. The space wherein new social and political debates about gender can freely emerge necessitates politico-cultural struggles, since at the heart of this process lies the right and power of forming group identity, expressing collective demands, and gaining legitimacy. Challenging sexual inequalities, marginalization of women, discriminations against gender "oddities," and criminalization of nonheteromarital sexualities involve addressing deep gender conflicts and call for a host of gender-based movements that transgress Islamic bound-aries—crisis-oriented movements that aim to improve women's lives but retain the theocratic state fail to eradicate sexual inequality.

To regard Islamist reformist women's emphasis on *ijtihâd* or reasoning signifying the democratization of Islamic cultural politics only relinquishes the struggle against Islam's politico-legal control of gender. Even a femi-nized *ijtihâd* does not negate Islamic imperatives in conceptualizing the goals and practices of the women's movement. As long as Islam is granted a focal role in defining Iran's social, political, or cultural identity, the Is-lamic ummat remains the indisputable constitutive social norm. Irrespective of its tolerance level, the dominance of ummat, denies individuals the right to autonomous and reflexive construction of identities and lifestyles.

The dual society reveals the need for the complete separation of religion and state. Contestations with the Islamic Republic over various forms of freedom highlight the need for the secularization of politics. Qualifying "democracy" and "civil society" with an Islamic prefix is a denial of free-dom. Separation of religion and state is vital for removing religious limi-tations on women's family and social rights. Without a secular state, women (and men) remain properties of Islam—they will not become free agents. In the absence of sovereign individuals, any discussion of "citizen-ship" and "citizens' rights" becomes hollow and meaningless.

Contrary to what scholar advocates of "Islamic feminism" allege, sepa-ration of religion and state does not mean that believers must abandon their beliefs if they are to demand sexual equality (see, for example, Na-jmabadi 1998b: 47). The separation of religion and politics allows individ-uals to formulate their liberation in terms they find most suitable. But, without the secularization of politics, "Islamic feminists" are affiliates of a state power that systematically denies nonbelievers and non-Muslims any role in cultural politics. Only after religion and state are separated, *and only then*, can secular feminists engage in a free dialogue with reformist Islamists. Because then, *and only then*, can a "feminist" reinterpretation of Islam constitute a personal belief system, without keeping other women subjected to Islamic laws. Otherwise, even if some women—or even equal numbers of males and females—define the terms of a gendered ummat, Islamic molds continue to limit the expression of individuality. We need to redefine "citizenship" to simultaneously treat all equally and recognize differences. We need a new definition of citizenship to include those who are not included as "citizens"—those who have to relinquish or conceal their identity to avoid being castigated by the ummat, those banished, or those tolerated "for the time being—the vulnerable survivors of the Islamic regime. This rewriting of citizenship requires the participation of all sectors of society in redefining the political system and inventing a new order that transcends *any* Islamic state.

Islamist women's reformism, at its best, remains a reform project for Muslim women. For Iranian women—or, more accurately, for gender relations in Iran—that is an insufficient and flawed project because it perpetuates the subjection of non-Muslims and nonbelievers to Islam. In the Shiite IRI, even Sunni Muslims are treated as de facto second-class citizens—a Sunni's conversion to Shiism is celebrated as a victory for Shiites; Sunnis have been subject to harassment; and several Sunni leaders have been murdered under suspicious circumstances (see, for instance, Rahmâni 1999). The Zoroastrian, Jewish, and Christian "Others" of Islam are recognized only if they align their actions with Islamic precepts. A Jewish woman, for instance, must wear the veil in public, though such practice is alien to her religious traditions. Bahaiis fare even worse as they are criminalized in Islam. Atheists are denied any formal existence—they can live as "bad Muslims" who, under the best circumstances, are tolerated *if* they do not overstep their boundaries. These people are subjected to a web of moral and ideological codes that denies their rights to freedom of thought and expression (Shahidian 1999f). Under these circumstances, to view Islamist women's reformism as a precursor to other forms of religious feminisms— for example, Jewish Iranian feminism or Christian Iranian feminism (Najmabadi 1998b: 50)—is wishful thinking at best.

CLASS AND THE CULTURAL POLITICS OF GENDER

I have argued that a separation of religion and state is vital for the development of an honest, candid, and courageous polity of gender, sex, and sexualities, a polity stripped of all the guilt and glory of metaphysics. I have also proposed that only dismantling the patriarchal triad could secure the emergence of public spaces where existing and emerging social groups can voice their needs and assert social identity. Social movements in Iran have already made the redefinition of state-society relationship a priority, as indicated by the vast ongoing discussions about *jâme'eh-ye madani*, or the civil society. These debates have particularly emphasized the role of culture in the reproduction of tyranny.

For gender politics, the recognition of the role of culture in society and politics is a welcome development, because it makes possible questioning of prevalent values and old assumptions. Yet, I consider it equally important to emphasize that patriarchy cannot be reduced to a cultural mistake, that combating patriarchy requires a redistribution of socioeconomic resources. Undoubtedly, these resources *also* include, yet are not limited to, cultural ones.

But no civil society is free from class relations and it would be fatal for the Left to abandon class politics as the struggle for democratic public spaces increases. As the struggle against sexual oppression grows, patriarchy is forced to make concessions. Though these tactical adjustments testify to women's strength, they also cause a dangerous condition for the movement. The political emergence of some women at these moments of struggle and compromise could be at the cost of marginalization of others. In the Islamic Republic of Iran, reformist Islamist women have gained the support of some leading clergy and statesmen. But their proposed demands have predominantly focused on the professional middle class women. Secular activists have been more concerned about working class women's demands, underlining the class implications of feminist politics. Working class women do share many problems with women of other classes—for instance, equal employment opportunity, equal pay, and daycare provisions—but these problems must be defined in the specific contexts of class experiences. Even inequalities that affect women across class are more pronounced for working class women. Many feminist demands cannot alter working class women's lives in a meaningful way unless class inequalities are addressed. Achieving equal rights in divorce, for instance, would be insufficient if working women's financial security were not guaranteed. Though the IRI's labor market does not favor women in general, working class women face considerably less job security than employed middle-class women do. For working class women, the struggle for overtime and job promotion is quite urgent: they enter the labor market as unskilled workers and remain at that level. They are the last to receive overtime, since they are less flexible than men on their working hours and may need special accommodation (e.g., shuttle services if they work into the night). Workingwomen are also rarely promoted in their jobs. Considering the dire economic conditions of these women, overtime and promotion are immediate economic concerns. Employed middle class women do not face these problems with the same urgency. Not only do they fare better in overall economic condition, but they can also move up the employment ladder faster because of their education. There are other demands that working class and middle class women do not share. For instance, workingwomen demand a retirement option after 20 years of work; employed middle class women do not favor this option. Or, middle class women fight against limitations on spatial mobility, such as the requirement for their husband's permission to leave the country or limitations on women's education abroad. These demands do not have immediate implications for the majority of working class women.

Working class women also share common interests with the men of their class. These include demands for increased wages and benefits, job security, and organizing. But compared to male workers, women have a lower chance of employment and promotion, and are paid less. Women's advancement in skilled jobs often faces resistance by not only their employers, but also by male workers who regard skilled female laborers a threat (Mohseni 1999: 124). According to the IRI labor laws, workers can be organized only in one form in each industrial unit. This means that the existence of an all-workers organization precludes women from organizing in autonomous women's organizations (128). Furthermore, the problems of working class women are not limited to the workplace. No women workers' struggle for sexual equality would be complete without targeting the reproduction of patriarchy in the families and culture.

People do not experience the various aspects of their social identities in isolation. Class, ethnicity (or, as referred to in Iranian political discourse, nationality), religion, and geographic differences (specificities stemming from provincial, urban characteristics, or rural and urban differences) simultaneously shape men and women's collective experience of gender. There is, then, a need for feminist politics that simultaneously addresses gender, class, and national or ethnic inequalities. This means a redefinition of Leftist politics to become more inclusive in its struggle without ceasing to fight for class equality. If anything, struggles against ethnic, religious, or regional injustices could enhance and strengthen class-based social movements. As long as these inequalities contribute to the perpetuation of class differences, real social transformation will not succeed without eradicating *all* forms of domination and exploitation.

TRANSCENDING BOUNDARIES

Perhaps one of the most significant developments in Iranian feminism in the past two decades has been the strong tendency to go beyond nativist interpretations and address global realities in a vernacular genre, rather than excluding them as "not ours." This is not, by any means, a new development in Iranian cultural politics, but it is nonetheless quite considerable due to the sensitivity of gender in Iranian politics, especially in the Islamic Republic.

Transcending national boundaries in gender politics has been a fiercely contested endeavor, however. At the same time that some women have sought to establish connection with global feminism, others have evoked cultural particularism to promote an "indigenous feminism." The former approach has favored a cultural relativist interpretation, arguing that though some observers may consider "our" ideas and practices oppressive, they are liberating in "our"—Islamic and Iranian—society. Many feminists around the globe have been reticent about this absolution of patriarchal practices under the aegis of "national" culture. The caution to avoid eth-

nocentric and cultural imperialist impositions on non-Westerners has put
many advocates of women's rights in a precarious position vis-à-vis Islamization of gender relations in Iran. That the continued struggles of secular
activists have been poorly reflected in most writings about women in Iran
has made the situation even more difficult. But Iranian secular feminists
have welcomed open, equal dialogues with both Iranians abroad and concerned non-Iranian feminists. There is a genuine interest to surpass national
boundaries and establish international solidarity among feminists, expressed in volumes of translations of feminist research, reflection of news
about women's conditions and activisms worldwide, and published and
private statements. These activists and scholars seek the solidarity of non-
Iranian feminists in the struggle against a relentless patriarchal regime. And
understandably so. But they seek more than support; they opt for challenging dialogues. Iranian feminists warn against overlooking sexist practices and beliefs on cultural relativist grounds; to them, such an approach
implies that "Though Western feminists would not tolerate a similar treatment, they think it is acceptable for us"—a message that contradicts the
good intentions behind Western-feminists relativism.

Surpassing geopolitical boundaries also involves Iranian exiles and immigrants. The relationship between activists among these groups and those
in Iran has overall been one of mutual support and sympathy. There has
been a lively flow of information across the border through formal and
informal channels. Such an interaction, to be sure, does not preclude dis-
agreements on strategies and tactics. The divisions among activists inside
Iran—especially on Islamist reformism, President Khatami, and the future
of the IRI—are also reflected among activists abroad and affect the inside-
outside interaction. I do not wish to discuss these differences in detail, as
I present a lengthier account in my forthcoming works. It suffices to mention here, however, that a main point of difference relates to the role of
Islam and the Islamic Republic in upholding sexual oppression. Activists
abroad are critical of those trends in Iran that opt to ameliorate women's
condition without questioning the legitimacy of the Islamic state. Concern
for specific grievance, critics abroad of activists in Iran argue, will bear
little fruit if Iranian activists do not address the patriarchal nature of the
Islamic state. So, combating Islamists' political power must always remain
a top priority of the women's movement. Though some push this argument
to the extreme and overtly or covertly accuse inside activists of colluding
with the Islamic system, the prevalent trend among outside activists seems
critical though accepting of reforms as tactical steps. Many activists abroad
realize quite well that struggle under the harsh conditions of the Islamic
state requires flexibility. Their concern (which I also share) does not so
much relate to tactical maneuvers as to the implications of tactics for the
overall goal. The critics' insistence is that the "liberties" developed in post-
revolutionary Iran are the accomplishment of women and men's struggle

against the Islamists' suppression, not the benevolence of the Islamic state. Thus, the alternative to a theocratic tyranny is not a less strict theocracy, but a secular democracy that vies to eradicate class, gender, and ethnic (national) inequalities. Needless to repeat, many within Iran also subscribe to this view.

Despite these differences, the relationship between activists outside and inside Iran is dominated by solidarity, cooperation, and mutual education. Exiled and immigrant Iranian feminists constitute a significant channel for the exchange between Iranian and non-Iranian feminists. I am not here referring solely to the constant flow of literature and information into and out of Iran. We have learned through our exile or immigrant years many valuable lessons about our homeland and hostland; we must bring this awareness over to home culture to redefine and reshape our future. Of particular relevance is our experience as "minorities," as people on the margins of our host societies. There is no guarantee for the role that we might be accorded in rehashing Iranian society and culture. Pessimistically or realistically, many of us consider an "exile after exile" (see Shahidian 2000). But we must intervene in the making of our tomorrow primarily because many in Iran voice similar concerns. To turn structural constraints to conjunctural opportunities—to echo Cornel West again—we must allow our exilic experience to inform our intervention in setting the margins of our future society.

I think it important to adopt that wide vision precisely at moments of uncertainty and ambivalence. At the time of any rupture, cultural borders become infinitely more flexible than at other times, making possible the absorption of novel ideas. Cultural politics at times of sociopolitical rupture need not follow the traditional past. We must think ahead, therefore, beyond today's limits. If we fail to think about that future, we won't prepare ourselves to shape it. We must set tentative goals. Only then can we take small though anticipatory steps. Else, we will be doomed to our Sisyphean punishment. The question, in other words, is for how long do we want to remain martyrs of our history rather than its makers? This is the time of recasting our lives, of creating new molds. What we make now will stay with us for times to come, affecting generations.

We must be brave. We must aim high.

Bibliography

Abbas-Gholizadeh, Mahboobeh. Sokhan-e Fasl: Cheguneh Bâyad Raft? ("Quarterly Discourse: 'How to Proceed?' "). *Farzaneh: Journal of Women's Studies and Research* 1–2 (1994a): 159–62.

———. "Quarterly Discourse: 'The Long Way Ahead.' " *Farzaneh: Journal of Women's Studies and Research* 1.1–2 (1994b): 61–66.

———.Châlesh Myân-e Khod va Digari dar Sâzmânhây-e Qeyr-e-dowlaty-e Zanân-e Iran ("Challenges Between Self and Other for Iranian Women's NGOs"). *Farzaneh: Journal of Women's Studies and Research* 7 (1995–1996a): 107–16.

———. Hameh Bâyad Râzi Bâshand: Arzyâby-e Avvallin Gozâresh-e Melly-e Zanân-e JII, dar Goftogoo'i bâ Khânomhâ Shahlâ Habibi va Doktor Parvin Ma'rufi ("Everybody Should Be Content: Assessment of the First National Report of the Women of the IRI, in an Interview with Mrs. Shahlâ Habibi and Dr. Parvin Ma'rufy"). *Farzaneh: Journal of Women's Studies and Research* 7 (1995–1996b): 139–46.

'Abdi, 'Abbâs, and Mohsen Goudarzi. *Tahavvolât-e Farhangi dar Iran. (Cultural Developments in Iran).* Tehran: Ravesh, 1999.

Abercrombie, Nicholas, Stephen Hill, and Bryan S. Turner. *The Dominant Ideology Thesis.* London: G. Allen & Unwin, 1980.

Abrahamian, Ervand. *Iran Between Two Revolutions.* Princeton: Princeton University Press, 1982.

Afary, Janet. "On the Origin of Feminism in the Early 20th-Century Iran." *Journal of Women's History* 1.2 (1989): 65–87.

———. "The War Against Feminism in the Name of the Almighty: Making Sense of Gender and Muslim Fundamentalism." *New Left Review* 224 (1997): 89–110.

Afshar, Haleh. "Islam and Feminism: An Analysis of Political Strategies." *Feminism and Islam: Legal and Literary Perspectives*, ed. M. Yamani. New York: New York University Press, 1996.

Afshari, Reza. "Egalitarian Islam and Misogynist Islamic Tradition: A Critique of the Feminist Reinterpretation of Islamic History and Heritage." *Journal of Critical Studies of Iran and the Middle East* 4 (1994): 13–33.

———. "An Essay on Islamic Cultural Relativism in the Discourse of Human Rights." *Human Rights Quarterly* 16.2 (1994): 235–76.

———. "An Essay on Scholarship, Human Rights, and State Legitimacy: The Case of the Islamic Republic of Iran." *Human Rights Quarterly* 18.3 (1996): 544–93.

Ahmady Khorasany, Noushin. Az Mahâfel-e Zanâneh tâ Tashakkolhây-e Mostaqell-e Zanân: Râhi beh Souy-e Jâmeʿeh-ye Madani ("From Women's Cliques to Autonomous Women's Organizations: A Path to Civil Society"). Spec. issue on women. *Farhang-e Towseʿeh* (1998a): 12–18.

———. Durnamây-e Jonbesh-e Ejtemâʿy-e Zanân: Enqelâb dar Shiveh-ye Zendegi ("The Future Outlook of the Iranian Women's Movement: A Revolution in Lifestyle"). *Negâh-e Zanân*, ed. N.A. Khorasany. Tehran: Nashr-e Towseʿeh, 1998b.

———. Negâh-e Moztarab-e Mard-e Irani beh Qarb va Zan-e Qarbi ("The Anxious Male Gaze at the West and Western Woman"). *Jens-e Dovom*, ed. N.A. Khorasany. Tehran: Nashr-e Towseʿeh, 1999b.

———. Feminizm-e Islami dar Negâhi beh Rouznâmeh-ye *Zan* va Majalleh-ye *Zanân* ("Islamic Feminism through the Prisms of *Zan* and *Zanân*"). *Andisheh-ye Jâmeʿeh* (1999c): 68–70.

Ahmed, Leila. *A Border Passage: From Cairo to America-A Women's Journey*. New York: Farrar, Straus and Giroux, 1999.

Akeb, Fatiha, and Malika Abdelaziz. "Algerian Women Discuss the Need for Change." *Women and the Family in the Middle East: New Voices of Change*, ed. E.W. Fernea. Austin: Texas University Press, 1985.

Akhavi, Shahrough. *Religion and Politics in Contemporary Iran*. Albany: State University of New York Press, 1980.

Âkouchakiân, Ahmad. Beh Souy-e Yek Didgâh-e Ravesh-shenâkhti va Nazariyeh-ye Dinshenâkhty-e Tahqiq va Towseʿeh-ye Zanân ("Toward a Religio-Methodological Approach to Research on Women in Development"). *Farzaneh: Journal of Women's Studies and Research* 8 (1997): 55–78.

Alexander, M. Jacqui, and Chandra Talpade Mohanty. "Introduction: Genealogies, Legacies, Movements." *Feminist Genealogies, Colonial Legacies, Democratic Futures*, ed. M.J. Alexander and C. T. Mohanty. New York: Routledge, 1996.

Ali ibn Abi Talib. *Nahjul Balagha: Sermons, Letters, and Sayings of Hazrath Ali*. Trans. M.A. Jafery. Karachi: Khorasan Islamic Center, 1971.

Alizadeh, Qazzâleh. Rouyâ-ye Khâneh va Kâbus-e Zavâl ("The Dream of the Home and the Nightmare of Destruction"). *Adineh* 19 March 1996.

Alvarez, Sonia E. *Engendering Democracy in Brazil: Women's Movements in Transition Politics*. Princeton, NJ: Princeton University Press, 1990.

Amir Ebrahimi, Masserrat. Tahavollât-e Farhangi Ejtemâʿy-e Javânân-e Jonub-e Shahr ("The Socio-Cultural Developments of the Youth in the Southern Districts of Tehran"). *Goft-o-gu* 19 (1998): 39–53.

Anderson, Benedict. *Imagined Communities: Reflections on the Origin and Spread of Nationalism*. London: Verso, 1991.

Anderson, Perry. "The Antinomies of Antonio Gramsci." *New Left Review* 100 (1977): 5–78.

Andors, Phyllis. *The Unfinished Revolution of Chinese Women 1949–1980*. Bloomington: Indiana University Press, 1983.

Archer, John, and Barbara Lloyd. *Sex and Gender*. New York: Cambridge University Press, 1985.

Ardalân, Parvin, and Forooq Kâkhsâz. Âqâ, Tâ Hâlâ Shodeh Hamsaretân râ Bezanid? ("Mister, Have You Ever Beaten Your Wife?") *Zanân* 18 (1994): 6–20.

Bâdâmchiân, Assadullâh. Bedoun-e Sharh [. . .] ("No Explanation Needed [. . .]) *Zanân* 19 (1994): 9–11.

Bakhtin, Mikhail. *Problems of Dostoevsky's Poetics*. Trans. C. Emerson. Minneapolis: University of Minnesota Press, 1984.

Bakhtin, Mikhail M. *The Dialogic Imagination*. Trans.C.E. and M. Holquist. Austin: University of Texas Press, 1981.

Bâqeriân, Mitrâ. Eshteqâl va Bikâry-e Zanân az Didgâh-e Towse'eh ("Women's Employment and Unemployment: A Developmental Perspective"). *Zanân* 1 (1991): 4–10.

Barnes, John Arundel. *A Pack of Lies: Towards a Sociology of Lying*. New York: Cambridge University Press, 1994.

Barrett, Michele. *Women's Oppression Today: The Marxist/Feminist Encounter*. London: Verso, 1988.

Bauer, Janet. "Sexuality and the Moral 'Construction' of Women in an Islamic Society." *Anthropological Quarterly* 58.3 (1985a): 120–29.

———. "A Long Way Home: Islam in the Adaptation of Iranian Women Refugees in Turkey and West Germany." *Iranian Refugees and Exiles since Khomeini*, ed. A. Fathi. Costa Mesa, CA: Mazda Publishers, 1991.

———. "Ma'ssoum's Tale: The Personal and Political Transformation of a Young Iranian "Feminist" and her Ethnographer." *Feminist Studies* 19. 3 (1993): 519–48.

———. "Conversations Among Iranian Exiles on Women's Rights: Implications for the Community-Self Debate in Feminism." *Journal of Critical Studies of Iran and the Middle East* 4 (1994): 1–12.

Bayat-Philip, Mangol. "Women and Revolution in Iran, 1905–1911." *Women in the Muslim World*, ed. L. Beck and N. Keddie. Cambridge, MA: Harvard University Press, 1978.

Behdad, Sohrab. "A Disputed Utopia: Islamic Economics in Revolutionary Iran." *Comparative Studies in Society and History* 36.4 (1994): 775–813.

———. "Islamization of Economics in Iranian Universities." *International Journal of Middle East Studies* 27.2 (1994): 193–217.

Beheshti, Ahmad. Sharâyet-e Mo'sser dar Behbud-e Zendegy-e Zanâsho'i ("Steps to Better Marital Life"). *Zan-e Rouz* 5 Oct. 1985b: 40–41.

Behfar, Mehri. 'Âsheqânehsarâ'i dar She'r-e Pârsi ("Love Poems in Persian Poetry"). *Golestâneh* 3–4 (1999): 30–38.

Behnood, Mas'oud. *Een Seh Zan: Ashraf Pahlavi, Maryam Firuz, Iran Teymoortâsh (These Three Women: Ashraf Pahlavi, Maryam Firooz, Iran Teymoortash)*. Tehran: 'Elm, 1995.

Bennoune, Karima. "Algerian Women Confront Fundamentalism." *Monthly Review* 46.4 (1994): 26–39.

Blom, Ida. "Feminism and Nationalism in the Early Twentieth Century: A Cross-Cultural Perspective." *Journal of Women's History* 7.4 (1995): 82–94.

Bocock, Robert. *Hegemony.* New York: Tavistock, 1986.

Bourdieu, Pierre. "The Specificity of the Scientific Field and the Social Conditions of the Progress of Reason." *Social Science Information* 14.6 (1975): 19–47.

———. *Outline of a Theory of Practice.* Trans. R. Nice. New York: Cambridge University Press, 1977.

Bourdieu, Pierre, and Jean-Claude Passeron. *Reproduction in Education, Society and Culture.* Beverly Hills: Sage, 1977.

Butler, Judith. *Gender Trouble: Feminism and the Subversion of Identity.* New York: Routledge. 1990.

———. *Bodies that Matter: On the Discursive Limits of "Sex".* New York: Routledge, 1993.

Calvert, Peter. *Revolution and Counter-Revolution.* Minneapolis: University of Minnesota Press, 1990.

Chafiq, Chahla. Islam, Pedarsâlâri, Chandgânegy-e va Chandgooneqy-e Mowqeʿiyat-e Konoony-e Zanân dar Donyây-e Islam ("Islam, Patriarchy, and Multiple Images of Women in Contemporary Muslim World"). *Women, Sexuality and Islam. Sixth International Conference of Iranian Women's Studies Foundation,* ed. G. Amin and H. Sarshar. Cambridge, MA: Iranian Women's Studies Foundation, 1995.

Chehabi, H. E. "The Impossible Republic: Contradictions of Iran's Islamic State." *Contention* 5 (1996).

Cherifati-Merabtine, Doria. "Algeria at a Crossroads: National Liberation, Islamization and Women." *Gender and National Identity: Women and Change in Muslim Societies,* ed. V. Moghadam. London: Zed Press, 1994.

Dallalfar, Arlene. "Iranian Women as Immigrant Entrepreneurs." *Gender and Society* 8.4 (1994): 541–61.

Daragahi, Haideh. Jensiyat va Akhlâq-e Islami ("Sexuality and Islamic Ethics"). *Women, Sexuality and Islam. Sixth International Conference of Iranian Women's Studies Foundation,* ed. G. Amin and H. Sarshar. Cambridge, MA: Iranian Women's Studies Foundation, 1995.

DuBois, Ellen Carol. "Women's Suffrage and the Left: An International Socialist-Feminist Perspective." *New Left Review* 186 (1991): 20–45.

Eagleton, Terry. *Ideology: An Introduction.* London: Verso, 1991.

Ebadi, Shirin. Hoquq-e Kudak: Negâhi beh Masâ'el-e Hoquq-e Koodakân dar Iran *(Children's Rights: A Study of Legal Aspects in Iran).* Tehran: Roshangaran, 1990.

———. Negaresh-e Sonnat va Moderniyat beh Barâbâry-e Zan va Mard ("Approaches of Traditionalism and Modernity to Equality between Women and Men"). *Jens-e Dovom,* ed. N.A. Khorasany. Tehran: Nashr-e Towseʿeh, 1999.

Ebtekar, Massoumeh. "Quarterly Discourse: Women's Studies: The Indispensable Cultural Factor." *Farzaneh: Journal of Women's Studies and Research* 1 (1993a): 1–4.

———. Sokhan-e Fasl: Cherâ *Farzaneh*? ("Quarterly Discourse: Why *Farzaneh*?"). *Farzaneh: Journal of Women's Studies and Research* 1 (1993b): 3–8.

———. "Va Sârâ Khandid": Talâshi barây-e Tabra'eh-ye 'Ahd-e 'Atiq az Ettehâmât-e Feministhâ (" 'And Sara Laughed': An Attempt to Exonerate the Old Testament from Feminists' Accusations"). *Farzaneh: Journal of Women's Studies and Research* 1 (1993c): 121–30.

———. Mabâny-e Fekry-e Sanad-e Pekan ("Intellectual Foundations of Beijing's Document"). *Farzaneh: Journal of Women's Studies and Research* 7 (1995–1996a): 131–38.

———. "Reflections on the Fourth World Conference on Women: The Process and the Issues." *Farzaneh: Journal of Women's Studies and Research* 7 (1995–1996b): 93–104.

Eftekhâri, Rosâ. Zanân va Pârlemânhây-e Jahân: 1945–1995 ("Women in Parliaments around the World: 1945–1995"). *Zanân* 27 (1995): 48–53.

Eisen, Arlene. *Women and Revolution in Viet Nam*. London: Zed Books, 1984.

Eisenstein, Zillah R. *The Radical Future of Liberal Feminism*. New York: Longman, 1981.

'Ellini, Mohsen. Zan dar Pooyeh-ye Târikh ("The Woman in the Historical Process"). *Zanân* 2 (1991): 6–8.

Esfandiari, Haleh. *Reconstructed Lives: Women and Iran's Islamic Revolution*. Washington, DC and Baltimore: The Woodrow Wilson Center Press and The Johns Hopkins University Press, 1997.

Eskandari, M. Dar Daheh-ye Enqelâb Negâhi beh Dah Sâl Talâsh-e Majalleh-ye *Zan-e Rouz* ("In the Decade Anniversary of the Revolution, A Glance at Ten Years of Effort by *Zan-e Rouz*"). *Zan-e Rouz* 17 Feb. 1988: 6–9.

Evans, Sara M., and Harry C. Boyte. *Free Spaces: The Sources of Democratic Change in America*. New York: Harper & Row, 1986.

Farhâdpour, Lili. *Zanân-e Berlin: Ravâyati Motefâvet az Konferâns-e Berlin ("The Women of Berlin: A Different Narrative about Berlin's Conference")*. Tehran: Jâme'eh-ye Iraniân, 2000.

Farid, Ahmad. Seyr-e Tahavvol-e Khânevâdeh dar Iran ("Development of the Iranian Family"). *Zanân* 8 (1992): 46–49.

Fausto-Sterling, Anne. "How to Build a Man." *Constructing Masculinity*, ed. M. Berger, B. Wallis and S. Watson. New York: Routledge, 1995.

Foran, John. "A Century of Revolution: Comparative, Historical, and Theoretical Perspectives on Social Movements in Iran." *A Century of Revolution: Social Movements in Iran*, ed. J. Foran. Minneapolis: University of Minnesota Press, 1994.

Foruzandeh, Mehrabân. Bohrân-e Shâdmâni ("The Crisis of Happiness"). *Hamshahri* Feb. 1992: 20–21.

Foucault, Michel. *Power/Knowledge*. New York: Pantheon, 1980.

Fraser, Nancy. *Unruly Practices: Power, Discourse and Gender in Contemporary Socialist Theory*. Minneapolis: University of Minnesota Press, 1989.

———. *Justice Interruptus: Critical Reflections on the "Postcolonial" Condition*. New York: Routledge, 1997.

———. "Rethinking Recognition." *New Left Review* 2nd ser. 3 (2000): 107–20.

French, Marilyn. *The War Against Women*. New York: Summit Books, 1992.

————. *Jang ʿAlayh-e Zanân ("The War Against Women")*. Trans. T.T. Maleki. Tehran: Nashr-e ʿIlmy, 1994.

Friedl, Erika. *Women of Deh Koh: Lives in an Iranian Village*. New York: Penguin, 1991.

Galasinski, Dariusz. *The Language of Deception: A Discourse Analytical Study*. Thousand Oaks, CA: Sage, 2000.

Ganji, Akbar. *Târikkhâneh-ye Ashbâh: Âsibshenâsy-e Gozâr beh Dowlat-e Demokrâtik-e Towseʿehgarâ (Ghosts' Darkhouse: Pathology of Transition to the Developmental Democratic State)*. Tehran: Tarh-e Nou, 1999.

Gaventa, John. *Power and Powerlessness: Quiescence and Rebellion in an Appalachian Valley*. Urbana: University of Illinois Press, 1980.

Geertz, Clifford. *The Interpretation of Cultures*. New York: Basic, 1973.

Giddens, Anthony. *Modernity and Self-Identity: Self and Society in the Late Modern Age*. Stanford, CA: Stanford University Press, 1991.

Goft-o-gu. Javânân va Moʿzal-e Jarâʾem-e Farhangi: Mosâhebeh bâ Kâmbiz Noroozi ("Youth and the Problem of Cultural Crimes: Interview with Kambiz Noroozi"). *Goft-o-gu* 19 (1998): 17–27.

Gorgi, Monir, and Massoumeh Ebtekar. "A Study of the Life and Status of Virgin Mary (Mariam), The Mother of Christ, in the Holy Quran: The Chosen Woman." *Farzaneh: Journal of Women's Studies and Research* 2–3 (1994): 67–80.

————. "The Life and Status of Fatima Zahra: A Woman's Image of Excellence." *Farzaneh: Journal of Women's Studies and Research* 8 (1997): 7–19.

Gramsci, Antonio. *Selections from the Prison Notebooks*. Trans. Q. Hoare and G.N.Smith. New York: International, 1971.

Grossberg, Lawrence, and Cary Nelson. "Introduction: The Territory of Marxism." *Marxism and the Interpretation of Culture*, ed. C. Nelson and L. Grossberg. Chicago: University of Illinois Press, 1988.

Group to Assess Future Ideas. Mardom darbâreh-ye Raʾis Jomhoor Shodan-e Zanân Chegooneh Fekr Mikonand? ("What Do People Think about Women's Presidency?") *Zanân* 35 (1997): 6.

Haddâd ʿÂdel, Qolâmali. *Farhang-e Berahnegi va Berahnegy-e Farhangi (The Culture of Nakedness and the Cultural Nakedness)*. Tehran: Soroush, 1995.

Haeri, Shahla. Of Feminism and Fundamentalism in Iran and Pakistan. *Contention* 4.3 (1995): 129–49.

————. Nâmeh (Letter to *Zanân*). *Zanân* 29 (1996): 56–57.

Hâj Seyyed Javâdi, Fattâneh. *Bâmdâd-e Khomâr (The Morning Hangover)*. Tehran: Alborz, 1996.

Hâjar, M. Zani dar Man ("Woman in Me"). *Jens-e Dovom*, ed. N.A. Khorasany. Tehran: Nashr-e Towseʿeh, 1999.

Hajjarian, Saeed. *Jomhouriyat: Afsoonzodaʾi az Qodrat (Republicanism: The Demystification of Power)*. Tehran: Tarh-e No, 2000.

Halliday, Fred. *Iran: Dictatorship and Development*. London: Pelican, 1979.

Hartmann, Heidi. "The Unhappy Marriage of Marxism and Feminism: Towards A More Progressive Union." *Women and Revolution*, ed. L. Sargent. Boston: South End, 1981.

Hartmann, Heidi, and Ann R. Markusen. "Contemporary Marxist Theory and

Practice: A Feminist Critique." *Review of Radical Political Economics* 12.2 (1980): 87–93.

Hartsock, Nancy. *Money, Sex and Power.* New York: Longman, 1983.

Hâshemi, Mohammad. Hoquq-e Ejtemâ'i-Siyâsy-e Zanân dar Chahâr 'Arseh ("Women's Socio-Political Rights in Four Arenas"). *Farzaneh: Journal of Women's Studies and Research* 8 (1997): 15–42.

Hassan, Riffat. "Feminist Theology: The Challenges for Muslim Women." *Journal of Critical Studies of the Middle East* 9 (1996): 53–65.

Haug, Frigga, Brigitte Hipfl, and Helga Dautermann. *Sündiger Genuss?: Filmerfahrungen von Frauen.* Hamburg: Argument-Verlag, 1995.

Hegland, Mary E. "Political Roles of Iranian Village Women." *Middle East Report.* January-February 1986: 14–19.

Heilbrun, Carolyn G. *Toward the Promise of Androgyny.* New York: Alfred A. Knopf, 1973.

Hejâzi, Banafsheh. *Zan beh Zann-e Târikh ("Woman According to History").* Tehran: Nashr-e Shahr-e Âb, 1991.

Higgins, Patricia J. *Going to Iran,* ed. Kate Millet. *Signs: Journal of Women in Culture and Society* 9.1 (1983): 154–56.

———. "Reply to Bergmann." *Signs: Journal of Women in Culture and Society* 12.3 (1987): 607–8.

Hoodfar, Homa. "The Veil in Their Minds and on Our Heads: The Persistence of Colonial Images of Muslim Women." *Resources for Feminist Research* 22.3–4 (1993): 5–18.

Hosseini, Shahrbânu. Sanduq-e Hamyâri va Fa'âliyat-e Mâ Zanân-e Kârgar ("Cooperative Funds and Our Activities as Working Women"). *Negâh-e Zanân,* ed. N.A. Khorasany. Tehran: Nashr-e Towse'eh, 1998.

Institute for Cultural Studies and Research. Barrasy-e Nahveh-ye Mo'ârrefy-e Zan dar Kotob-e Darsy-e Dowreh-ye Ebtedâ'i–1368 ("Analysis of Women's Roles in Primary School Textbooks–1989"). *Zanân* 11 (1989): 2–7.

Irani, Sholeh. Da'vây-e *Zan-e* Rouz va *Sobh* bar sar-e Chist? ("What Are *Zan-e* Rouz and *Sobh* Fighting for?") *Avaye Zan* 26–27 (1996): 36–40.

Jacobs, Sue-Ellen, and Christine Roberts. "Sex, Sexuality, Gender, and Gender Variance." *Gender and Anthropology,* ed. S. Morgen. Washington, DC: American Anthropological Association, 1989.

Jaggar, Alison M. *Feminist Politics and Human Nature.* Totowa, NJ: Rowman & Littlefield, 1983.

Jalali Naeini, Ziba. Vâqe'garâ'i dar Goftâr-e Feministi dar Iran-e pas az Enqelâb ("Realism in Feminist Discourse in Post-Revolutionary Iran"). *Goft-o-gu* 16 (1997): 27–35.

Jay, Martin. *Marxism and Totality.* Berkeley: University of California Press, 1984.

Jayawardena, Kumari. *Feminism and Nationalism in the Third World.* London: Zed, 1986.

Jenson, Jane. "Both Friend and Foe: Women and State Welfare. *Becoming Visible: Women in European History,* ed. R. Bridenthal, C. Koonz and S. Stuard. Boston: Houghton Mifflin, 1987.

Johnson, Kay Ann. *Women, The Family and Peasant Revolution in China.* Chicago: University of Chicago Press, 1983.

Joyce, James. *Ulysses.* New York: The Modern Library, 1961.

Kadivar, Jamileh. *Zan (Woman)*. Tehran: Ettelâʿât Publication, 1996.

Kandiyoti, Deniz. "Bargaining with Patriarchy." *Gender and Society* 2.3 (1988): 274–90.

———. Introduction. *Women, Islam and the State*, ed. D. Kandiyoti. Philadelphia: Temple University Press, 1991a.

———. "Islam and Patriarchy: A Comparative Perspective." *Women in Middle Eastern History: Shifting Boundaries in Sex and Gender*, ed. N. Keddie and B. Baron. New Haven, CT: Yale University Press, 1991b.

Kar, Mehrangiz. Jâygâh-e Zan dar Qânun-e Keyfary-e Islam ("Women's Status in Islam's Punitive Law"). *Zanân* 11 (1993): 16–25.

———. *Zanân dar Bâzâr-e Kâr-e Iran (Women in Iran's Labor Market)*. Tehran: Rowshangarân, 1994.

———. 1995. Mâdaran Cheh Mikhâhand? ("What Do Mothers Want?") *Zanân* 26 (1995): 38–44.

———. Barây-e Hefz-e Jân-e Zanân, Âyâ Hanooz Ham Zarurat-e Ta'sis-e "Khâneh-hâh-ye Amn" Ehsâs Nemishavad? ("To Protect Women's Lives, Is the Need for "Safe Houses" Still Unrecognized?") *Zanân* 29 (1996a): 2–3.

———. "Women and Personal Status Law in Iran: An Interview with Mehrangiz Kar." *Middle East Report* 198 (1996b): 36–38.

———. *Hoquq-e Siyâsy-e Zanân (Women's Political Rights)*. Tehran: Roshangaran & Women's Studies, 1997a.

———. Ezdevâj-e Dokhtarbacheh-hâ Qânuni Ast! ("Little Girls Can Legally Marry!") *Zanân* 36 (1997b): 16–18.

Karam, Azza M. "Veiling, Unveiling and Meaning of "the Veil": Challenging Static Symbolism." *Thamyris: Mythmaking from Past to Present* 3.2 (1996): 219–36.

Karimi-Hakkak, Ahmad. Negâhi bar Movaffaqtarin Român-e Irani dar daheh-ye Gozashteh ("A Glance at the Most Successful Novel of the Past Decade"). *Iran Nameh* 15.3 (1997): 447–70.

Katzenstein, Mary Fainsod. *Faithful and Fearless: Moving Feminist Protest Inside the Church and Military*. Princeton, NJ: Princeton University Press, 1998.

Keddie, Nikki R. *Roots of Revolution: An Interpretive History of Modern Iran*. New Haven: Yale University Press, 1981.

Kermânshâhi, Zeynabussâdât. Jâygâh-e Zan dar Fiqh-e Keyfary-e Islam ("Women's Status in the Islamic Punitive Fiqh," Part 1). *Zanân* 13 (1993a): 56–60.

———. Jâygâh-e Zan dar Fiqh-e Keyfary-e Islam ("Women's Status in the Islamic Punitive Fiqh, Part 3). *Zanân* 16 (1993b): 38–44.

———. Âyâ Kasb-e Ejâzeh az Showhar dar Omur Lâzem Ast? ("Is It Necessary to Have the Husband's Permission?") *Zanân* 13 (1993c): 60.

Keshâvarz, Nâhid. Harim-e Hassâs-e Eshteqâl-e Zanân ("A Sensitive Issue: Women's Employment"). Spec. issue on women *Farhang-e Towse'eh* (1998): 42–45.

Keyhânniâ, Asqar. *Zan-e Emrooz, Mard-e Dirooz: Tahlili bar Ekhtelâfât-e Zanâshoʾi (Today's Woman, Yesterday's Man: A Discussion of Marital Problems)*. Tehran: Roshangaran and Women's Studies, 1996.

Khan, Shahnaz. "Veil as a Site of Struggle: The Hejab in Quebec." *Canadian Woman Studies* 15.2,3 (1995): 146–52.

Khâni, Faribâ. Kenâr-e Daryâ bâ Moshkelât-e Khânomhâ ("On the Beach, with Women's Problems"). *Zanân* 36 (1997): 8–14.

Khoi, Esmail. Gozâreshi Vizheh beh Yek Doost ("A Special Report to a Friend"). *Ketâb-e Jom'eh* 7 Feb. 1980: 13–20.

———. *Edges of Poetry*. Trans. A.K.-H. a. M. Beard. Santa Monica: Blue Logos, 1995.

Khomeini, Rouhullah. Dar Jostojooy-e Râh az Kalâm-e Imam ("In Search of the Pathway by Imam's Word"). *Zan (Women)*. Vol. 3. Tehran: Amir Kabir, 1982.

———. Vasiyatnâmeh-ye Siyâsi-Elâhy-e Rahbar-e Kabir-e Enqelâb-e Islami ("The Political-Celestial Testament of the Great Leader of the Islamic Revolution"). *Ettela'at-e Siyâsy-Eqtesâdi* 21 Apr.–21 June 1989.

Kiâni Sâbet, Mozhgân. Naqd-e Sokhanrâny-e Khânom-e Mehrangiz Kar ("Critique of a Lecture by Mehrangiz Kar"). *Zanân* 14 (1993): 42–49.

Knauss, Peter R. *The Persistence of Patriarchy: Class, Gender, and Ideology in Twentieth Century Algeria*. New York: Praeger, 1987.

Koran. Trans. N.J. Dawood. New York: Penguin, 1988.

Kousha, Mahnaz. "Women, History and the Politics of Gender in Iran." *Journal for Critical Studies of Iran and the Middle East* 1 (1992): 25–37.

Kozol, Wendy. "Fracturing Domesticity: Media, Nationalism, and the Question of Feminist Influence." *Signs: Journal of Women in Culture and Society* 20.3 (1994): 646–65.

Kruks, Sonia, Rayna Rapp, and Marilyn B. Young, eds. *Promissory Notes: Women in the Transition to Socialism*. New York: Monthly Review P, 1989.

Kuhn, Annette. *Women's Pictures: Feminism and Cinema*. London: Verso, 1994.

Laclau, Ernesto, and Chantal Mouffe. 1987. *Hegemony and Socialist Strategy: Towards a Radical Democratic Politics*. Translated by W. Moore and P. Cammack. London: Verso.

Lâhiji, Shahlâ. *Simây-e Zan dar Âsâr-e Bahram Beyza'i, Filmsâz va filmnâmehnevis (The Image of Woman in the Works of Bahram Beyza'i, Director and Screenwriter)*. Tehran: Roshangaran, 1993.

Lâhiji, Shahlâ, and Mehrangiz Kar. *Shenâkht-e Hoviyat-e Zan-e Irani dar Gostareh-ye Pishtârikh va Târikh (The Quest for Identity: The Image of Iranian Women in Prehistory and History)*. Tehran: Roshangaran, 1992.

Lerner, Gerda. *The Creation of Patriarchy*. New York: Oxford University Press, 1986.

MacKinnon, Catharine A. "Feminism, Marxism, and the State: Toward a Feminist Jurisprudence." *Signs: Journal of Women in Culture and Society* 8.4 (1983): 635–58.

Mahdi, Ali Akbar, and Abdolali Lahsaeizadeh. *Sociology in Iran*. Bethesda, MD: Jahan, 1992.

Matin, Mahnaz. "Ettehâd-e Melly-e Zanân," Fasli Tâzeh dar Mobârezât-e Zanân-i Iran ("The National Union of Women: A New Chapter in the Iranian Women's Movement"). *Bâzbiny-e Tajrobeh-ye Ettehâd-e Melly-e Zanân (The National Union of Iranian Women Revisited.)*, ed. M. Matin. Berkeley: Noghteh Books, 1999.

Mazdâpour, Katâyoon. Nourooz, 'Eyd-e Ashiyâ', 'Eyd-e Zanân ("Nourooz: Celebrating Objects, Celebrating Women"). *Zanân* 28 (1996): 30–33.

McLellan, David. *Ideology*. Minneapolis: University of Minnesota Press, 1995.

Melucci, Alberto. *Challenging Codes: Collective Action in the Information Age*. New York: Cambridge University Press, 1996a.

———. *The Playing Self: Person and Meaning in the Planetary Society*. New York: Cambridge University Press, 1996b.

Milani, Farzaneh. *Veils and the Words: The Emerging Voices of Iranian Women Writers*. Syracuse, NY: Syracuse University Press, 1992.

Miliband, Ralph. *Socialism for a Sceptical Age*. London: Verso, 1995.

Miller, Judith. *God Has Ninety-Nine Names*. New York: Simon & Schuster, 1996.

Ministry of Islamic Culture and Guidance. *Osul-e Siyâsat-e Farhangy-e Jomhury-e Islamy-e Iran (Principles of Cultural Politics of the IRI)*. Tehran: Bureau of Planning, Ministry of Islamic Culture and Guidance, 1992.

Mir-Hosseini, Ziba. "Stretching the Limits: A Feminist Reading of the *Shari'a* in Post-Khomeini Iran." *Feminism and Islam: Legal and Literary Perspectives*, ed. M. Yamani. New York: New York University Press, 1996.

Moallem, Minoo. "Ethnic Entrepreneurship and Gender Relations Among Iranians in Montreal, Quebec, Canada." *Iranian Refugees and Exiles since Khomeini*, ed. A. Fathi. Costa Mesa, CA: Mazda, 1991.

Moghadam, Khadijeh. 2000. Ta'âvonihây-e Zanân. Az Harf tâ 'Amal (Women's Cooperatives: Theory to Practice). In *Jens-e Dovom* (97–101), edited by N. A. Khorasany. Tehran: Nashr-e Towse'eh.

Moghissi, Haideh. *Populism and Feminism in Iran: Women's Struggle in a Male-Defined Revolutionary Movement*. New York: St. Martin's, 1994.

———. Feminism-e Popolisti va 'Feminism-e Islami': Naqdi bar Gerâyeshhây-e Nomohâfezehkârâneh-ye Feministhây-e Irani dar Qarb ("Populist Feminism and 'Islamic Feminism': A Critique of Neo-conservative Tendencies among Iranian Academic Feminists"). *Kankash: A Persian Journal of History, Culture, and Politics* 13 (1997): 57–95.

———. *Feminism and Islamic Fundamentalism: The Limits of Postmodern Analysis*. London: Zed, 1999.

Mohammadi, Majeed. *Jâme'eh-ye Madani beh Manzaleh-ye Yek Ravesh (Civil Society as a Method)*. Tehran: Qatreh, 1997.

———. *Jâme'eh-ye Madany-e Irani: Bestarhây-e Nazari va Mavâne' (Iranian Civil Society: Theoretical Bases and Obstacles)*. Tehran: Nashr-e Markaz, 1999.

Mohseni, Maryam. *Motâlebât-e Zanân-e Kârgar* ("Workingwomen's Demands"). *Jens-e Dovom*, ed. N.A. Khorasany. Tehran: Nashr-e Towse'eh, 1999.

Mojab, Shahrzad. "Islamic Feminism: Alternative or Contradiction?" *Fireweed* 47 (1995): 18–25.

———. Zan bar Masnad-e Ijtihâd: Navid-e Zanvarâneh Shodan-e Mardomsâlâry ("Women at the Seat of Ijtihad: Promise of a Feminine Democracy"). *Arash* (1999): 48–52.

Mokhtâri, Mohammad. *Ensân dar She'r-e Mo'âser (The Human in Contemporary Poetry)*. Tehran: Toos, 1992.

———. *Tamrin-e Modârâ (The Practice of Tolerance)*. Tehran: Vistar, 1998.

Molyneux, Maxine. "Mobilization Without Emancipation? Women's Interests, the State, and Revolution in Nicaragua." *Feminist Studies* 11.2 (1985): 227–54.

Moossavi, Nastaran. Seyri dar Mardsâlâri ("Patriarchy at a Glance"). Spec. issue on women *Farhang-e Towse'eh* (1998): 68–71.

————. Dar Vâdy-e Motâle'ât-e Zanân ("In the Field of Women's Studies"). *Adineh*. Feb. (1999): 36–37.

Moti', Nâhid. Tahavvol-e Naqsh-e Zan-e Roostâ'y-e Iran dar Fa'âliyathâ-ye Zerâ'i ("Changes in Woman's Role in Agricultural Activities"). *Zanân* 14 (1993): 19–23.

————. Jâme'ehpaziry-e Jensi: Mâne'i barây-e Towse'eh ("Gender Socialization: A Barrier to Development"). *Zanân* 19 (1996): 28–33.

————. Feminism dar Iran: Dar Jostojoy-e Yek Rahyâft-e Bumi ("Feminism in Iran: In Search of an Indigenous Approach"). *Zanân* 33 (1997a): 20–25.

————. Zan-e Khânehdâr, Negarân-e Sâlhây-e Piri ("The Housewife, Worried about Old Age"). *Zanân* 36 (1997b): 34–38.

————. Defâ'i Mardâneh az Feminism ("A Manly Defense of Feminism"). *Zanân* 40 (1998): 39–44.

Mouffe, Chantal. "Hegemony and Ideology in Gramsci." *Gramsci and Marxist Theory*, ed. C. Mouffe. Boston: Routledge & Kegan Paul, 1979.

Mousavi, Kâzem. "Simây-e Zan dar Nezâm-e Islami": Naqdi bar Ketâb-e *Simây-e Zan dar Nezâm-e Islami* "Ta'lif-e Ayatollah Ahmad Âzari-Qomi (" 'Women's Visage in the Islamic System' ": A Review of the *Women's Visage in the Islamic System* by Ayatollah Ahmad Âzari-Qomi." *Zanân* 17 (1994): 36–40.

Myerhoff, Barbara. *Number Our Days*. New York: Touchstone, 1980.

Najmabadi, Afsaneh. Sâlhây-e 'Usrat, Sâlhâye Rooyesh ("Years of Destitution; Years of Growth"). *Kankash* 12 (1995): 171–206.

————. Degarguny-e 'Zan' va 'Mard' dar Zabân-e Mashrutiyat ("Change in 'Woman' and 'Man' in the Discourse of Mashrutiyat"). *Negâh-e Zanân*, ed. N.A. Khorasany. Tehran: Towseeh, 1998a.

————. Feminism va Mazhab: Peyvandhâ va Gosasthây-e Târikhi va Nowpardâzihây-e Konouni ("Feminism and Religion: Historical Links and Ruptures and Contemporary Reinterpretations"). *Arash*. Aug.-Sept. 1998b: 46–50.

Najm-e-'Erâqi, Manizheh. Shakhsiyat-e Zan: Az Pendâr tâ Vâqe'iyat ("Women's Nature: Illusion and Reality"). *Negâh-e Zanân*, ed. N.A. Khorasany. Tehran: Nashr-e Towse'eh, 1998.

Najm-e-'Erâqi, Manizheh et al., eds. *Zan va Sinemâ (Women and Cinema)*. Tehran: Rowshangarân and Women's Studies, 1998.

Nouroozi, Kâmbiz. Hoquq-e Zanân: Tarh-e Mas'aleh'i Digar ("Women's Right: Raising another Issue"). *Zanân* 67 (2000): 20–21.

Paidar, Parvin. *Women and the Political Process in Twentieth-Century Iran*. New York: Cambridge University Press, 1995.

Parham, Bagher. Hezb-e Tudeh va Kânoon-e Nevisandegân-e Iran ("The Tudeh Party and the Iranian Writers' Association" Part 1). *Ketâb-e Jom'eh* 31 Jan. 1980a: 10–14.

————. Hezb-e Tudeh va Kânoon-e Nevisandegân-e Iran ("The Tudeh Party and the Iranian Writers' Association" Part 2). *Ketâb-e Jom'eh* 7 Feb. 1980b: 9–12.

————. Hezb-e Tudeh va Kânoon-e Nevisandegân-e Iran ("The Tudeh Party and the Iranian Writers' Association" Part 3). *Ketâb-e Jom'eh* 14 Feb. 1980c: 9–15.

———. Hezb-e Tudeh va Kânoon-e Nevisandegân-e Iran ("The Tudeh Party and the Iranian Writers' Association" Part 4). *Ketâb-e Jom'eh* 21 Feb. 1980d: 19–30.

———. Hezb-e Tudeh va Kânoon-e Nevisandegân-e Iran ("The Tudeh Party and the Iranian Writers' Association" Part 5). *Ketâb-e Jom'eh* 28 Feb. 1980e: 57–64.

———. Hezb-e Tudeh va Kânoon-e Nevisandegân-e Iran ("The Tudeh Party and the Iranian Writers' Association" Part 6). *Ketâb-e Jom'eh* 7 Mar. 1980f: 8–13.

Pourzand, Lili. Khânom, Cherâ Siyâh Mipooshid? ("Madam: Why Do You Wear Black?") *Zanân* 22 (1994): 4–17.

Qâ'eni, Mohsen. Kotak Zadan-e Zan Yeki az Âsâr-e Ryâsat-e Mard ("Wife Battery: A Result of Men's Command in the Family" Part 1). *Zanân* 18 (1994a): 54–59.

———. Kotak Zadan-i Zan Yeki az Âsâr-i Ryâsat-e Mard ("Wife Battery: A Result of Men's Command in the Family" Part 2). *Zanân* 19 (1994b): 68–72.

Qâ'eni, Sadât. Velâyat-e Pedar: Mafhoom va Dâmaneh ("Father's Guardianship: Meaning and Scope"). *Zanân* 36 (1997): 18–21.

Qahremâni, Mahvash. Jâme'eh-ye Madani va Khânevâdeh ("Civil Society and the Family"). Spec. issue on women *Farhang-e Towse'eh* (1998): 32–34.

Rahmâni, Taqi. Ahl-e Tasannon: Aqaliyati Mazlum ("The Sunnis: An Oppressed Minority"). *Iran-e Farda* 6 Oct. 1999: 8–9.

Rahnavard, Zahra. Zan, Islam va Feminism ("Woman, Islam, and Feminism"). *The Journal of Foreign Policy (In Persian)* 9.2 (1995): 523–48.

Rahnema, Ali, and Farhad Nomani. *The Secular Miracle: Religion, Politics and Economic Policy in Iran.* London: Zed, 1990.

Rahnema, Saeed, and Sohrab Behdad, eds. *Iran after the Revolution: Crisis of An Islamic State.* New York: I.B. Tauris, 1995.

Rajaee, Farhang. "Islam and Modernity: The Reconstruction of an Alternative Shi'ite Islamic Worldview in Iran." *Fundamentalisms and Society: Reclaiming the Sciences, the Family, and Education,* ed. M.E. Marty and R.S. Appleby. Chicago: University of Chicago Press, 1993.

Ray, Raka. *Fields of Protest: Women's Movement in India.* Minneapolis: University of Minnesota Press, 1999.

Research Group on Women's Issues. *Âncheh darbâreh-ye Hoquq-e Ezdevâj Bâyad Bedânim (What We Should Know About Marriage Law).* Tehran: Roshangaran & Women's Studies Publishing, 1996.

Rodinson, Maxim. *Islam and Capitalism.* Austin: University of Texas Press, 1981.

Rofugarân, Faribâ. Negâhi beh Ta'rif-e 'Zan' va 'Mard' dar *Loqatnâmeh-ye Dehkhodâ* ("Review of the Definitions of 'Woman' and 'Man' in the *Dehkhodâ Dictionary*"). *Jens-e Dovom,* ed. N.A. Khorasany. Tehran: Nashr-e Towse'eh, 1999.

Rokni, Maral. Mo'arrefi va Naqd-e Ketab: Jang 'Alayh-e Zanân ("Book Review: The War Against Women"). *Faslnameje Zan* 2 (1996): 89–96.

Rowbotham, Sheila. *Woman's Consciousness, Man's World.* Baltimore, MD: Penguin, 1973.

Royanian, Simin. Ta'amoli bar Gozâresh-e Khânom-e Nayereh Tohidi az Konferâns-e Chin ("Considerations on Ms. Nayereh Tohidi's Report of the China Conference"). *Zan dar Mobarezeh* 2 (1995): 1–2, 7.

Royer, Michelle. "Deconstructions of Masculinity and Femininity in the Films of Marguerite Duras." *Feminine, Masculine and Representation*, ed. T. Threadgold and A. Cranny-Francis. Boston: Allen & Unwin, 1990.

Rushdie, Salman. "Imaginary Homelands." *Imaginary Homelands: Essays and Criticism 1981–1991*. New York: Penguin, 1991.

Sa'edi, Gholamhossein. Namâyesh dar Hokoumat-e Namâyeshi ("Performance in a Performing Government"). *Alefba* 5 (1984): 1–9.

Sa'idzâdeh, Mohsen. [. . .] Va Ammâ Pâsokh-e Mâ ("[. . .] And Our Reply"). *Zanân* 14 (1993): 50–57.

———. Zanân; Farâtar az Khatar ("Women: Beyond Danger"). *Jâme'eh-ye Sâlem* 58 (1997).

———. Zanân dar Jâme'eh-ye Madani Cheh Andâzeh Sahm Dârand? *("What Share Have Women in Civil Society?")*. Tehran: Nashr-e Qatreh, 1998.

Sabbah, Fatna A. *Woman in the Muslim Unconscious*. New York: Pergamon P, 1984.

Sacks, Karen. "Engels Revisited: Women, the Organization of Production, and Private Property." *Women, Culture, and Society*, ed. M.Z. Rosaldo and L. Lamphere. Stanford, CA: Stanford University Press, 1974.

Safari, Fâtemeh. Jensiyat va Akhlâq ("Sexuality and Morality" Part 1). *Payâm-e Zan* 21 Apr. 1999a: 36–41.

———. Jensiyat va Akhlâq ("Sexuality and Morality" Part 2). *Payâm-e Zan* May 1999b: 41–45.

———. Jensiyat va Akhlâq ("Sexuality and Morality" Part 3). *Payâm-e Zan* June 1999c: 36–41, 55.

———. Jensiyat va Akhlâq ("Sexuality and Morality" Part 4). *Payâm-e Zan* July 1999d: 40–46.

Saidi, Ghulam Husayn (Gholamhossein Sa'edi). *Othello in Wonderland and Mirror-Polishing Storytellers*. Trans. M.R. Ghanoonparvar. Costa Mesa, CA: Mazda, 1996.

Sami'i, Âtusâ. Az 'Zan-Poush' tâ Zan: Honar-e Namâyesh-e Zanân, Gozar az Sonnat beh Modernism ("From 'Dressed-as-Woman' to Woman: Women's Theater from Traditionalism to Modernity"). *Jens-e Dovom*, ed. N.A. Khorasany. Tehran: Nashr-e Towse'eh, 1999.

Sanasarian, Eliz. *The Women's Rights Movement in Iran: Mutiny, Appeasement, and Repression from 1900 to Khomeini*. New York: Praeger, 1982.

Sanday, Peggy. "Female Status in Public Domain." *Women, Culture, and Society*, ed. M.Z. Rosaldo and L. Lamphere. Stanford, CA: Stanford University Press, 1974.

Sargent, Lydia, ed. *Women and Revolution: A Discussion of the Unhappy Marriage of Marxism and Feminism*. Boston: South End, 1981.

Sattâri, Jalâl. *Simây-e Zan dar Farhang-e Iran (The Image of Woman in Iran's Culture*. Tehran: Markaz, 1994.

Schild, Verónica. "New Subjects of Rights? Women's Movements and the Construction of Citizenship in the 'New Democracies'." *Cultures of Politics, Politics of Cultures: Re-visioning Latin American Social Movements*, ed. S.E. Alvarez, E. Dagnino, and A. Escobar. Boulder: Westview Press, 1998.

Sciolino, Elaine. "The Chanel Under the Chador." *New York Times* 4 May 1997: 47–51.

Scott, James C. *Weapons of the Weak: Everyday Forms of Peasant Resistance.* New Haven, CT: Yale University Press, 1985.

Segal, Lynne. "Whose Left? Socialism, Feminism and the Future." *New Left Review* 185 (1991): 81–91.

Shâditalab, Zhâleh. Towseʿeh va ʿAqabmândigy-e Zanân ("Development and Women's Underdevelopment"). *Zanân* 23 (1995): 4–11.

Shafiʿi, Rouhi. Khâhary-e Jahâni, dar Jostojoy-e Esterâtezhi ("International Sisterhood in Search of a Strategy"). *Zanân* 32 (1996): 26–28.

Shahâbi, Mahmood. Afrâd dar Cheh Senni Ezdevâj Mikonand? ("At What Age Do People Marry?"). *Zanân* 11 (1993): 44–49.

Shahidian, Hammed. "National and International Aspects of Feminist Movements: The Example of the Iranian Revolution of 1978–79." *Journal for Critical Studies of Iran and the Middle East* 2 (1993): 33–53.

———. "Islam, Politics, and Problems of Writing Women's History in Iran." *Journal of Women's History* 7.2 (1995): 113–44.

———. "Iranian Exiles and Sexual Politics: Issues of Gender Relations and Identity." *Journal of Refugee Studies* 9.1 (1996a): 43–72.

———. *"Our" Reflections in "Their" Mirror: Depiction of Iranian Exiles in the Iran of the Islamic Republic.* Paper read at Crossroads in Cultural Studies: An International Conference at University of Tampere, Tampere, Finland, 1996b.

———. "Women and Clandestine Politics in Iran: 1970–1985. *Feminist Studies* 23.1 (1997a): 7–42.

———. "The Politics of the Veil: Reflections on Symbolism, Islam, and Feminism." *Thamyris: Mythmaking from Past to Present* 4.2 (1997b): 325–36.

———. Châleshhây-e Jonbesh-e Mostaqell-e Zanân ("Challenges of an Autonomous Women's Movement in Iran"). *Cheshmandâz* 18 (1997c): 41–65.

———. Feminism dar Iran dar Jostojoy-e Chist? ("Feminism in Iran: In Search of What?") *Zanân* 40 (1998): 32–38.

———. "Saving the Savior." *Sociological Inquiry* 69.2 (1999a): 303–27.

———. "Gender and Sexuality among Iranian Immigrants in Canada." *Sexualities* 2.2 (1999b): 189–223.

———. Nesbigarâ'y-e Farhangi: Châlesh yâ Kornesh dar barâbar-e Setam ("Cultural Relativism: Challenging or Kowtowing to Oppression?"). *Jens-e Dovom,* ed. N.A. Khorasany. Tehran: Nashr-e Towseʿeh, 1999c.

———. Âqâz-e Pâyân: Beh Ou keh Goft: 'Mikosham, Mikosham [. . .]' ("The Beginning of End: To the One who Said: 'I'll Kill, I'll Kill [. . .]'). *Noghteh* 9 (1999d): 4–6.

———. Barâbâri, Âzâdi, Demokrâsi: Jonbesh-e Zanân dar Kârzâr-e Ejtemâ'i ("Equality, Freedom, Democracy: Women in Struggle). *Jens-e Dovom,* ed. N.A. Khorasany. Tehran: Nashr-e Towseʿeh, 1999e.

———. "Islam's 'Others': Living Out(side) Islam." *ISIM Newsletter* 5 July 1999f.

———. "Sociology and Exile: Banishment and Tensional Loyalty." *Current Sociology* 84.2 (2000): 81–106.

Shâhmorâdi, ʿAzizeh. Kelisheh-hâ, Abzâr-e Bâztowlid-e Nezâm-e Mardsâlâri ("Clichés: Tools for Reproducing Patriarchy"). *Nigâh-i Zanân,* ed. N.A. Khorasany. Tehran: Nashr-e Towseʿeh, 1998a.

———. Mozakkar va Mo'annas: Âri; Mardâneh va Zanâneh: Nah ("Male and Female: Yes; Masculine and Feminine: No"). *Negâh-e Zanân*, ed. N.A. Khorasany. Tehran: Nashr-e Towse'eh, 1998b.

Shah-Rokni, Nâzanin. Namâyeshgâh va Seminâr-e Hejâb ("Hejâb Exposition and Conference"). *Zanân* 26 (1995): 8–9.

———. Rang Âzâd Shod, Ammâ [. . .] ("Color Is Free, But [. . .]"). *Zanân* 67 (2000): 2–8.

Shahshahani, Soheila. *Chahâr Fasl-e Âftâb: Zendegy-e Ruzmarreh-ye Zanân-e Eskânyâfteh-ye 'Ashâyer-e Mamasani (Âftâb's Four Seasons: Daily Life of the Women of Stabilized Nomads of Mamassany)*. Tehran: Tous Publications, 1987.

———. Cherâ Khâvar-e-miyâneh, Cherâ Zan? ("Why Middle East, Why Woman?") *Zanân* 1 (1991): 18–20.

———. Hoviyat-e Zanân-e Irany-e Moqim-e Paris ("The Identity of Iranian Women in Paris"). *Iran-e Farda* 9.2 (1997): 45–50.

Shâmbayâti, Giti. Agar Mikhâhim dar Dehkadeh-ye Bozorg-e Jahâni Hal Nashavim [. . .] ("If We Want to Survive in the Global Village [. . .]"). *Zanân* 16 (1993a): 10–12.

———. Kargar-e Khâneh, 'Arusak-e Âqâ! ("Housemaid, Mister's Doll!") *Zanân* 18 (1994): 24–27.

———. Bâztâb-e Masâ'el-e Zanân dar Shabakeh ("Reflections of Women's Concerns on the Net"). *Iran Nameh* 15.3 (1997): 471–77.

Sharifi, Firoozeh. Mowqe'iyat-e Zan dar Nezâm Edâry-e Iran ("Women's Position in Iran's Administrative System"). *Zanân* Jan.-Feb. 1991: 4–9.

Sherkat, Shahlâ. Cheshmeh-ye Âgâhi Agar Bejooshad ("If the Stream of Consciousness Springs Forth"). *Zanân* 1 (1991a): 2–3.

———. Nakhostin Bâztâb ("Initial Reflection"). *Zanân*, Jan.-Feb. 1991b: 2–3.

———. Sâl-e 'Usrat, Sâl-e Rooyesh ("Year of Destitution; Year of Growth"). *Zanân* (1993): 2–3.

Shirazi-Mahajan, Faegheh. "A Dramaturgical Approach to Hejab in Post-Revolutionary Iran." *Journal of Critical Studies of the Middle East* 7 (1995): 35–51.

Shokri, Shokoh, and Sâhereh Labriz. "Tamkin." *Zanân* 1 (1991): 58–63.

———. Mard, Sharik yâ Re'is? ("Man: Partner or Boss?") *Zanân* 2 (1992): 26–32.

Shotter, John. *Cultural Politics of Everyday Life: Social Constructionism, Rhetoric and Knowing of the Third Kind*. Toronto: University of Toronto Press, 1993.

Skocpol, Theda. "Social Revolution and Mass Military Mobilization." *Social Revolutions in the Modern World*, ed. T. Skocpol. New York: Cambridge University Press, 1994.

———. Mabâd Ân Rouz! ("May That Day Never Come!"). *Sobh* 74 (1997a): 4.

———. Sâdeq Sabâ Kist? ("Who Is Sâdeq Sabâ?"). *Sobh* 74 (1997b): 63.

Soroush, Mohammad. Negâh: Negâhi Doubâreh va Nou: Pazhoheshi Fiqhi-Ejtemâ'i dar Mozou'-e Negâh va Masayel-e Ân ("Looking Revisited: An Investigation of Fiqh and Social Dimensions of Looking and Its Complications"). *Payâm-e Zan* (2000): 4–9.

Stacey, Judith. *Patriarchy and Socialist Revolution in China*. Berkeley: University of California Press, 1983.

Stokes, Susan C. *Cultures in Conflict: Social Movements and the State in Peru.* Berkeley: University of California Press, 1995.

Sztompka, Piotr. "The Social Function of Defeat." *Social Movements as a Factor of Change in the Contemporary World,* ed. L. Kriesberg, B. Misztal and J. Mucha. Greenwich, CT: JAI, 1988.

Tabari, Azar, and Nahid Yeganeh, eds. *In the Shadow of Islam: The Women's Movement in Iran.* London: Zed, 1982.

Tabatabaie, Kia. "Human Rights of Women." *Farzaneh: Journal of Women's Studies and Research* 7 (1995–1996): 83–91.

Tâheri, A. Az Kojâ beh Kojâ Farâr Mikonand Een Dokhtarân ("These Girls Flee from Where to Where?") *Zanân* 58 (1999): 6–13.

Tajussaltaneh Qajar. *Khâterât-e Tajussaltaneh (Tajussaltaneh's Memoirs),* ed. M. Ettehâdyeh (Nezâm Mâfi) and S. Sa'dvandiân. Tehran: Nashr-e Târikh-e Iran, 1983.

Tâleqâni, A'zam. Sokhanrâny-e Khânom-e Tâleqâni ("Mrs. Tâleqâni's Lecture"). Spec. double issue on women's role in poverty alleviation and sustainable development *Payâm-e Hâjar* 221–222 (1995): 3–8.

Tavakoli, Nayereh. Cheshmam Rowshan! Nakonad Tow Ham Feminist Shodeh'i? ("What? Don't Tell Me You've Become a Feminist, Too?") *Negâh-e Zanân,* ed. N.A. Khorasany. Tehran: Nashr-e Towse'eh, 1998.

Taylor, Verta. *Rock-a-bye Baby: Feminism, Self-Help, and Postpartum Depression.* New York: Routledge, 1996.

Tibi, Bassam. *Islam and the Cultural Accomodation of Social Change.* Tran. C. Krojzl. Boulder: Westview, 1991.

Tohidi, Nayereh. Gozâresh az Didâr-e Zanân-e Jahân dar Pekan ("A Report on the Meeting of Women of the World in Beijing"). *Zanân* 25 (1995): 2–8.

———. Nâmeh (Letter). *Zanân* 29 (1996): 56.

———. Âyâ Zan va Mard Dow Jens-e Mokhâlef Hastand? ("Are Female and Male Two Opposite Sexes?"). *Zanân* 34 (1997a): 20–23.

———. 'Feminism-e Islami': Châleshi Demokrâtik yâ Charkheshy Theokrâtik? (" 'Islamic Feminism': A Democratic Challenge or a Theocratic Reaction?"). *Kankash: A Persian Journal of History, Culture, and Politics* 13 (1997b): 96–149.

Treblicot, Joyce. :"Two Forms of Androgynism." *"Femininity," "Masculinity," and "Androgyny,"* ed. M. Vetterling-Braggin. Totowa, NJ: Rowman & Littlefield, 1982.

Vakili, Valla. *Debating Religion and Politics in Iran: The Political Thought of Abdolkarim Soroush.* Studies Dept.: Occasional paper ser. 2. New York: Council on Foreign Relations, 1996.

Vološinov, V.N. *Marxism and the Philosophy of Language.* New York: Seminar, 1973.

Walby, Sylvia. *Theorizing Patriarchy.* Cambridge, MA: Blackwell, 1994.

———. *Gender Transformations.* New York: Routledge, 1997.

Watson, Helen. "Women and the Veil: Personal Responses to Global Process." *Islam, Globalization and Postmodernity,* ed. A.S. Ahmed and H. Donnan. New York: Routledge, 1994.

Weber, Max. "The Social Psychology of the World Religions." *From Max Weber: Essays in Sociology,* ed. H.H. Gerth and C.W. Mills. New York: Oxford University Press, 1981.

Weeks, Jeffrey. *Sexuality*. New York: Tavistock, 1986.

West, Candace, and Don H. Zimmerman. "Doing Gender." *Gender and Society* 1 (1987): 125–51.

Williams, Raymond. "Base and Superstructure in Marxist Cultural Theory." *Problems in Materialism and Culture*. London: Verso, 1982.

Worsley, Peter. *The Three Worlds: Culture and World Development*. Chicago: University of Chicago Press, 1984.

Wuthnow, Robert. *Meaning and Moral Order: Explorations in Cultural Analysis*. Berkeley: University of California Press, 1989.

Yâdgâr-Âzâdi, Minâ. Qezâvat-e Zan ("Women's Judgeship"Part 1) *Zanân* 5 (1992a): 20–26.

———. Qezâvat-e Zan ("Women's Judgeship" Part 2). *Zanân* 5 (1992b): 17–25.

———. Ijtihâd va Marja'iyat-e Zanân ("Ijtihad and Women as Leading Clerics"). *Zanân* 8 (1992c): 24–32.

Yalfani, Mohsen. Dournamâ'i dar barâbar-e Kânunhây-e Farhangi ("The Outlook before Cultural Centers"). *Cheshmandaz* 2 (1987): 2–8.

Young, Iris Marion. *Justice and the Politics of Difference*. Princeton, NJ: Princeton University Press, 1990.

Zâhedi, Shamsussâdât. Mowqe'iyat-e Zanân dar Jâme'eh-ye Dâneshgâhi ("Women in Universities"). *Zanân* 21 (1995): 2–12.

Zâhedi, Zohreh. E'âdeh-ye Heysiyat-e Havvâ ("Reclaiming Eve's Dignity"). *Zanân* 16 (1993): 2–6.

Zahir-Nezhâd Ershâdi, Minâ. Mâjerây-e Kashf-e Hejâb ("The Story of Women's Unveiling"). *The Journal of Foreign Policy (In Persian)* 9.2 (1995): 795–834.

Zanân. Fâezeh Hashemi Cheh Migooyad? ("What Does Fâezeh Hashemi Say?") *Zanân* (1996a): 8–17.

———. Nâhid Shid: Cherâ Âmad, Cherâ Raft? (Nahid Shyd: Why Did She Come? Why Did She Leave?) *Zanân* (1996b): 18–19.

———. Natijeh-ye Entekhâbât: 10 beh 231 ("Election Results: 10 to 231"). *Zanân* (1996c): 60–62.

———. Mohemtarin Masâ'el-e Zanân Iran Chist? Miz-e-gerdi bâ Sherkat-e Farideh Farrahi, Mehrangiz Kar, va 'Abbâs 'Abdi ("What are Iranian Women's Most Important Problems?") Round table discussion with Farideh Farrahi, Mehrangiz Kar, and 'Abbas 'Abdi. 33 (1997a): 12–18.

———. Mohemtarin Masâ'el-e Zanân Iran Chist? Miz-e-gerdi bâ Sherkat-e Shirin Ebadi, Alireza 'Alavitabâr va Nâhid Moti' ("What are Iranian Women's Most Important Problems?") Round table discussion with Shirin Ebadi, Alireza 'Alavitabâr, and Nâhid Moti'. 34 (1997b): 12–19.

———. Mohemtarin Masâ'el-e Zanân Iran Chist? Miz-e-gerdi bâ Sherkat-e Qolâm'abbâs Tavassoli, Homâ Zanjânizâdeh va Nasrin Mosaffa ("What are Iranian Women's Most Important Problems?") Round table discussion with Qolâm'abbâs Tavassoli, Homâ Zanjânizâdeh, and Nassrin Mosaffa. 35 (1997c): 28–35.

———. Mohemtarin Masâ'el-e Zanân Iran Chist? Miz-e-gerdi bâ Sherkat-e Mansureh Ettehaiyeh, Zhâleh Shâditalab va Mohammad Hâshemi ("What are Iranian Women's Most Important Problems?") Round table discussion with Mansureh Ettehaiyeh, Zhâleh Shâditalab, and Mohammad Hâshemi. 36 (1997d): 26–32.

————. Mohemtarin Masâ'el-e Zanân Iran Chist? Miz-e-gerdi bâ Sherkat-e Zahrâ
    Shojâ'i, Soheilâ Safâ'i, va Seyed Ziâ Mortazavi ("What are Iranian Women's
    Most Important Problems?") Round table discussion with Zahrâ Shojâ'i,
    Soheilâ Safâ'i, and Seyed Ziâ Mortazavi. 37 (1997e): 50–57.
————. Tanhâ Zan-e Kâbineh Kist va Cheh Migooyad? ("The Only Woman of the
    Cabinet: Who Is She and What Says She?") 37 (1997f): 2–5.
Zan-e Rouz. Zan- Mard Mojudi Fâqed-e Shakhsiyat-e Haqiqi va Hoquqi
    ("Woman- Man A Being Devoid of Real and Legal Status"). 19 Apr. 1985:
    3, 58.
————. Âqây-e Modir 'Âmel, Zanân-e In Enqelâb beh Sedâ va Simâ Mo'tarezand!
    ("Mr. Chairman of the Board, the Women of This Revolution Complain
    Against the Sound and Vision!"). 11 Nov. 1989: 3–4.
Zeinali, Mohammad Hossein. Ezdevâj-i Movaqqat (Temporary Marriage). Tehran:
    Surah, 1998.

Index

About the Author

HAMMED SHAHIDIAN is Honorary Research Fellow at the Faculty of Social Sciences, University of Glasgow (2001–2002). He teaches Sociology at the University of Illinois at Springfield, where he was honored with the University Scholar Award. He is also a research associate at the UIS Institute for Public Affairs. Focusing mainly on gender and political activism and Iranians in exile, Shahidian has published in *Qualitative Sociology, Current Sociology, Sexualities, Sociological Inquiry, Feminist Studies,* and elsewhere. He serves on the Editorial Board of *Sexualities.*